★

My Creative Year in the Army

MY CREATIVE YEAR IN THE ARMY

David Madden

THE UNIVERSITY OF TENNESSEE PRESS
Knoxville

First Edition.

LIBRARY OF CONGRESS CATALOGING-IN-PUBLICATION DATA

Names: Madden, David, 1933- author
Title: My creative year in the army / David Madden.
Description: First edition. | Knoxville, Tennessee : The University of Tennessee Press, 2026. | Summary: "David Madden escaped from a life of poverty in Knoxville by joining the merchant marines. This book documents his early years as a developing writer and his enlistment in the military in Cold War America. He ends up all over the country and in far-flung places in the world just as the Korean War threatens to break out into worldwide conflict. Along the way, the book has a lot to say about midcentury Knoxville and the life of an ambitious young writer, already beginning work on what would become the novel Cassandra Singing, among other works" — Provided by publisher.
Identifiers: LCCN 2025054200 (print) | LCCN 2025054201 (ebook) | ISBN 9798895271001 paperback | ISBN 9798895273418 adobe pdf | ISBN 9798895273319 epub
Subjects: LCSH: Madden, David, 1933- | Madden, David, 1933 — Childhood and youth | Authors, American — 20th century | United States. Army — Military life | LCGFT: Autobiographies
Classification: LCC PS3563.A339 Z46 2026 (print) | LCC PS3563.A339 (ebook)
LC record available at https://lccn.loc.gov/2025054200
LC ebook record available at https://lccn.loc.gov/2025054201

Contents

Illustrations

MY CREATIVE YEAR IN THE ARMY

I BECOME A GOVERNMENT ISSUE AT FORT JACKSON, SOUTH CAROLINA

Historically speaking, I was inducted into the Army on February 26, 1954, at the age of twenty. Alone in the tent, when we cautiously entered as into unknown territory, sat an odd young fellow on a top bunk, wearing an old-timey brown leather helmet. He had not been among my friends and neighbors on the Greyhound bus out of Knoxville.

As men rushed to take possession of the bottom bunks, I dove onto the nearest, the one below the dangling man. Malodorous bare feet, long as my forearm, hung down, without the slightest muscle twitch. I swung back out and onto my feet, hoping one other bottom bunk remained. All were inhabited.

Around his moist red lips, the baby-faced fellow's blond whiskers were too thin and short to shave. His eyes, brown as the richest clay loam, stared into Kingdom Come.

The I LIKE IKE button pinned to his black Navy surplus jacket gave me the impression that he probably could not tell me who Ike was.

Why I already had a faint feeling that I would write about him someday was not then at all clear to me.

After only five hours' sleep, I was yelled out of bed at 4:30 a.m. to take a battery of tests for eight hours without a break. Craving irony, I took the Officer Candidate School qualification test, and was shocked that I proved to be the stuff officers are made of. But I was not at all sure I wanted to be an officer as one way of making Army life easier.

That evening, the helmeted farm boy was gone, but his chicken-coop smell hovered.

The next afternoon after chow, we were issued uniforms, mine as oversized as the light blue uniform I had been handed the day I became an usher at the Bijou theater.

Entering the tent, I almost stumbled into a recruit who was bent over splattering his new fatigue trousers with what his stomach was rejecting. Who stood up was that farm boy, whose white nameplate stitched above his breast pocket was blank.

At the first glint of light next morning, a twerp of a corporal waltzed into the tent, shouted us out into the street, and lined us up with about 300 guys out of other tents close by.

When the buttocks and elbows that moved directly in front of me straightened up, the corporal ran up to a guy and turned him around, revealing the farm boy with the rank bare feet. Stuffing cigarette butts into the shirt pocket of his uniform, the boy, whose name plate now read ROOKS, said, "Gonna roll me a few."

Lying on the bottom cot at Fort Jackson Reception, Orientation, and Processing Center, listening to spooky wind in the pine tree hovering over the tent, I imagined Cassie McDaniel lying in the yellow wrought iron antique bed she had shared with her big brother Lone when they were younger, her imagination conjuring him coming home on his Triumph motorcycle from wildly racing around Harlan, Kentucky with his gang, the Hellhounds, then lying on his narrow cot beside her queen-sized bed, moonlight awash over his black leather jacket and boots, fearful that the army would prevent me from being able to write their story for bleak weeks to come.

★

BOOT CAMP AT CAMP GORDON, AUGUSTA, GEORGIA

In March 1954, for boot camp, I got transferred to Camp Gordon, southwest of Augusta, Georgia.

Training began after very little ceremony. A gung-ho, very tough captain in the Rangers instructed us hyper-melodramatically on how to perform well on the obstacle course, scaring us about the terrors of combat, therefore of the necessity to be combat-ready.

Bright and early the next morning, as about two hundred of us recruits filed into a barn-like room to learn hands-on what an M1 rifle is made up of, word raced through us like greased lightning that the Ranger had been arrested in Augusta for molesting a little boy.

I had long enjoyed Henry Reed's poem "The Naming of Parts," so I was inspired by the rifle assembly session to memorize it and recite it in chow line.

> And this you can see is the bolt. The purpose of this
> Is to open the breech, as you see. We can slide it
> Rapidly backwards and forwards: we call this
> Easing the spring. And rapidly backwards and forwards
> The early bees are assaulting and fumbling the flowers:
> They call it easing the Spring.

When we returned for the after-lunch session, a handsome young chaplain pranced into the enormous room who looked and sounded as if he were about to perform the easy task of convincing his captive congregation that, as he declared, "the chain of command comes down from God and goes all the way down to your squad leader," which meant down to my old classmate, Gene McClamrock, a Knox High football hero. "And America is the only nation that can make that claim!"

His cigarette commercial phraseology offended me as a devout agnostic who was fond of Jesus as a real life hero, but when the chaplain invited, expecting none, questions of clarification, I, imagining that he must hunger for the kind of religious contention I used to enjoy with former monk and fellow actor Brendan Liddell, now a jet pilot, asked point blank, "What if what we are commanded to do turns out to be an abomination in the sight of God?"

Before the chaplain could stop spluttering, a comrade behind me tapped me on the shoulder and asked me, "What the fuck's a 'bomb the nation'?"

The flack my disrespectful question brought down on me from both the training staff and the recruits over the next few weeks intensified the fellow-feeling I already had for Martin Luther, who suffered severe harassment for nailing his 95 theses to the door of Wittenberg's Castle Church.

While Boot Camp training disabled me from being able to write about the lives of Cassie and Lone and their momma and daddy up on Sharp's Ridge in north Knoxville, I imagined them obsessively.

In the barracks, I couldn't even concentrate enough to delve deeper into Albert Camus' *The Plague* that I had dipped into now and then on visits to Professor C. P. Lee's cabin high up on Chilhowie Mountain. Now, plagued by the military ambience, I was ready to renew the effort.

So, I walked down 26th Infantry Division Road to the Service Club and into the library where listening to Beethoven, Brahms, and Sibelius on earphones, I felt the aura of the Lawson McGhee Public Library in uptown Knoxville, and of the University of Tennessee music department building in an old mansion on Cumberland Avenue, and the aura of Boston Public Library in Copley Square, where in that setting earphone listening seemed high-toned.

★

"HUT, TEW, TREE, HOR, MADDEN KEEP IN STEP!"

Intrusions of Boot Camp activities into the realm of the imagination allowed only for creating short, compressed pieces, "epiphanies" I knew to call them, from James Joyce's creations of them in *A Portrait of the Artist as a Young Man*. In the Post Library, I wrote,

This is the era of swift progress.
Wheels turn more intricately,
with an efficiency to dazzle
even the somber intellect of Marx.
Conspiracy renders rank the air
and tons of hatred go up
in the smoke of secret experimentation —
not for life's lost cause
but for the winning hand of death,
whose very scythe science has honed,
until the face of death comes veiled
in man's own noxious smoke —
the exhaust fumes of civilization.

Where lies the country
Laughter can make whole,
Where tears be spent on trifles,
A place to lie down in peace and wonder
unafraid, where thoughts spring

not from fear and ignorance
but from passionate respect for beauty?

Even in UT's required ROTC sessions, a rebellious inclination that may have been congenital often rendered me unable to keep in step. Marching in the actual Army often inflicted pain that was not always excruciating but certainly unusually fatiguing, causing me to lag behind so often that the corporal who called cadence changed his tune to "Hut, tew, treet hor, Madden keep in step!"

Having failed to convince military doctors that the after-effect of the surgery—three incisions on each foot to transplant bones and to fuse the ones in my big toes to prevent their curling upward — so afflicted me that I should not do marches and that I could only be a liability in battle, I finally persuaded the doctor at least to affix metatarsal bars to the footpad part of the bottoms of my combat boots, like the ones I wore as a boy of 14, augmented back then with metal leg braces, enabling me to affect sometimes a limp in kinship with Lord Byron and with club-footed Philip Carey in W. Somerset Maugham's masterpiece *Of Human Bondage* and with Herbert Marshall, who lost a leg in World War I and who portrayed Maugham himself in the movie adaptation of his novel *The Razor's Edge.*

After I experienced a scary lapse of consciousness one afternoon, another door out of the Army possibly opened. Reporting the event, I tried but failed to con a new military doctor into thinking I was perhaps a little demented. His only response was a faintly benign smile.

I was one of five government issues on weekend leave strutting along Broad Street in Augusta with that aura of soldiers on the prowl for pretty girls, reminding me of the merchant seamen's swagger when ashore.

Alone, I explored the city landscape, crossed its bridges over the Savannah River.

The very idea of there being a historical Arsenal structure inside a city right near Augusta College set my imagination astir.

I wrote to Raven, "It's impossible to communicate with these fatheads with words of more than four letters and even those are mutilated, slurred, mouthed, mumbled, chopped, and hardly distinguishable. One has the weird feeling that mankind may be regressing to early linguistic stages in which the grunt is most expressive, but far from adequate to define relativity."

Dickie had served a couple of years in the army stockade in Hamburg, Germany for taking a camera out of supply where he worked to shoot his German girlfriend Eva to send her picture back home to us, and the camera had some sensitive military film already exposed in it. Eva's father had been a high-ranking Nazi officer. Dishonorably discharged, Dickie had brought Eva over here and gotten into some hometown trouble, and she'd returned to war-torn Berlin.

I'll never forget, as the saying goes, the time I eagerly walked through Mammy's house and out into the backyard to see Dickie after his six months cutting cotton under the gun in a Texas prison.

Dickie's face was darkly handsome, his voice quite fine.

Reclining in a hammock under a mimosa tree, he was smoking a cigar. To make him feel a part of his brother's life as young writer, I told him that his appearing at the screen door suddenly in a merchant seaman's uniform during the war years had inspired my romantic aspiration to go to sea. He tapped the long ash off his King Edward cigar, which seemed to cause a mimosa blossom to waft down, gave the hammock a swing, looked me in the eyes and said, "Why, Bud, I ain't never been in no Merchant Marine."

In my response to news that Dickie got caught passing a string of bad checks across Texas, I sermonized in a very long letter to him, a sort of "You must change your life" exhortation, to draw upon a line from Rainer Maria Rilke.

Reading a letter from Dickie, I heard Groucho Marx's voice talking to Chico. "Hi Bud, Just a few lines to let you know I received your letter and was glad to hear from you.

"No, I didn't resent the sermon you gave me as I guess I deserve it in a way — but I think I finally found what I wanted after so long a search. As you probably know I've married again and this time to a very sweet girl indeed. So, I know from here on out my life is cut out and whatever I do shall be for her.

"Say bud could you do your bud a great favor? I would appreciate it if you could send me some cash as I'm out of cigs and things, and I hate to ask Mother and them because they need what they have and as I'm not allowed to receive packages here it'll have to be a money order. So, if you could spare it please do —

"Well the place they have me sent is not so bad — it's just like the Army except of course no passes "ha" "ha" and say when can you come and see me?

"Well bud write me soon, as I like to hear from you. Your Bud, Dick, James Richard Madden 10650."

His response was "Thanks a lot for the dough. I can't begin to tell you how much a little comes in handy to a fellow in my position and might someday I can repay you some way."

One thing I like to remember about Dickie is that he always repaid me money he borrowed, and so did Daddy, but neither little brother John nor Phil, my own uncle, ever did.

★

THE FARM BOY WHO STOOD UP ON THE FIRING RANGE

Some people, some events made me feel as if I were re-reading one of my own short stories, or at least the kind of tale I was likely to write. The story of Private Rooks turned out to be one of those tales.

A regimental colonel and a major were conducting a general inspection.

The major, who looked like Errol Flynn, kept picking up the barrels of the M1's — (a piece of our "piece") — going over to the window, squinting up at the sun through the bores.

In the same casual way, the major came to me and squinted up mine, but the quiet, slow way he said, "Good God!" at the window behind my back made the shaved hairs prickle on my neck and my ears burn.

"Sergeant, gig this man for this dir-ty ri- fle. If he had fired it, it would have blown his face off. I'd like to look at that face."

I turned to face him, and he executed a near about-face, gave me a hard look, yelled at me to render the proper salute, and I rendered something that made him say again, "Good God!"

When he sidestepped over to Rooks, Rooks snapped to and rendered the proper salute.

"That's more like it."

Then he stepped back to me and backed off from me several separate times and shook his head and said to the colonel, "Sir, wouldn't you say to even court-martial something like that would be a crime?"

The colonel nodded like a big-time wholesaler looking at a crop he'd counted on buying but that a blight had hit overnight.

Then the major stepped over to Rooks again and looked at his rifle that I had stayed up late cleaning for him, neglecting my own, and said to Sergeant Harmon, "Sergeant, it might be a good idea if you sort of assigned Private Rooks to watch over Madden. Who's his squad leader?"'

"Private McClamrock, sir."

The major moved far down the line, and the tone of his voice talking to my old Knox High classmate Gene McClamrock seemed to blame him for my conduct.

As they passed by me, leaving the barracks, I heard the colonel say to Sergeant Harmon, "You better hold that helmet down with both hands. Looks to me like that Eagle's got some eggs to get back to."

They all laughed, good ol' boys, turning Sergeant Harmon's face pleasure pink, while I enjoyed the pride of knowing it was me who he had detailed to paint helmets for thirty other officers in the regiment, his own custom made with the eagle.

He ordered me to report for evening KP for failing properly to maintain government property, my filthy rifle.

After they told us that tomorrow, we would be crawling under live machine gun fire, Rooks moved around slow-motion telling everybody that his big brother had stood up on the machine-gun range and got killed, and that he was going to do the same thing.

The guys thought that was the funniest thing they'd ever heard, but Sergeant Harmon, who had come back from Korea a year ago and had seen a few things, called me in and told me to stick with Rooks-like skin on a snake. "He's in your care."

So that would be me crawling along beside him under fire.

Bright and early in the damned morning, my face down on the hard dirt and gravel, I tried to get my breath to push forward again, when somebody screamed.

Turning my head sideways, I looked up at Rooks standing like a giant within two feet of me, his head turned up to the sky that was clouding for rain, like he was trying to decide whether it would start to fall before or after dark and he didn't want to get caught in a rainstorm on the road home.

The machine guns stopped, and five NCOs rushed Rooks at the same time from different ends of the firing range just as I got a good hold on his legs and pulled him down, expecting to get an armful of blood. I was astonished that those live rounds had missed him.

As they dragged him off, each one repeatedly asking him why he did it,

Rooks muttered something about not believing they'd really use live bullets after the time his little brother got killed "for standing up on the rifle range." Well, as it turned out, they may as well have been blanks.

The moon, the stars, the sun, clouds, rain. The moon that had always illuminated my imagination hovered still over the military landscape. Lights out all over the post, I often stepped outside onto the second story stair landing to gaze at the stars, the names of which I preferred not to learn, wishing to regard them as nameless, mysterious in origin millions of years ago.

For days, the assault of the sun rendered the coming of clouds, even briefly, a blessing. The heat was so awful, we sweated so much, they gave us salt pills. I tried not to remember the heat in Manhattan when I walked the foot-scorching sidewalks bare-headed as a messenger for Nitie-Nite Pajamas.

Everybody prayed for rain because upcoming next week was practice on the grenade range.

But the fact was that it was a very hot day. In South Carolina, that seemed to be always the fact.

The smell of the heat in "the jungle," barracks, dayroom, and mess hall made the feeling and smell of my sweat-damped uniform seem the same. Sweat and scents applied to my armpits, hair, and face lured mosquitos to suck blood.

"Colder than a witch's tit, ain't it, muddafughah?"

"Hey, Tubbs!" sounded like Sergeant Turl's voice.

Among the grenade range pits, I saw no one. The round dome of a helmet liner, one I had painted myself several weeks ago, rose up out of a hole in the ground, and then came Sergeant Turl's eyes and his grin just before he sprang up from what was probably a kneeling position. Turl stood knee-deep where several grenades had burst. He saluted and fell backward, and all of us sitting under the linden trees, the branches swaying in the stout wind, laughed.

Lieutenant Crigger in the tower reached for the mike. "Sergeant Turl, you *will* stop that clowning around down there."

Turl got up and walked toward the pits, stumbling theatrically in the holes. When he got to one pit, he stepped off as if onto solid ground and when he started dropping, shot up his arm and pinched his nose as if into the deep end of a pool.

Lieutenant Crigger looked up at the sky, then started coughing and blowing into the mike to overcome the impulse to laugh at Turl's familiar antics.

Crouching behind him, grasping him under the armpits, Field First Sergeant Tubbs tried to help Turl up, until he realized Turl was playing rag doll and dropped him, too tired to contribute any physical exertion to Turl's compulsive horseplay. But when Turl, still holding his nose, tried to paddle to the surface of an imaginary deep pool, Tubbs could hardly get his breath for laughing.

In the weeks I had watched him, Turl clowned his way down to corporal and back up to Sergeant. His clowning started, I heard Sergeant Harmon tell First Sergeant Simms, the first day under fire in Korea. Turl got hysterical and couldn't stop laughing, and when they told him about it later, he latched onto it, doctors said, as a survival gimmick.

When he stood up, his face was straight. "Tubbs, you collect rare rocks?"

"Yeah." Tubbs was going along with it.

"Here." Turl flipped up Tubbs' breast pocket, crammed a piece of shrapnel in it, and with a swipe of his thumb pressed the flap down again. "Merry Christmas, one week early."

"On your feet, you dead beats!" Lieutenant Crigger in the tower yelled over the PA system.

Turl did a Groucho Marx walk — drop down, spring up — around the thick wall of sandbags that divided the pits.

We quick-timed it toward the waiting line, and the platoons that had already gone through scrambled for the trucks where only four of them would be able to sit in the cab with the driver.

"Hustle! Hustle!"

At the sound of Lieutenant Crigger's low, bored voice, the stragglers approaching the pit did a hop-skip and quickened their pace.

"All right, men, you heard and saw the demonstrators and the first platoon that survived the test. You should know exactly what to do. But if I really thought you did, I'd . . . " Lt. Crigger turned his head from the mike and I faintly heard him say to the NCO up in the tower with him, "Ringler, what's that truck up to?"

Turning my head, I saw a truck coming toward the training area out of the curving line of pine trees and stop beside the other trucks. A tall trainee got out, wearing shiny new, too-tight-fitting fatigues, the nameplate blank.

"Who is that man, Sergeant?"

Field First Sergeant Tubbs yelled up to the tower. "Regimental sent him over, sir. A hospital re-lease. They want him to qualify with this company.'"

"All right, Sergeant, fill up one of the lines with him. . . . Now, men, listen to me." Lieutenant Crigger shifted into the standing tall posture. "Every syllable. You are on the grenade range."

"Who dropped a rose?" Turl said, in a loud whisper.

"If you don't know that by now, you shouldn't be here. And if I were one of the cadres on the ground, I know damn well I wouldn't want you here." After one man in the first round had laughed, not knowing that to Lieutenant Crigger it was not funny, nobody laughed. "You see before you ten pits. In each pit is a cadre, holding a live grenade. You are one man in a line of ten other men. You have been told what line to stand in. Are you standing in it? Are you standing in it?"

"Yes, sir!" We all sounded off.

"I wants to bless you." He grimly imitated Sergeant Ringler, who sat on the wooden railing of the tower, his helmet liner resting on the broken ridge of his nose, his boots resting on the bottom slat. They say that last summer Ringler bitched his group through the grenade range in a stiff wind, and the tower keeled over, and he sprained his wrist. Now every chance he got, he was up in the tower, balanced on the rail, defying fate.

"First line, enter the pits!" Lieutenant Crigger suddenly slapped the railing. "Hustle! Hustle! The rest of you honchos stay, stay back of that wire. Sit!" I heard the men shoosh to the ground, cartridge belts clinking. "You men in the pits. Take a good look at your cadre. He's real, made of flesh and blood, not a dummy put there to scare you. He wants to go on living, even if you don't, so — Sergeant Turl!"

"Yes, sir?"

"Where's your man?"

Turl looked around. "I don't know, sir. Want me to try lost and found?"

"Field First!"

"He's coming, sir. Went to stack his rifle."

I kicked gently at the sanded incline and looked at the rise where the helmeted heads moved behind the protection bank under the wire. A head rose up above the wire and a leg cocked to step over, and who stepped over was Rooks.

I wanted to yell to the lieutenant that this man was from the psycho ward, inclined to behave dangerously, but as Rooks loped down to the pit, I realized that they must have cleared him for return to training, right where he left off, skipping a rerun of the machine-gun range probably. The day after he went to the hospital, the company was full of cute remarks about the kid who thought he was too good to crawl on his belly.

Stumbling into the pit next to mine, he didn't even grin at me. I looked him full in the face for some sign of recognition, guarantee of sanity, but Rooks' eyes didn't register me. "Hi, Rooks."

"Hi." Rooks blinked.

"I'm going to go over it once more, men!"

The voice from the tower startled Rooks, and he turned and shaded his eyes, looking up into the blistering sun, grinning, as Turl reached out and pulled Rooks into his pit.

"On the count of one, you will, as a body, as a body, take into your right hand the pineapple, the grenade, which the cadre on your right will hand you. If you are left-handed, you will simply execute the marvelous maneuver of shifting it to your left hand. On the count of two, you will hook your index finger in the pin ring, in the pin ring. On the count of three, on the count of three, you will pull the pin out. On the count of four, you will cock your hand back, and in your head, you will count to three. On the count of five, on the count of five, I said on the count of five, you will throw that grenade as far as you possibly can, and then, without any encouragement from arithmetic, you will crouch down behind the barrier. The sound you hear will be that of a live, a live grenade, exploding as a direct result of your having pulled the pin."

"When in doubt, bug out." Turl snickered. Rooks was quiet in there with him, his pit cheek-to-cheek with mine.

I wondered what had gotten into Lieutenant Crigger, who usually allowed no embroidery of instructions, even on the dry run, and decided that Turl's clowning, along with Sergeant Ringler's "I wants to bless you," had reached his manager-of-a-dry-goods-store soul.

Not looking, I imagined Rooks on the other side of the sandbagged walls, his eyes still on Lieutenant Crigger, his hand shading his eyes. I tensed.

"One more item. If, I say if, and goddam it, I mean if, one of you panics, I mean you jerked the pin out and it suddenly dawns on you that you've set loose what can blow your arm off and your eyeballs sky high, and you panic, you freeze, and you can't throw, drop it, drop it, and let the cadre pick it up. Not you. You stay perfectly rigid, and let the cadre pick it up. Two heads, four arms, four feet, and a live grenade on the floor of a four-by-four pit is a mistake. So, remember. You've pulled the pin, you can't throw, so you drop it."

"Come Saturday, short-timer,'" I heard Turl say to Rooks, "let's me and you get drunk as two waltzing piss ants."

"Now. Ready on the right? Ready on the left! Ready on the firing line! One."

My cadre handed me the grenade.

"Two!"

I hooked my finger in the pin ring.

"Three!'"

I pulled the pin.

"Four!"

"Goddamn you!" I heard Turl scream at Rooks.

I threw the grenade and dropped with my cadre behind the front wall.

"Five!"

"I'm sorry. He said, 'Drop it on four,'" I heard Rooks say.

"No!" Turl commanded. "Do not attempt to pick it up, Rooks! Rooks! Gotdamn!"

Turl fell on the grenade, rolled over, and pitched it up out of the pit, got up, and blessed Rooks out, jumping up and down, Rooks just standing there, rooted to the spot, looking at him out of no-seeing eyes as the grenade exploded.

In a dream that night, I listened to a voice saying, "I cannot *go* into the pit, I can only *be* there."

At noon the next day, I visited my buddy Rooks in the violent ward. I had never known a spark of violence out of him myself, but the Army seemed to like it that way.

Rooks' face looked exactly the same as when he dropped the grenade on the range.

We played Chinese checkers, best three out of five.

Loser in that game, I never saw Rooks ever again.

★

WHY I REFUSED TO SIGN SENATOR McCARTHY'S LOYALTY OATH

Mornings, it was world famous Military Police Private G. David Schine who often pointed us into the swamps for survival training, or into the woods for bayonet practice, and halted traffic as we emerged from training exercises deep in the boondocks, then waved our truck through the intersection. One morning, he halted a tank convoy so we could march to the firing range.

With delicious irony, I finally qualified as marksman.

We fell in on the parade ground in front of the dayroom door, where the Sergeant Major often delivered commands on the raised porch the size of Momma's flowered plastic apron. Between that porch and us, two small trees shuddered in the wind, awash in the shimmering of their thousands of flickering silver tongues, inspiring me to imagine Cassie seeing the same image from her sickbed through a dusty windowpane up on Sharp's Ridge in North Knoxville. My imagination often worked immediately on reality that way.

I was eager to gag down my chow, then race half the company for the soft chairs in the dayroom to watch G. David Schine in civvies on CBS national news testify in the Senate Army-McCarthy hearings, his dearest friend Roy Cohn and their mentor Wisconsin Republican Senator Joseph R. McCarthy witnessing.

"Now, Private Shine, I'm afraid I must ask you a question which . . . " twinkle-eyed Counselor Welch would start in on him.

The sun was in my eyes, but I squinted the Sergeant Major into focus as the Company Commander himself stepped out of the dayroom-mailroom and received the report from the Field First. "All present and accounted for, Surp!"

I was present but still, within weeks of the end of the basic training cycle, not fully accounted for.

Listening to the soothing, intimate whisper of the tiny new leaves, I heard little of what Lt. Moyers said, only phrases, "You will sign it . . . You *will* report to the orderly room. . . . You *will* render the proper salute . . . You *will*. . . ."

Sometimes I did. Often when I didn't, it was from mere inattentiveness. Sitting or walking in the blistering South Carolina sun, sometimes I was sitting in memory by one of the huge windows in the Lawson McGhee Library on Summit Hill in Knoxville, listening to Schoenberg's string sextet "Transfigured Night" while watching people on the walkway outside, pass in cars, come out of, go into buildings, Roberts Funeral Home or the Library Grill or the Induction Center, which happened to be nearby, as if they were one of several annexes to the Library. Even then, I often said aloud Lord Byron's line from *Childe Harold's Pilgrimage*, "I stood among them, but not of them, in a shroud of thoughts which were not their thoughts." Laved in waves of sunlight, the gray people of the streets were lovable and serene.

In formation or sitting at weapons demonstrations, I often withdrew into that sort of haze, listening to some inner music that neutralized everyone within my vision, or into a line of poetry, Stephen Spender's "I think continually of those who were truly great."

"Dismissed!"

The men broke not for the barracks immediately but for the porch, as though it was mail call.

Corporal Simms, the fat-assed, smart aleck company clerk, handed out sneer-stained sheets of paper to hands that reached up, hands made even more anonymous by the glazed boredom that passed over his eyes.

Field Sergeant Tubbs leaned against the wall on the tiny porch behind Simms, smoking, his eyes shut, taking the sun, his copy of James Jones' bulky *From Here to Eternity* crammed into his breast pocket, making him look like the best red-headed lay in the whorehouse were it not for the one amputated tit. The movie version with Burt Lancaster and Deborah Kerr had washed up on the beach of popular acclaim in 1953.

From *Here to Eternity* aroused my fear of the stockade, even before I came under the power of the military, and Ernest Borgnine beating Frank Sinatra in the stockade seemed to be routine behavior that aggravated my fear of ending up in the stockade myself. Memories of Dickie and John imprisoned inclined me to foresee myself in prison one of these days.

On the other side of the door, one foot on the porch, the other on the second step down, Sergeant Turl sprawled on the railing at the head of the wooden steps, his chin on his hands, his eyes sharpshooting each man as he received his sheet of paper, on target each time.

"One left." Simms favored me with an even more lethal sneer and a direct look. "Always said you wasn't right, Madden."

"It's to sign, not draw dirty pictures on." Sergeant Turl's smile was unattractive.

"I'm all drawed out for today."

Shutting his eyes, he shook his head as if he saw lucidly the lewd drawings I had made for him all day long in the rifle pits on the backs of scorecards and target sheets to keep from having to pull targets.

Along with five others on that detail who didn't work, but slept in the dark behind pillars in the pit, I was superfluous, but I wouldn't have been were it not for a facility that had people looking over my shoulder since grammar school and that won me an art scholarship, which I turned down, in high school, and kept me painting white-bordered blue bands around helmet-liners most of the rainy days when the rest of the company was lying in the mud simulating rifle range procedures.

If only I had had time, I could have made a fortune drawing my comrades' girlfriends from their wallet snapshots or drawing their own ugly mugs to send back to their sweethearts.

Walking to my barracks, dodging without looking at the clothesline that had swatted me just under my left eye one dark morning, leaving a blue scar that still shows up in mirrors, I scanned the document they had given each of us.

Executive Order 10450, issued by President Dwight D. Eisenhower, April 1953, expanded the Attorney General's list of subversive organizations, adding the proviso that members of the United States armed forces could not join or associate with any group on the list under threat of dishonorable discharge from military service.

As I read the list of un-American organizations, I felt hot chills on the back of my neck skitter down my back as I realized that, among the ones I fervently despised, I felt affinities for, sympathized with many of the "un-American organizations" listed, by name if not by intimate knowledge. For instance,

Abraham Lincoln Brigade
American Christian Nationalist Party

American National Socialist League
American Patriots, Inc.
American Peace Crusade
Jewish People's Fraternal Order
Labor Council for Black Rights
League for Common Sense
League of American Writers
Maritime Labor Committee to Defend Al Lannon
United Black and Allied Veterans of America
Walt Whitman School of Social Science, Newark, N. J.
Young Communist League
And more. . . .

"Have you ever been a member of or sympathized with the beliefs of any of the following organizations?" I felt that Attorney General Herbert Brownell, under the forceful influence of anti-communist crusader Senator Joseph McCarthy of Wisconsin, asked me, personally.

"Yes," I kept muttering.

"If not, sign below. . . ."

Staring at the empty space that called loudly for a signature, I felt that I was about to step into unknown regions of military quicksand.

"What we supposed to do, Sergeant?" I asked Platoon Sergeant Harmon.

"Madden, don't you ever listen?"

"The trees were blowing."

When he spoke, I tried hard to listen because his resonant voice always spoke very low, even when he called us all together for a talking-to, less loud even out on the parade ground where other platoon sergeants were cultivating sore throats. When we didn't fall out fast enough, he'd wait until we all got in formation, then say quietly, but darkly in the dawn darkness, "Again."

"Tell him, Squad Leader McClamrock."

With an exasperation that drew a little on my reputation for recalcitrance in Knox High where he had been a football hero and was in the same home-room with me, and drew a great deal on his experiences of me during the past weeks as barracks aide, McClamrock commanded, "You *will* take ten minutes to study the paper, then at exactly 1400, the orderly room will call each barracks in order to report to the orderly room. You *will* ask the company clerk to see the Sergeant Major, you *will* render the proper hand salute and request permission to see the Company Commander. Thus: 'Sir, Private Madden E-2 requests permission to see the Company Commander.' He will then grant you permission to see the Company Commander. You will knock at his door, he will admit you, you *will* march in, halt, smartly render the proper hand salute, and address the Company Commander in this manner: 'Sir, Private E-2 Madden reporting to the Company Commander, as ordered, sir.' You *will* then sign the oath in his presence, wait till he excuses you, come to attention, render a salute, do an about face, and bug the fuck out."

"Now let's see, I go to the orderly room. . ."

"Madden, you can go take a flying fuck at a rolling donut!" He did a precise about face and strutted off. Even so, I still sort of liked that good ol' boy.

Sitting on my bunk, I read the form again, much more carefully, even the little numbers and printers' signs. "Sympathize with. . . ." That's what got me. I'd never joined anything in my life so far and expected never to join anything during the rest of it, but I had lined up a long list of sympathies in twenty years.

And for the past three years in high school and college I had read sympathetically about Marx and Lenin, Communism, and socialism, and was at that time in the midst of reading Bernard Pares' *A History of Russia*.

And I had talked. Quite often, quite a lot.

I looked around. Nobody was reading. Everybody was talking — standing, sitting, leaning, lying on cots in the bright light that came through the windows, waiting to get called.

I decided to poll the masses. "Hey, Sneed, you read this thing?"

"Hell, it's a loyalty oath, ain't it?"

"*Did* you?"

"Who needs to *read* it? *I* ain't no commie."

"But you might sympathize with some organization. . ."

"Watch your mouth, Madden."

"How do you know, if you don't read it?"

"Just shove off, git me?"

"Hey, Dunlap, what do *you* think of the Klan?"

"How come?"

"Just wondered."

"I ain't *against* it. My Daddy's *in* it."

"Then you aren't gonna sign it?"

"Sign what?"

"The oath."

"Man, I kill your ass, you talk like 'at."

"But the Ku Klux Klan is listed here as a subversive, un-American organization, right along with the Communist Party."

"You lie, man."

"Read it."

"I don't *need* to read it. I'm a loyal mulifuckin' American, Madden! You gonna gimme the red ass if you don't get away from me!"

Feeling extracted from the group, I sat on my bunk, the sun in my lap, the form glaring up into my eyes.

The bitch box growled, somebody who understood spittle-spew with a dialect responded, and the others followed him, clomping down the stairs. Some of the last ones noticed, frowning, that I had not risen from my bunk.

"Attorney General's consolidated list includes also wartime German, Japanese, and Italian-influenced organizations as well as white nationalist groups."

I was not reading the form again and again to make up my mind, I had made my decision as soon as I just glanced at the form, ducking under the clothesline, because I wasn't going to lie. I just felt sad that all these guys would, without blinking, readily sign such a form, and it infuriated me that Senator McCarthy had been able directly or indirectly to bully the Attorney General and the Army into demanding that kind of oath on top of the simple oath I had readily taken orally the day I was inducted.

McClamrock was the first one back. Seeing me, knowing I hadn't gone down, he sort of walked around a couple of times in circles down at that end of the floor, then ambled over to Sergeant Harmon's room, knocked, and was invited in.

Harmon came out and looked down the polished floor at me.

"You. Madden." I barely heard his quiet voice.

"Sir?"

"What are you doing?"

"Sitting. Thinking."

"Don't you know you supposed to report to Company Commander?"

"Yes, sir. I'm waiting till the line goes down. Thought I'd go last." Of four platoons, 50 men each.

"Everybody's supposed to fall out by now. Move it." I got up and walked past him, nodding. "How come you want to be last?"

"It might take some time." I stopped halfway down the steps and looked up at him. I liked the way he stood, holding a cadre baton, wearing the helmet liner I had decorated with the eagle, I just didn't like what his stance expressed. In the background, McClamrock's face peered at me through Harmon's right arm, akimbo.

Outside, other guys on my floor sat on the concrete steps, having reported.

"What happens when you go in there?"

They told me, nonchalantly. It didn't mean anything to them one way or another.

"I wonder if everybody has to do this all over Camp Gordon."

They just looked at me.

Sitting on the curb, I looked down the long row of barracks on each side of the street, seven companies, islands isolated from each other. Our cadre walked around, wearing helmets I had painted.

Men had started watching me. When I saw the last man come out of the orderly room, I stood up, and it seemed that they, sprawled on the concrete stoop, had all begun to speculate about me.

In the four weeks, I had gotten involved in situations, confrontations, discussions that aroused their dormant imaginations. I had a handful of fairly good we're-in-the-Army-together type friends, mostly boys who had come down on the bus with me from Tennessee, no strong friendships though, so that when they scented that I was about to do something unconventional, they faded back into khaki.

Though they knew nothing yet about what I was going to do, I felt as though I was passing in review as I walked past the three front stoops of the barracks to the orderly room.

"Where you been, Madden?" When Corporal Simms spoke, the company clerk turned and looked at me, while the Sergeant Major pretended clumsily not to notice, waiting for me to do something wrong. The elaborate instructions former classmate McClamrock had given me blurred.

"They said I was supposed to come over here with this form."

"And what was the first thing you was supposed to do, soldier?" Sergeant Major didn't look up.

"Get your permission to see the Company Commander?"

"How?"

I came to attention, rendered the proper hand salute. "Sir, Private E-2 Madden requests permission to see the Company Commander."

"Permission granted. You may go in. Knock to be admitted."

I felt as silly as when I did something nearly as elaborate to get into Tommy Jackson's basement when I was nine, so I could belong to the Spy Smasher Gang, the result being that I got tongue-tied and ejected, then spent the rest of the summer in fear the Spy Smasher Gang would run me down and beat me up.

I knocked.

"Enter."

I entered, approached the Company Commander's desk, rendered the proper salute. "Sir, Private E-2 Madden requests permission to see the Company Commander."

His shoulders winced, but his eyes were on the green inkblot, where the other forms, signed, lay sprawled. "You say that to the Sergeant Major outside. Don't you know what you're supposed to say to *me*?"

"Sir, Private E-2 Madden reporting to the Company Commander as ordered."

"At ease. Sign the oath, then you're dismissed."

"What do you do if you can't sign it, sir?"

He looked up. "What's keeping you from signing it?"

"It'd be a lie, if I did."

"Look, Madden, sign the damned thing and save us all a lot of grief."

"I can't."

"You won't?"

"I won't, if I can't — I mean, sir, I'm not going to lie about something like that."

He willed a zone of silence. "Okay, dismissed."

Walking back to the barracks past the men, it seemed all four platoons had come out onto the concrete steps. But they couldn't have known yet.

Since grade school, I had persistently defended democratic rights, especially in school, even before I learned that the Constitution was the source, and I defended other rights I did not actually have from any source, but only thought I had or thought I should have had, and I had advocated moral and ethical rights that had no legal basis, and now in the army, I was always vaguely aware of that ambience of rights in my mind.

Hearing cries of "Fall out!" I joined the formation on the company parade ground for retreat.

To qualify for a place in chow line we were forced to leap up for the bar and do ten chin-ups. If we failed, we had to do ten Augusta pushups which you had to do until you looked like you were about to fuck the muddy puddle of water, then you touched the water, then you dropped into it. Your filthy fatigues had to be clean the next morning or your name went on the roster for KP duty. I dealt with calisthenics in the army the way I did all during public school, including high school, where when I was forced to run laps in the gym with the class, I peeled off out the door and down the steps, and at UT in mandatory ROTC, by faking, finessing, or dodging behind the government issue in front of me. And so forth.

Colson, squad leader in another platoon, did thirty chin-ups, while we waited until the chow line was empty inside and the cooks and mess-men came to the windows to watch. Colson made the other guys mad, but I liked the sight. Colson played the game so well they made him squad leader, but he hated the Army and everything about it. He rose above it, alone, on that high bar — a little guy, shorter than I am, and I'm just half an inch taller than most short fellows.

Colson was doing what I had sworn to myself I would do that cold night hitch-hiking back home from a weekend at my old professor C. P. Lee's cabin up on Chilhowee Mountain, where I had gone alone to think and had come down resolved to do my best. Colson, in a simpler, less self-conscious way, seemed to feel, though perhaps never thought, the same way.

Although I dislike most athletics, except running and swimming, solitary contests of an individual against his own best, I always managed to make the leap and haul my body up to the count of ten chin-ups.

But my fatigues that evening, as on many evenings before, were already dirty with soot from the huge stoves I had to clean. So, I found my name on the KP roster yet again, and the cook ordered me to ride the range — clean the black coal stoves and polish them. That was at about one o'clock, and when I got back to the barracks all lights were out, and orders were for every man to be in bed if he wasn't taking a leak or a crap.

So, I had no clean fatigues to put on that morning when we fell out for reveille. Consequently, with that logic that overleaps contingencies, I was put on report for being out of uniform — "uniform" meaning a clean, pressed suit of fatigues.

After supper, having missed David Schine's continuing TV testimony before the Senate Armed Services Committee, I reported yet again for punitive KP, was ordered to ride the range again, and rode it, deriving some satisfaction from the fact that I wore Raven's panties as silent protest, hoping the mess sergeant would release me in time for me to wash my fatigues before lights out.

A futile hope. All the barracks were dark as I, soot-stained, crossed the parade ground in the moonlight.

Passing a lone birch tree, I gave the white bark a glancing kiss like the little girl, hair-lipped Rosemary, in my first really literary story, "Seven Frozen Starlings," a kiss like the one I gave a birch tree in that last climb to C.P.'s Lee's cabin up on Chilhowee Mountain, a romantic gesture of empathy with something outside the world of human affairs.

I didn't sleep all night. Not because I anticipated KP again tomorrow night for appearing in the morning in greasy black fatigues — that was a clear and obvious gloom. What would happen to me for refusing to sign the loyalty oath was beyond my fertile imagination, absolutely a blank.

"All presen'coun'for, surp!" uttered Sergeant Harmon the next morning, with a salute like flicking a sweat bee off your brow, stiff-legged, ass-cheeks clenched, his back bowed backward.

"Fall out!"

But at chow, I found out that not everybody was all present and accounted for in the rest of the regiment.

Standing in the chow line, I saw the new company cook skipping jauntily over to the serving line. "I'm from Knoxville," he whispered, "and I know many people that tell tales about you, Maddog Madden."

After he turned to his pots and pans, I heard a gunshot-like sound but only faintly thought he might have fired at me and missed.

With a fake yawn, some wit behind me in line explained. "Some bolo done lost a toe."

Ten minutes or so later, an affable fellow sat down at our mess table, eager to tell us some shocking news. "This ol' boy begged for a pass to go see his wife, having a baby. Com'ny Commander refused permission — guy was a general fuck up anyway — so last night he gets this telegram that his wife's dead, baby too, killed her dropping it, so iss morning iss old boy 'ports Sergeant Major, says, 'Private E-2 whatever's name requests permission to see Com'ny Commander.' Permission granted, he knocks at the door, carrying his M1, see, in the proper military manner, and Company Commander says, 'Enter,' and he goes in, says, 'Private E-2 whatshisname reporting, sir,' rendering the proper salute, you know, and when the C.O. looks up, the M1's right on target. Blowed som'bitch head right off."

Made me sick-sad to listen. I felt sad for both the young recruit and the Company Commander, with some left over for all of us inhabitants of the military empire.

But what depressed me was the way the guy, a boy about my age, told it, like it was an anecdote he had heard the good ole boys at the service station tell.

But it was only half hour ago, in the next company down the street, though it seemed foreign in a way, because when you're living every minute of your life within the confines of a tiny piece of ground, like a penitentiary exercise yard, which you flee immediately after you're dismissed, the next area down the parade ground looks like a town on a map. So, in a way, it could have been a tale about two men in Columbia.

At formation after chow, the platoon sergeant reported. "All presen'coun'for, surp."

"Private Madden, step out!" I took two steps forward. "Platoon Leaders! Pull your men out!"

Standing at attention, I felt my platoon pulling away from me on the sand toward the swamps, where David Schine, MP, would halt them to let trucks pass, then permit them to lock-step march across.

"If I die on a Russian front, wrap me up in a Russian cunt. Sound off, hut, two, sound off, hut, two, three, four, hut, two, three-four! Madden, keep in step."

Sometimes I sang it, sometimes I didn't, sometimes I liked listening to the thumping rhythm of it, sometimes it gut-struck me.

Having felt each phase of the withdrawal, until they were all gone, I stood there in the middle of the company area, like a needle stuck at the end of a record, the wavy lines breast-stroking toward a red label.

"Madden!" Startled, I listened to the bitch-box over the dayroom door. "Report to Orderly Room, on the double!"

Quite possibly it was about my dirty fatigues. But I was already on report again. What more effective than a vicious circle — ride the range tonight and still have no chance to wash my other fatigues until the weekend.

"Private Madden reporting, as ordered, sir."

Sergeant Major didn't look up. "As you were, Private Madden."

"Would that I were, Sergeant."

Sick of this ritual — like delivering the same promo for Cas Walker's Grocery Stores when I was a teenage radio announcer — I turned and started reading the bulletin board.

"Where's Madden?" Company Commander's voice penetrated the plywood wall.

"Right here, sir. Report to Company Commander, Madden."

"Private E-2 Madden reporting to Company Commander as ordered, sir."

He didn't look up. I sneered.

"At ease."

Relaxing, feet apart, hands behind my back, I was not at ease.

"Sign it, Madden."

"I can't, sir."

"Why not? Everybody else signed it."

"If I were everybody else, sir, I'd have signed it, too."

"What does that mean?"

"Sir, I'd feel foolish explaining it even to me."

"You *act* foolish. You're the only one in my company, Madden. Maybe the only one in the regiment, even all Camp Gordon."

"I don't follow you, sir."

"Now what's *that* supposed to mean?"

Was he listening for disrespectful puns now?

"The point is that I cannot sign it, and that's got nothing to do with the company, the regiment, the post, the nation. . . . Sorry, sir, I'm just trying to stress." I didn't like tormenting him.

"Do you know what will happen to you, if you insist on doing this?"

"No, sir." Very true.

"I don't neither." He smiled. I smiled. He stopped smiling. What were we smiling about? "Wait outside."

"Thank you, sir." I rendered my best about face, possibly adequate, and stepped outside.

"Don't hang around in the orderly room, Madden." One of the clerks waved me out.

"Company Commander told me to wait here."

The Company Commander came out of his office. "Madden. In here."

Inside, I snapped to attention, saluted.

"Stop saluting me. Look, there's a space at the bottom for telling why, if you refuse to sign. Fill it in, and may God have mercy on your soul."

His wit scalded my cheeks.

He handed it across the desk. I took and looked at it. "It's only two little bitty spaces, sir."

"Madden, I have a short fuse, and you lit it last night." As I took the form from his hands, he commanded, "Dismissed."

Upstairs in the barracks, I was about to reach for a pen, when the bitch box screeched my name and the command to report to the office.

A jeep was parked out front.

"Get your ass in this jeep." The driver seemed to love saying that, one of his sayings.

At regimental headquarters, a young second lieutenant told me to find a seat and wait. I waited on a bench against the wall, a bare window behind me, in a room full of desks and doors, remembering the summer I was nineteen, only a year ago, when I was mail clerk and messenger for Nightie Nite Pajamas on the top floor of the Empire State Building.

One day, I arrived late because I was trying out for a part in a play, *Bernadine* by Mary Chase, directed by Guthrie McClintock, the husband of the venerated actress Katherine Cornell. My very nice boss fired me. As I was leaving, I turned in the doorway and shouted, thinking of the ladies who worked there under tough conditions, their sweating butts sticking to the plastic seats of their office chairs, "Workers of the world unite! You have nothing to lose but your chains!"

I had sat down beside a ragged copy of *Time.* Inside was a profile story on the ogre Wisconsin Republican Senator Joseph McCarthy, including a photograph of his dark, sinister visage — the sound of that phrase was apt — answering a reporter's questions at a news conference in Washington on February 26, 1954, wrapping one ankle around the chair leg, while twisting the other to tilt the chair on the floor that was scarred from many other, similar events. Reporters questioned the Senator about his controversy with Defense Secretary Charles Wilson and Army Secretary Robert Stevens.

Well aware that McCarthy blamed the Korean disaster on the State Department, I recalled that in 1950, in Wheeling, West Virginia, on Lincoln's one hundred and forty-first birthday, Senator McCarthy meant to catch my attention, among millions of other citizens, when, glowering at us radicals out of dark Mafia-looking eyes, he held up a list, and declared in his gutturally nasal, whiny voice, mildly equivalent to atomic radioactive fallout, "I have here in my hand a list of 205 members of the Communist Party, still working and shaping policy in the State Department." A quick, easy, successful way to get famous overnight, cameras rolling.

Publicly, McCarthy viciously attacked General Zwicker for not firing another general who honorably discharged a known communist. "You are not fit to wear that uniform, General."

Before I showed up in uniform, that episode and others that followed had caused President Eisenhower finally to break with McCarthy, declaring that "McCarthy is making the same plea of loyalty that Hitler made to the German people. . . . Using the pretense of fighting Communism."

From 1950 to 1954, McCarthyism had been on the march, making the cover of *Time* twice. He charged President Truman and us Democrats with being "soft on Communism." Truman declared that McCarthy was "the best asset the Kremlin can have."

McCarthy nailed Secretary of State Dean Acheson with a sledgehammer. After graduation, feeling unready to live and work in Manhattan, I had headed for Washington, DC in the summer of 1951. Walking past Secretary of State Dean Acheson's office every morning from my room on 23rd street, I was influenced by McCarthy's claim that the State Department was full of homosexuals and communists, implying that Acheson, "a pompous diplomat in a striped suit with a phony British accent," was one of them, igniting rumors. One morning, as I passed Secretary of State Dean Acheson on the sidewalk, his mustache twisted up, revealing a toothy smile, he intoned, "Hello, young man."

McCarthy and I invaded the US Army precincts in the same month, March 1954, when he went to war with the Secretary of the Army in public on TV accusing him of harboring communists. So, when I refused to sign the loyalty oath that he had bullied the Army into forcing upon me, the Army and I declared war on Senator McCarthy.

As I reminisced about Iva Lee and me meeting in secret places and imagined scenes between Cassie and Lone and Blackie almost simultaneously, a jeep pulled up, scattering gravel that pinged on the window and skittered over the outside of the wall, boots struck the steps sharply, the flat of a hand slapped open a swinging door. In strode a cocky little bird colonel's white mustache and pure white hair, red scalp tinting it from beneath. I enjoyed the way he walked, just like James Cagney. I smiled, as though we knew he was only acting and that everyone within eyeshot photographed him to show their grandchildren. His face was red, too, but that was temporary, and exploding into words as he zeroed in on an office door seemed to help, "Second one this month!" The door slammed on cue. Then I suspected that his showy routine was all for my sake alone, and that scared me.

A few minutes later, he came out, calmed down, but determined, and a Clark Gable-looking major and a shiny young second lieutenant were laughing, tied up in knots, the young one tighter.

"Private Madden." I followed the voice and felt someone shut the door behind me. The young second Lieutenant and I were alone in a small, bare office.

"Sit down, David."

I sat in a sturdy chair in the middle of the room, feeling just as if I were David and not Private E-2 Madden.

He began to do a walk such as important people do in the movies, hands behind his back, pursing his lips. I tried not to laugh, but beneath fear, I did enjoy his grade C performance and got in the mood for mine. I always enjoy people having a good time doing roles, especially when they're still shaping it up, trying it out. Years later he might perfect his own, as the Colonel had his.

"David, I'm Lt. Lambert of S-2 office, which in your case has to do with security clearances. You can help me do my job better if you would tell me a little bit about yourself — in your own words."

In my own words, I told him more than a little bit about myself, stressing that I aspired to publish a novel by the time I got out of the Army.

"Good, very good. That gives me a handle on you. Now, again, in your own words, tell me the reason why you have refused — declined — to sign the US Attorney General's loyalty oath, so to speak."

"It can be in my own words?" I had gone too far, but he was oblivious.

Giving him my reasons, I was beginning to feel a little like Captain Queeg complaining about the missing strawberries in *The Caine Mutiny Court Martial* — "Kay. About that loyalty oath." — when he said,

"Thank you, David. That's helpful. Now, the Colonel would appreciate it if you would write out a statement, for the record, as it were. Mind doing that?"

Mind? Not at all.

When I went into the army, Stephen Daedalus' credo in *A Portrait of the Artist as a Young Man* had long been my own. "I will not serve that in which I no longer believe, whether it call itself my home, my fatherland, or my church." Stephen aspired to the priesthood of high art, and so did I. From age 16, I had also honored James Joyce's *Ulysses* as the highest art of fiction.

It was a reluctant Christmas gift from Mammy, the year Momma gave me *The Portable Thomas Wolfe*, for my birthday, with a little less reluctance.

The driver took me back to the company area, and, as my mother liked to say, I said, "Just pour me out here."

In the barracks, silent as a tomb, astraddle my dark green footlocker, using the green pen with which Professor Daniel had armed me as I had set out to become a merchant seaman, I wrote, in green ink, in my very own words, a P. S. to the loyalty oath.

Sensing that grim Senator McCarthy was reading over my shoulder, I summoned up all of the tightest logic and the gravest, most high-toned, formal style of which I was capable, very much aware that this was a major moment in my intellectual life in the army.

"April 15, 1954

"To whom it may concern:

"I am making this statement of my own free will, not because I know that every man in the Army shall be investigated anyway, but because I wish to make known that which I have believed and now believe, so that I may not be reproached later for harboring in secret what I have said publicly or written in the past, and because I believe in intellectual honesty among my fellow men and despise intellectual hypocrisy and irresponsible allegiance to or belief in causes, ideals, religions, governments, etc.

"I know that this statement will be misinterpreted almost as freely as the Holy Bible, for as no man has ever been able to communicate to his fellow men in the exact manner he has wished, and knowing that no man can ever be sure enough of himself, since, like all beings, he is constantly changing in space and time, I cannot state exactly what I am, or was, or will be, nor can I expect those concerned to find in these words what cannot be more explicitly stated even by a superhuman intellect.

"I think it is said in the Declaration of Independence (one of the greatest documents ever written, the sentiments in which I respect very highly) that "All men are created equal." In some respects, this is true, but it is by no means altogether true. What they did not do in such an important declaration of belief cannot justly be expected from this humble statement.

"Thus, where there is interpretation, there is misinterpretation, and the two must be allowed to prevail side by side, since no man today can say exactly what he years ago meant and let stand unqualified.

"There is yet another reason why I wish to make a statement of my beliefs. I believe that the human rights provided for me and my fellow citizens by the Constitution are possibly coming to a time when their safekeeping will be endangered. To what extent I do not know. And I believe that never before in the known history of mankind, as I know it, has there ever been a set of laws more humanely and justly conceived and then executed than those incorporated in our Constitution. Believing that, I now hope not only to do my utmost as a citizen of this country to protect those rights, but more importantly, I now intend to exercise them within the confines of my needs as a thinking, searching individual. I am doing that now, and I do not think that any of my foregoing remarks will obviate or contradict my preceding professions.

"It is, then, also my right not only to express my beliefs, but to discover whether I may exercise the privileges that as a member of the U.S. Army it is my duty to defend. It is also my right as a natural born citizen to refuse to say anything, and if I did not think that my right to speak still prevails, I would refuse. There are people in this country who will not speak because they fear their right to do so is already in danger. I do not myself know the status of our rights, but by writing this I shall soon find out.

"I am and always have been a loyal citizen of these United States. But how can loyalty be the same thing for one man as it is for another? Each man in his own individual process of learning comes to know what kind of actions and beliefs are expected of him if he is to be loyal to his country.

"Though some of us are never actually taught loyalty, we nevertheless go through life loyal to our country, just as the child who didn't learn the alphabet moves through life speaking to us. Thus, what I learned about loyalty, from whatever source, as I grew up, is by no means the same for my brother or my buddy.

"As I know the meaning of loyalty, I have been loyal, and from what I am able to see of the future I will be loyal when I die, whether it be on a battlefield or of old age.

"But what of tomorrow? A crucially relevant question. I do not know what I will be doing seconds from now, much less 5, 10, or 20 years later. Today, is it not possible for me to pledge loyalty to the future unless I qualify such a pledge, and if I do, how can it be, by being more sincere, less binding, less truthful? Today I believe America to be the greatest country in the world, especially insofar as the morality of its methods in achieving its ends compared with other countries is concerned. But I have many disagreements with some of those methods and aims, as it is each American's right and as many Americans do exercise that right.

"On the other hand, Russia is perhaps one of the worst countries in the world as regards its methods. I cannot criticize Russia's aims, because I don't think anyone has defined them accurately enough; and the fact is that the end results are too far away to see. I cannot see why Russians should be hated any more now than they were when they were our allies — for then as in the past since 1921 or so their aims and methods were not dissimilar from those we denounce today.

"If in the future this country were to be taken over by leaders whose methods and aims repulsed me morally, I would possibly not be what some people would term, or what I now term, loyal.

"But of course, how can I or any man know what he would do? Any man who says he will be, he will do, he will think this or that 10 years later is either a fool or a person who has little sense of his own intellectual or moral existence.

"There are those who might say that I am forcing the issue, but to me this is a very real problem, which I don't feel I can solve by merely signing my name to a sheet of paper.

"If the day were ever to come when the United States would cease to command my respect, I believe I would possibly cease to be a citizen of the U.S. as it would exist at that particular point, and then work and fight for a restoration of the good that would have been lost and the establishment of even better good.

"Currently, I feel that I owe my mind and my actions to mankind for its advancement toward finer, more ideal endurance first and to my country later, but it seems that since this country now commands my highest respect, the two obligations go hand in hand.

"At this point, I wish to state that I, in the process of my intellectual, moral and spiritual growth, have in public, by word of mouth and in unpublished written matter, expressed sympathies with ideas or perhaps organizations possibly listed on the attached form.

"As I learn more each day, my ideas either change partially, completely, or are amplified and clarified, and my corresponding beliefs are either intensified or weakened. Thus, what I said or wrote at one point may not hold true now. I would venture to say that among those who know me, I may be known as a liberal, as a person with controversial ideas and beliefs. I will not attempt to list those ideas and beliefs because I feel they deserve and demand lengthy explanation.

"Also, it must be said that frequently in discussions with friends and acquaintances, I employ a certain method of argument, to wit, assuming an opposite view from my own to get or extract remarks from those with whom I am discussing a given issue or topic that they otherwise may not make.

"Some of my ideas and beliefs have reference to a time in the future when the conditions might be more conducive for a certain thing to occur. For instance, at one time I might believe that socialism — 'from each according to his ability to each according to his need" — is good, better than capitalism, but that the former would not work until the latter slowly evolves into it. That is not the same as saying, 'I believe communism should replace capitalism now.'

"I elaborate on all I have said because I think language can be a deadly weapon against him who uses it either improperly or among those who might turn it against him. Unfortunately, no language is accurate enough to defend me or any man in an ambiguous situation such as this.

"Now, I have also stated on the attached form that I have known individuals officially known as suspect. My relationships with them (several persons) are no more unique than those formed between them and my fellow students in the University. I have never been alone with them except in a scholastic respect. In my opinion, they are very moral, respectable individuals who have unfortunately been misinterpreted by irresponsible or uncomprehending individuals and thereby labeled subversive. In other words, I have had no more to do with them than have 500 other students. None of their ideas have adversely affected me. I refer to them merely because some of my ideas coincide with theirs and I do not wish to invite unnecessary trouble that might occur without regard to this statement.

"On the form, I referred to membership in the Seafarers International Union (SIU), which I understand has been labeled subversive by some other unions and other organizations and individuals; the record, however, will show that it opposed communist organizing of seamen. My relationship with the SIU has had to do with sailing on their ships to the sum of 9 months' sea time. I respect them for the fine work they are doing for seamen everywhere, raising wage and living standards, and protecting them from possible abuse from management.

"In conclusion, I wish to state that I have absolutely nothing to hide and feel I can withstand with positive results the most thorough investigation, should that be necessary. It is my desire to complete honorably my two-year enlistment term after which to return to civilian life, continuing to serve my country as a responsible citizen within the limits of my capacity.

"Pvt. E2 David Madden."

The bond I had for years felt with Martin Luther was tending toward ironclad. Luther resoundingly declared, perhaps on my behalf, "Here I stand. I can do no other."

I knew that the Army might judge me guilty by association. Before McCarthy's shadow fell upon the Army, thirteen "White Collar Radicals" at TVA working out of Knoxville and professors at UT and were investigated.

As I wrote that testimonial, I was aware that hovering around in my memory was the somber, rather cold, thin, deep dark-eyed instructor Samuel Haskell Baron, Russian born, who taught me in a newly added Russian history class the year before I took the traditional induction oath. That same year, 1953, while I was at sea bound for Hawai'i, my severe early American history teacher Charlotte Stevens accused Baron of being a communist and a Knoxville paper charged him with having communist leanings and associates.

I was closer to my philosophy teacher Howard Lee Parsons, a Presbyterian minister, who was extremely liberal and often attacked, defended by Professor Willis Moore, also my professor, who taught me to appreciate Charles Sanders Pierce's philosophy of pragmatism, despite my romantic sensibility, and Josiah Royce's philosophy of community, despite my elevation of the individual.

★

"MADDEN! TAKE OFF YOUR MASK, MADDEN!"

My private Jeep for the day, it seemed, was waiting out front. My driver took me back to battalion headquarters, where, having been told that Lt. Lambert was in conference, I left my handwritten statement on a clerk's desk.

"Where to now?"

My driver looked straight ahead, not responding.

In a clearing in the forest, the members of my company were not horsing around as usual. They were standing and lying all around a small white cement building under the trees, weeping.

A small door in the white building opened and Private Jacobs staggered out, his hands over his face as if ashamed of weeping, and Sergeant Turl came out behind him, his own eyes red.

"Fall in, Madden!"

I followed Sergeant Turl into the building, lit only by light coming through a window, making me feel as if I were in a very narrow, stinking cave.

Settling a gas mask over his face, he handed me one. "Put it on."

Suspecting that I was about to die, I snapped it on.

He threw a canister against the scorched wall, making a plume of smoke hiss out, as it spun on the floor.

The order he was giving me sounded something like, "Take off the mask!"

I shook my head and said "no" in a voice I hardly recognized as my own.

I finally understood when he yelled, "Madden! Take off your mask, mud-dafuggah! That's an order!"

Shaking my head negatively, I backed away from him, in the grip of my childhood memory of the gas chambers at Auschwitz and turned to dash out of the cement shack.

The masked man turned me around, pulling my mask off with a histrionic flourish.

Gas choked me, stung my eyes, and I dropped the mask.

"Put your fucking mask on, Madden!"

"What?"

In a panic, he grabbed me by the neck and hauled me out of the building.

"Why didn't you put your mask back on, you dumbass shit?"

"I thought you were going to kill me, Sergeant."

"Not today, lamebrain." He doubled over laughing, and my comrades and the other cadre joined in, wiping their eyes. "It's gas test day, you sawed off little nitwit."

"Oh." I wiped my eyes, nodding, a shit-eating grin on exhibit.

My terror of Auschwitz, the nuclear bombing of Hiroshima, and capital punishment had been profound since long ago, and pervaded my subconscious, rising often to consciousness. They were pervasive sources of emotional upheaval, imaginative elaboration, and intellectual scrutiny even when I was not conscious of them.

★

ON LEAVE AT THE VAN VACTORS

"Cassandra Singing," as a one and as a three-act play, was the play I worked on most steadily in the Army.

I had not written movie scripts, but in the post library, I wrote in green ink a draft of my television adaptation of Henry James' "Europe," a short story that I had read a month or so before I trudged into the Army era of my life. The task I set myself was to create live television equivalents for the psychological traumas of the British heroine who yearned to go to Europe. The characters reminded me of Chekhov's *Three Sisters*.

When I asked the Sergeant Major whether I could keep a rented typewriter in my footlocker, he said, "Hell no."

The next day, surprisingly, he told me that the Company Commander had told him to tell me that I could use the typewriter in his office at night to type my script. So, I did, but thought the C. O.'s generosity was odd.

I hoped to get help placing "Europe" from my friend and Raven's old lover, rather exotic-looking Bill Howell, of the Knoxville Howell Nursery family, a radio announcer on WKGN soon after I left who had a beautiful voice. As a TV director, Bill was best-known at that time for his work on *CBC Playhouse* and the cult favorite adventure series, *Johnny Chase: Secret Agent of Space*.

All my leaves were somewhat similar, so fragments from all of them gives an impression of the contrast between life in the army and the lively few days in the Knoxville milieu.

On leave in late March, I set out to find Daddy. An hour of searching the uptown streets of Knoxville did not turn up the sight of my elusive Daddy ambling along, drunk. I walked along the part of Central where the third-rate stores in very old buildings were, where Daddy often stepped inside to buy a bag of peanuts, and there he was in the doorway about to step down on the sidewalk, not seeing me.

I followed him and he left a trail of peanut hulls that he casually dropped, not tossed, loving fresh peanuts the way I remembered. My coming up beside him caused him to glance over at me, and he handed me a peanut in a shell.

In Lawson McGhee Public library, I took a notion to reach back and list the books I had read before the Army reached out and took hold of me. They were stored in barrels with my nomad Momma's stuff in the garage that Mammy's new husband Cap had built for his new lime-colored Lincoln Mercury Zephyr, which turned out not to fit among all the boxes and barrels and pitiful furniture. As chapters in my literary life, the effect of those books also was active during my time in the Army, mostly in my unconscious, affecting my moods, attitudes, behavior, and my new reading and my new writing.

Having visited my family first, I showed up at the threshold of the Van Vactors' bedewed in a light summer shower.

Assembled, Raven, Ginger, Dave, Davie, Walton, Brendan, and Vera, tuning up, were like the voices of the instruments for overtures to an opera, "Carmen," "The Magic Flute," "Romeo and Juliet," suddenly bursting into performance.

We brought up, took on, covered, many subjects, personal and public, sometimes sex and intellectual utterance in the same sentence.

"If you've heard of the Private Schine controversy, you may be interested in the analogy between my case and his (oh, pardon me, Ginger — his case and mine). I knew that Gerard David Schine, better known as G. David Schine or David Schine, heir to a hotel chain fortune, became a central figure in the Army-McCarthy hearings in his role as the chief consultant to the Senate Permanent Subcommittee on Investigations.

"I reckon you all saw the *Time* magazine cover that shows Roy Cohn's pouched mouth open at a mike, his dear bosom lawyer friend Schine just behind, almost touching him. That both Schine and Cohn were Jewish was basically interesting because, as you know I have become more and more interested in Jews, in many ways.

"The Army accused Cohn, McCarthy's main darling, of trying with threats to get special treatment for Private David Schine, also McCarthy's aide, at Camp Gordon. If I don't run into him off duty, I'm inclined to go looking for him.

"Couldn't you become an officer and outrank the poor little rich guy?" Ginger sometimes rears back when she nails a point with a smile, arms crossed.

"Though I'm qualified for Officer Candidate School, I *ain't* gonna go. So far, what training I can't back out of, I do as well if not better than most. I just hope I can refrain from slapping the piss out of a few of those smart-ass, psychopathic sergeants, and corporals. But sometimes I become aware that I'm acting like a soldier, and it scares me stiff."

I felt an urge to snap Dave, standing before the fireplace, out of his abstract stare. "Dave, I hope the symphony's next performance is as fine as the one I saw last night. By the way, I have not forgotten that you offered to commission another libretto from me."

"Well, David, don't forget, it's an open invitation."

"Raven, you still listen to the exotic singer Yuma Sumac?"

"Not much these days, but I've always cherished your telling me she looks like me."

"And your perfect imitation of her deep, exotic voice."

"The voice of the Incas," said Ginger, her eyes fixed upon me across the room. "David, I'll never forget the look on Eleanor Stieber's face the time you showed up on the landing of the stairs in your jock shorts."

"When I baby-sat Davie, I always used to think a midnight noise downstairs meant a possible break-in."

"We were all bunched at the bottom of the stairs loudly saying goodnight, when — "

A time or two when descending the crimson carpeted stairs, I remembered that night. I was sleeping in Raven's twin bed, Raven having gone off to New York, after baby-sitting young Davie, when loud voices and laughter woke me and I went downstairs in my jock shorts and into the arms of one of the world's most famous opera singers, Eleanor Stieber, who had sung Samuel Barber's musical setting of James Agee's prose poem "Knoxville: 1915" that very night, conducted by her friend Dave Van Vactor. She said Dave and Ginger had told her about me and she was eager to hug me. And I was happy she hugged me, tight, memorably.

I had heard and read about Knoxville born and raised James Agee for years, especially for that lyrical prose poem about himself as a child lying on a quilt on the grass at twilight. I was often achingly nostalgic myself for the evenings when my family and I lay on quilts on the grass on too-hot summer nights in Knoxville in the front yard, high hedges framing us, protecting us from the scrutiny of neighbors who knew we were a suicide family or had heard the other story that a co-worker had shot Gran'paw Charlie.

I finally got around to reading my hometown fellow poet-novelist-high grade journalist James Agee's novella *The Morning Watch* when it showed up in my copy of *Thirteen Great Stories by 13 Master Storytellers*, a ragged Dell paperback. I admired Agee's hyper-lyrical style, and as an agnostic, I identified with his adolescent protagonist's agonized doubts about Christianity.

Brendan had been listening to me tell, acting all the parts, the story of "Cassandra Singing."

"David, I know you read almost nothing before *God's Little Acre*. But I don't think you ever told me what inspired you to write stories?"

"Movies." I saw an expression of remembering on Vera's face. "From about age five to fourteen, I idolized the gods and goddesses of the Silver Screen, Hedy Lamarr, Vivien Leigh, Eleanor Powell," I had told Vera on one of our walks at twilight through a black neighborhood to Knoxville College for Negroes to see foreign movies in a series they offered. "Long, long before I read that first novel, Brendan, the mainline inspiration to my creative and intellectual activity had been movies. From childhood on, movies had affected my sensibility more powerfully than any other art. My affinity for images, voices, music were all expressed in movies, while radio conveyed images, with voices and music that also enhanced the effects of movies."

The soaringly melodious background music in the movie *The Outlaw*, derived from Tchaikovsky's *Sixth Symphony*, enhanced by Freddie Martin's rendition "Now and Forever," became one of my great romantic favorites on a visceral level, enhanced further, differently, by the censorship of the movie, released in 1941, re-released not until 1946 when I was thirteen. The scene in which Billy the Kid seemed to be dying and Jane Russell crawled in the bed to keep him warm was the target of the censorship.

Russell's sexual appeal and pretty-faced Beutel's Billy the Kid were alluring in the extreme. But Billy the Kid and Jesse James had a place in my crowded pantheon of dark heroes because of movies about them, starring Robert Taylor and Tyrone Power.

"Movies inspired my first literary actions, 'Across the Snow,' my retelling of the movie versions of Jack London's *Call of the Wild*, starring Clark Gable, and 'Blue Waters,' my retelling of *The Spanish Main*, starring Maureen O'Hara and Paul Henreid. I asked Peggy Dean, who was taller than I and was very briefly my girlfriend, to read "Blue Waters," and she lost the damned thing. Her father, who was a cop, shot himself.

"Under the spell of the pace and dialog and music of the movies, I wrote many scenarios before I ever read a book, rooting my storytelling compulsion in the visual."

Raven raised her left eyebrow. "I'd much rather act on the stage than on celluloid."

Ignoring Raven, I kept my blue-eyed stare upon Vera. "I always associated books and their movie adaptations with each other, the voices and printed names of the trailers dramatizing the fame of the authors as book jackets did."

A knowing nod was often Vera's most effective response.

"I never cared that music was the one art I had no ability to create. Sorry, Dave. It's just that I enjoyed knowing it was mysteriously above me. That different instruments played different notes simultaneously in a composition impressed me."

I had explored all classical music, while enjoying some of each of the other types, especially folk songs.

My love of classical music took hold when I was a child while listening every week to the background music of the old Saturday serials, that we called chapter plays, especially Mendelsohn's' "Hebrides" or "Fingal's Cave" Overture and listening on the radio to Rossini's "William Tell Overture" to the opening of "The Lone Ranger" was thrilling every time.

I liked overhearing movie background music when I was backstage in the usher's dressing room. Warner Bros. Max Steiner, especially for Bogart movies. *Casablanca, The Big Sleep*, and *Passage to Marseille* impressed me most.

I first heard "Rhapsody in Blue" when Alan Alda's daddy Robert Alda played it in the movie *Rhapsody in Blue*. And the first time I really heard "Night and Day" was when Cary Grant as Cole Porter played it in the movie by that name.

To move onto another subject, Brendan asserted the superiority of his general knowledge over my own. "It was Socrates who famously declared that 'the unexamined life is not worth living.'"

My response caught him off guard. "Greater than that is Madden's 'the unimagined life is not worth living.'"

"The movie version having impressed me, I recorded Hemingway's short story 'The Killers' on a 78rpm disc next door to Iva Lee's house — her neighbor had a recording outfit — changing my voice for the narration and each of the six characters."

I was always flattered when Ginger wanted to know more. "So do you include Hemingway in your pantheon of literary heroes?"

"In *A Farewell to Arms* Ernest Hemingway's economical, impressionistic style more than the subject of war attracted me and taught me. I, too, would like to make 'a separate peace.'"

"I'll take *Kiss Me Deadly* by Mickey Spillane." Walton gulped the last of his martini down to the speared olive.

"*Passage to India* by E. M. Forster enhanced the long-sustained lure of exotic India that I saw in many movies, especially *Black Narcissus* and *The Rains Came*."

I loved the way Ginger turned quickly to Dave and leaned forward. "Instead of doing Spain all over again, Dave, let's consider finally going to India."

"They don't guarantee you'll make it back." Long-legged Walton had slouched back in the straight chair again. "So, otherwise, David, what in the world are you doing in the Army?"

"On his deathbed, Buddha said to his followers, 'Go and seek thine own salvation with diligence,' which is what I've been doing."

Walton sat up straight and delivered: "An idea in mind, such as Hegel's thesis-antithesis-synthesis, and Jean Paul Sartre's exquisitely succinct, 'Existence precedes essence,' is as tangible as an erection in hand."

Dave chuckled a little, Ginger and Raven soared into laughter, Vera curled an eyebrow, Brenden lidded his eyes and shook his head, Davie piped up with, "No shit?" and I wrote down what Walton had said on the envelope of the most recent rejection slip from the *Paris Review*.

Then, I set out to share with Walton my excitement on reading about differences between Mahayana and Hinayana Buddhism.

With Harvard hauteur, he informed me that I had misread my source.

His arrogance that night became a fixed revision of my concept of his character. But generally, I continued to enjoy the feeling of awe he aroused in me.

"I also read *The Bhagavad-Gita, The Song of God*, written 25 centuries ago, translated by Swami Prabhavananda and Christopher Isherwood, with Aldous Huxley's introduction. The gospel of Hinduism seemed another way to supplant Christianity. I struggled to identify somehow with Arjuna, the sleepless, bow and arrow warrior in his bronze chariot about to slaughter some folks, and with Krishna's wise advice to him. And I failed fully to embrace 'desirelessness,' renunciation of what I craved in this world — other contradictory ideas, for one thing."

Odd that Isherwood, the author of *Goodbye to Berlin*, on which John Van Druten based the play I *Am a Camera*, starring Julie Harris that I saw in 1951 soon after pure-damn adoring her as Frankie in Carson McCullers' *The Member of the Wedding* and accosting her at the stage door of the Ethel Barrymore Theater to vow that I would someday write a play for her, should be leaping back to circa fourth century before Christ to guide me via his translation into "an exposition of Vedanta philosophy." The Gita is part of an epic poem, prophetic, a gospel, in the core of which lies four doctrines: the phenomenal world of matter and of individualized consciousness . . . is the manifestation of a Divine Ground, the existence of which we can realize "by a direct intuition." Henri Bergson's *Introduction to Metaphysics* came to mind. "Man possesses a double nature, a phenomenal ego and an eternal Self. . . . Man's life on earth has only one end and purpose: to identify himself with his eternal Self and so to come to intuitive knowledge of the Divine Ground."

To achieve that goal, one must practice self-abnegation and charity. Mahayana Buddhism regards the divine Ground as Mind or the Pure Light of the Void. I struggled with the first part because of its Old Testament fixation on battle, on Arjuna the warrior, and with the second part because its simplicity was like slipping on ice by twilight.

"Vera, I read the Bhagavod-Gita in an upstairs room in a Tourist Home that time I searched for you in Union, South Carolina when you were visiting your aunt. Inspired, I wrote a poem about it."

Khrisna's exhortations clear the cobwebs
of Christ's imperfections here manifest
in all aspects of human behavior I behold.
My understanding of society, of life,
Flows dark, subterranean here in the sunlight
Where innocent shapes move on Sunday walks.
These things I see men call the good, simple things.
There seems nothing amiss here, no cause
For shame, guilt, the philosophers' accusations.
One might call these moments true reality
For the time being, and thoughts of known
contradictions quite unnecessary.
But my mere sense-presence here in a peaceful town
Is no more real than my thoughts, which turn
To famine in India, death in Siberia, war in China.

The juxtaposition of *The Bhagavad-Gita* to *The Lonely Crowd* by David Riesman, Nathan Glaser, and Reuel Denny was exhilarating, as if I breathed a crystalline mountain air. Those three fellows taught me to consider individuals as inner-directed, outer-directed, or other-directed.

"David, what did you think of the Andre Segovia record I lent you?"

"Andre Segovia surprised me, Dave, playing Bach on a guitar, the instrument I always thought was the province of Hank Williams and such fellows. After I made a drawing of a fellow seaman playing the Stella guitar that I had bought in Galveston but never learned to play a decent note on, he gave me his own recording of Segovia.

"Walton, have you ever listened to Virgil Thomson's *The Mother of Us All* and *Four Saints in Three Acts*, words by Gertrude Stein? I've never heard anything like it, distinctly different. I met Thomson one night here. Both he and Dave were friends with Leonard Bernstein. By the way."

"Sure, I was present, age five, when my father dragooned the whole family to a performance. In Tokyo he was General McArthur's assistant, you know."

"Dave, I want you to know that I listen to classical music whenever and wherever I can. It suffuses my creative consciousness as I work on 'Cassandra Singing,' especially Ravel's *Introduction and Allegro*. That's ironic given that Cassie sings folk songs along with what she makes up and has little access to classical music.

"Last week, listening to Stravinsky's *Rite of Spring*, I was inspired to describe my life and art using musical terms: largo, bitonality, allegretto, fugue, counterpoint, dominant chord, double stop, sonata, thematic transformation, tone, 12-bar blues."

Dave broke his pose before the fireplace to turn and dust his cigarette into the embers, then turned to all of us. "Stravinsky has affected us all."

"Almost out of loyalty to classical composers, I detest country music even though I put both kinds out 'on the big wind,' my term for radio, when I was a disc jockey. Juke boxes and disc jockeys, including myself, created a background to my experiences with Jenny and Iva Lee."

As a sort of celestial master of ceremonies, silently, and aloud when alone, I often intoned the names of composers and compositions. And the nationalities of the composers had always affected my responses to the music, creating a symphony of auras of France, Germany, Italy, Russia, Norway, Sweden.

With Dave's guidance, and chosen on my own, composers most powerfully affected my changing temperament.

"I could tell a story associated with my life for each piece of music, but I must restrain myself, except to say that I play my favorites in the Service Club's listening room."

I used to look into Dave's study, open to the living room, late at night, babysitting Davie, while Ginger was with him when he was conducting a concert. I listened to many compositions for the first time on his tape-recorder and his turntable.

Dave made a point of playing for me *Concerto for The Left-Hand* because Maurice Ravel wrote it for Paul Wittgenstein, a concert pianist who'd lost his right arm in WWI. I listened to Paul Hindemith's *Mathis der Maler*. And Dmitri Shostakovich's most famous work, the "Fifth Symphony."

Ginger turned to me, curious. "David, how did you come to take such an interest at such a young age in local and world events?"

"My knowledge and attitude about major world events came most powerfully to my consciousness through images, *Life* and *Time* photographs, in the newspapers I carried every afternoon and too early on Sunday, movie theater newsreels, and images that radio newscasts conjured up."

"You talk about your family and friends and neighborhood places more often than anyone I know. What — ?

"What Ernest Hemingway said about places — 'and finally only the names of places had dignity' — describes somewhat my own feelings. Returning to Knoxville from life in New York, at sea, in the Army, I usually made pilgrimages to places that a kind of sacred nostalgia keeps vibrantly alive, obsessive, what I sometimes called 'a terrible nostalgia.'"

Hoping to make a direct connection with Dave's own creative process, I caught him as he turned from poking the logs in the elegant fireplace. "Dave, I've adapted to my fiction a technique from Prokofiev's music for Eisenstein's epic movie *Ivan the Terrible*. He composed it in consultation with Sergei Eisenstein in an effort to make the sound follow the eye as it takes in the images. I think movies are closer to poetry than to stage plays."

"Sorry, David. I don't get it." Dave flicked the ash off his cigarette into the fireplace.

The next day, nostalgic, I visited some of the places I've always loved most. The Bijou Theater, the Market House, of course, but even the paper routes I carried from age 9 to 17, the Sharp's Ridge, including the home of my first fervent love Jonnie Lou Gilmer, whose daddy, a postman, was a drinking partner of my daddy, along with Tennessee Williams' daddy. And Daddy's mistress Mary's house was on one of my routes in Lincoln Park.

Flipping through the 1953 Bell telephone book for the address of the Chapman Highway Drive-In, I was shocked to discover about eight pages announcing the existence of about 200 churches in Knoxville, a city of around 130,000, in which about 25 theaters threw moving pictures on screens after church lets out. It is a chilling thought, that at about 12 o'clock each Sunday some 40,000 people rose with a great rustle to intone the Lord's Prayer in strict unison.

Even cemeteries lured me in. Impressively stone gated and iron fenced Old Gray Cemetery embraced the grave of reconstruction governor William "Parson" Brownlow, behind whose great stone monument Daddy found the bootleg whiskey he had called for on the telephone.

The impact of my many memories in numerous movie theaters in Knoxville, Washington, DC, New York, and Boston had a powerful effect upon my writing. I enjoyed awareness of the ring of about 20 neighborhood movie theaters in Knoxville, among them nine drive-in theaters, at the four points of the compass, orbiting, embracing the city, five uptown theaters the reeling heart of it.

After getting off work at the Bijou, I sometimes went to Roxy's 3 features and burlesque show. I saw the harridan who managed it bearing down upon me in the flickering darkness. "The Roxy prohibits playing pocket pool during the burlesque."

"So, after the strip tease pocket pool is allowed?"

In the Tennessee, the jewel theater, Iva Lee delved under her coat in my lap, rousing the nosy old lady down the row to take offense.

A new one was The Tower, which appealed to my love of towers. I turned the old tower at the dismantled water plant into my own sanctuary below my house on the bluff across from the East Tennessee Packing House that my namesake David Madden owned, where the cries of cows being slaughtered invaded my dreams.

Momma sold tickets at the short-lived Lake Theater set in a triangle, woods at the top, railroad on the right, Sevier Avenue on the left, irony overall, in that Daddy's big sister's family used to live in a house on that site when Momma was sick, and Aunt Kathleen's husband threw John and me out for adding to the noise Bobbie and Betty Anne always made when he needed sleep after working nightshift at David Madden's Packing House down the street.

My excessive love of Pecan Logs attacked me in the Broadway Theater so severely, the lady manager called Mammy and Cap came to get me and the man in the next apartment carried me into Momma's bed, where she administered my first and final enema.

Dickie's favorite place for picking up girls, mostly underage briar jumpers from Sevierville and Greenup, was the raunchiest theater in Market Square, the Crystal.

Dickie's maybe wife Flora stayed with us on Atlantic and on Henegar Street and danced in the front yard and showed her extraordinarily hairy vagina as I walked past where she lay propped up in bed reading the Sunday funny papers in the bed across from Momma's.

John's favorite movie was Disney's sentimental *Song of the South* that combined live actors and animated characters, showing an ideal South, in which Negroes were content.

Dickie may never have mentioned the title of a movie to me.

Momma went to the movies alone, usually, to take a load off her feet.

Mammy and Cap went very seldom, keeping the television on "from here to eternity," Momma said, when she visited or settled in for a while now and then, between jobs in Nashville and Chattanooga or between one house or apartment and a new one.

Reading their letters, I often turned from listening attentively to Momma's energetic, sometimes merry voice to Dickie's resonant, laconic voice.

"Well, how's the Army treating you? I will say I feel for you for being in such a hellhole. Almost went to Fort Jackson myself once — but conned them out of it.

"I'm learning to weave chairs and couches of all things — but it pays pretty good outside I hear. So, when I get out . . .

"Been reading quite a bit. Such as novels of Thomas Wolfe that I can find and am on one by e. e. Cummings — very well written. Suggest you get 'The Enormous Room.'

"Well David mom said you'd like to read one of my poems so I'll enclose one.

HURRICANE
Man builds himself proud palaces
that rise ornate with curves
and silver toned bells;
he churns the water with a thousand spells.
He hurls his mirage far across the sky
with patient gesture and glib surmise.
He searches Nature to her farthest cells,
then like Poseidon among his shells,
he pats his belly and contended sighs.
And then a finger reaching from the sea
hurls his palaces to casual dust,
scatters the suns of many a golden year
and dresses his glory in age old rust
while he, like Adam, cowers,
a refugee stripped of his Eden,
naked and cold with fear.

I sensed the hand of the con man in those lines.

"What do you think about John being on the radio? You wouldn't even think it, would you. I wrote and told him a few pointers and said I'd bet he had lots of gal friends. And he wrote and said he had none. What the "H" is the matter with that guy anyway?

"Say by the way, I'd like to meet this girl friend of your girl. Does she live in Knoxville — and what does she look like? Write and tell me."

Dickie exhibited to the world either a half-hearted sneer about things generally or a distinct leer about sex.

"Well, that's it for now, must go now, movie night in the old hell hole. Write me real soon as I enjoy your letters.

"I guess its Eva again — that girl puzzles me no end. First, she wants to come back, and now another 'Dear John' tonite. Oh well. I've always been unlucky when I pick wifes. Such is life in the Far East as the saying goes.

"Say bud you said something in your last letter about your gal Vera having a very cute trick for a friend — sure sounds interesting — maybe you ought to write her and give me a big build up — for when I get out. Couldn't write her because married no can do. Which by the way you wouldn't have to tell her — guess old gay blade — Madden — will go on the rampage again. Of course I can promise you I wouldn't do anything rash — with anyone you put me onto. You know me — two or three weeks build up and then to the bed, "da" "da". Well David write me real soon and let me know what's up — poem next time. Your Bud, Dick."

He gave the impression of being a very lecherous boy and man, but one day he shocked me by confessing that "I never did and never will make love to a woman without marrying her first."

Sometimes within days after meeting her.

"Well old buddy write me soon and often.

The best to you from your Bud, Dick."

★

THE JEW WHO BOXED HIS TORMENTOR

Seemingly as isolated as Devil's Island, even from the six other companies on our street, even from the next one over, I got news now and then from far away Israel.

Having been a fervent supporter of Israel since carrying the Knoxville *News-Sentinel* that revealed photographs of the liberated concentration camps and told the ongoing story of the Arab-Israeli Civil War, I had profoundly sympathized with the Jews. So, I was infuriated when I read that Jordanian soldiers stationed at the walls of the old city of Jerusalem had begun to snipe at residents of the city, killing a young Israeli woman near the Jaffa Gate.

In Philosophy Club at UT, I had often argued the injustice of the Rosenberg's sentence. Stark in my consciousness was the case of Julius and Ethel Rosenberg, communists convicted of espionage for the Russians, often in the news. The Rosenbergs were executed — partly because they were Jews, I was convinced.

The year before, when I was a merchant seaman at sea in-route to Antofagasta, Chile, waiting on the dock for the launch back to the oil tanker, I was shocked to see photogravure sepia-toned photographs of their corpses in their coffins in an old newspaper lying on the dock in Tal Tal, which thrived on the sale as fertilizer of white excrement of seabirds and bats scraped off the rocks.

Now that the Rosenberg controversy was a dead issue, I felt a compulsion to know the facts. I had written to Washington requesting a copy of the Rosenberg Trial that ended in their execution as spies for the Soviet Union. November 3, the Justice Department responded in the negative. So, I appealed on November 18 with a card to the Court of Appeals. The Government Printing Office responded quite quickly to my request for a transcript of their trial.

When I opened the thick, brown-covered government document, a few fellows at the tail end of the chow line, asked, "What you reading *now*, Madden?"

When I said, "Transcript of the Rosenberg trial," in a voice that assumed they knew who the Rosenbergs were, since a fair number in the company had had a few years of college and didn't want to betray their ignorance, they shut up abruptly.

I was always eager to follow any news about the fate of the Jews everywhere. March 17, 1954, Arabs boarded an Israeli passenger bus in the middle of the day and massacred eleven and injured two passengers.

After chow, I asked my Jewish comrade Jacobs whether he'd heard about the bus attack.

"Of course."

Jacob's ugliness by conventional standards, the huge hook nose embedded in cheeks severe acne embossed, reminded me of the *L. P. St. Clair's* scapegoat, Jack Torri, self-exiled from Argentina who the men tormented by calling him Peron, his deadly enemy, all during my last trip in the Merchant Marine, to Aruba, Panama, and Chile. I saw contrasting parallels between *my* function in the Army also for others — taking risks on behalf of all — and Jack's function as scapegoat for heavily discontented men at sea. I wondered whether Jacobs' trouble with some of the men just for being ugly, Jewish, and aloof and my rebellious conduct helped our comrades defuse their own explosive dissatisfactions.

I had seen a few guys from the hiring hall and from the old ship a few weeks after that last voyage and they had told me that when Evita died, Jack Torri bragged to them that he might now return to Argentina. Taking shape in my imagination was a novel about Jack called "The Naked Ambassador," because he always disembarked dressed like a diplomat, armed with a shiny briefcase and a gold-headed cane, and returned to the ship and his tormentors under that homburg hat, wearing that double-breasted suit without a wrinkle.

And now to some vague extent I had similar feelings about David Schine and Roy Cohn as Jewish pariahs, a role I sometimes felt I myself was playing on ships and in the Army.

Jacob no longer waited for his turn at the chin up bar beside the chow line. He would just break out of wherever he happened to be in the line and walk over to the mud puddle — hollowed out in the shape of a woman, where Sergeant Turl stood mock leering — and do four pushups, collapse into the mud, wait for Turl to tell him to get up, which wasn't until someone dropped off the bar below "ten," then, "On your feet, Hercules," and Jacob would get up and go to the back of the line, without changing the one expression with which he faced the world.

Somehow this ritual took the fun out of ridiculing him, and every abusive wisecrack was a damp pop.

One day, seeing company scapegoat Jacobs walking into view on the sidewalk of the street behind the company area, I wondered why he wasn't in chow line, vaguely aware of his absence from the dining hall lately. He seemed to keep walking on by.

"Hey, Jacobs!" Butch, our handsome, amiable bully, was fixated on Jacobs. "Hey, Jacobs! Jacobs! Get your heinie over here and do your daily Augusta pushups, boy!"

Jacobs kept walking, on out of sight, Butch still almost hysterically screaming, as if at a phantom.

Just when Butch had turned on Tim, a sub-scapegoat, Jacobs was suddenly in our midst, just standing there among us.

"Hey, Butch. Lookie here who's here."

"Hey, it's the creature from the black lagoon, in 3D, hook nose, pockmarked face and all!" Butch yelled, as if he had created Jacobs out of thin air.

My impulse was to stand beside Jacobs against Butch, as I remembered having sided with Jack on the *LP St. Clair* on the Panama Canal-Chile voyage. Awareness of such parallels lent a kind of artistic design to my life.

"No fighting." Nearly whispering, sergeant Harmon too was suddenly among us.

"Sergeant, are there any boxing gloves in the storeroom?"

I saw that Jacobs saw that nobody could quite discern what he had just said, so he repeated it, and had to repeat it a third time, finally causing boxing gloves to show up quite readily on his fists and on Butch's.

Jacobs maintained a relaxed, cool demeanor, but Butch kept up a rather half-hearted dance in place.

Sergeant Harmon waved them over to him. "Now, Butch, get it out of your system. After this, no more harassing Jacobs. Not funny. Now touch gloves and go to your corners."

Butch turned and strutted over to the men in chow line. Jacobs didn't realize that I was in his corner, so he didn't come over by me, didn't even look at me.

Sergeant Harmon blew his shrill military whistle, inspiring Butch to charge Jacobs, who stood stock-still. Before Butch could lay glove one on Jacobs, Jacobs laid one, then two, then three, and a rapid series on Butch.

One witness expressed everyone's astonishment. "Fucker frailed hell out of him."

I kept seeing Montgomery Clift in fist fights with company bullies in "From Here to Eternity" and in "The Young Lions."

"He beat the living shit out of ol' Butch" was what the witnesses said time and again throughout chow-time and until lights out.

I was mindful of the first day of sixth grade at Lincoln Park Elementary hitting on Carroll Crowe, who had taken moderate bullying from me and others the previous year. He jumped me and taught me a hard-earned lesson about how bullying can turn out.

And a few months later, I saw my own bully Buddy Smith coming at me through a field and tried to placate him by saying, "See, I got a burr haircut like yours, Buddy," and when he punched me on one cheek, I, a fervent Christian at the time, piously turned the other cheek, and he swatted that one too, so I flew into him and he staggered away well-beaten.

★

MOMMA'S LIVELY LETTERS

Momma was only 44 the year I went into the Army. Getting letters from her flooded my consciousness with a hovering sense of the home place, for us the hub of Knoxville, for me a star in my own literary firmament. "Good ol' 206 Henegar Street." Built in the 1920's, it started out being three small, low-ceiling rooms, which had become a cozy four-room cottage by 1952.

To give myself a lingering impression of the power of Momma's fifty or so letters she sent to me while I was in the army, I gathered together various passages, repeated motifs from her letters, with no attempt to create a consistent timeline, as if sewing a patchwork quilt.

"Dear David, Haven't been able to stir up a job for Dick yet for when he gets out. I promised him, and now I can't seem to get to first base. Have been going to see Dick 3 or 4 times a week, and this official and that official, about his trial — till I am a nervous wreck. The trial is in the morning, and I feel like I'll fall apart before then. I am so afraid Dick is going to get a longer sentence. They checked and found out about him being in that Colorado prison in Canon City and his air force prison time in Hamburg and the dishonorable discharge all goes against him.

"I could take your old man and beat his ears off. He carried Dick's official papers for two weeks and not a thing did he do. Honestly if he lives another year I'll be surprised. I met him to get the papers back and he looked 55 yrs. old, and I'll bet he doesn't weigh 130. I feel sorry for him and again I could wring his neck. So, there will be no help from Jimmy Madden. Your Dad has never sent Dickie a penny.

"If I get Dick the job, I am going to get an apartment for him and John and me. If only we could *all* be together again.

"I guess John wrote and told you he's been discharged out of the Marines again. They caught up with him being in before, underage, and that one-time underage in the Navy. I don't think he will ever live in Knoxville for too long and can't say that I blame him. He loves Los Angeles most, like I love Cleveland. But he seems to be doing alright and looks healthy. Was so sorry he missed you. I look for him to hitchhike over to see you.

"He says he wants to turn over a new leaf, so he has started at Fulton Hi, taking radio speech and is narrator on Station WKCS, the voice of Fulton High. This week he narrated the Galveston Tidal Wave of 1900 and each week some different disaster. He has his own program like you did at WKGN. Next week he is going to learn to operate the console and have a crack at news commentator. And he is going to have the leading part in *Mr. Roberts* at Fulton High if they can tone the language down fitten for childish ears. So watch to your laurels old boy as your little brother seems to have a flair too.

"Dearest David, If you don't come to Knoxville this weekend, while I'm in town, I hope I can get sense enough to mail you your foot braces.

"Ruth said to tell you Hello and that you were still her best beau. But it always seemed to me you would prefer Ruby, if not for her bucked teeth, I reckon.

"Anyway, I will be thinking of you. And how Dr. Luttrell came down to the alley, where your dad was helping me walk, and spanked me and put me to bed 20 min. before you arrived screaming your head off!

Because Dickie's and John's birthdays were in wintry February and mine was in warm July, Momma combined birthday parties for the three of us. Yes, and every year that solution had rubbed an old sore spot.

"Honey, I sure hated to see you go back so soon. Seems I only had glimpses of you. Hope you find out soon where they intend to send you. *Do not* wait till you get down with your feet. If you can't take it, let me know and I'll try to get you out. Maybe I can write to Senator Kefauver. Ha! I am anxious to hear how your feet are standing up, whether they have improved, and if you want me to appeal to handsome Governor Clement to get you out before I go home — *2 wks* I hope. This is the time. Election is coming up and favors are easier to get. Write pronto and tell me!!!

"Honey I hope you can come home soon as your trouble with the investigators is straightened out. Let me know, as I am so worried about it. Accused of being a Red, who ever dreamed? Just anxious to hear if you wanted me to go to the Gov. for you or even maybe Senator Kefauver to make the Army assign you to a real job.

"P.S. Please keep your views on communism to *yourself.* You might land in the clink!

"Dear David, I'm sorry there had to be dissention between you and Phil on your philosophy of life that Sunday. I have had to act friendly on the surface to keep peace but that doesn't make me feel right down inside.

"I met Roy, a handsome jewelry salesman from N.Y. Cocktails, movies, dinner, lunch, and Sonya Henie ice show—'for 3 days.' Roy said I was just like a kid I was so enthralled. It was certainly out of this world."

Painful, sad to realize that I have never seen Momma like that.

"Roy is here for the weekend. We ate waffles and maple syrup till it ran out our ears and then walked up to the War Museum. We spent 2 hrs and still had 3 rooms to go. He does everything so thoroughly. My feet are killing me. He is in his room writing his boss (he said) and me in mine writing you. Then we are going for a ride to the Parthenon. . . . Then we are going to eat dinner, and I'll help him with his necktie line. We do inventory, then take out the obsolete styles. He is a pleasure to know. Manners to the 9th degree and very well educated — a Mason too. My 20 min. break is up. Will write later. Bye now."

"Dear David, Had a very sweet letter from Roy today and that helped my sad streak some. Haven't seen anyone here that is available that I would wipe my feet on. I guess every year I get less desirable and more particular.

"Mother got a letter from Bob last week and she sent it on to me. Imagine. Poor guy thought she might tear it up and wrote IMPORTANT PLEASE READ on the outside. But I should have known my marriage with Bob could never last. Plus to live and die in Terre Haute didn't seem like the berries to me.

"David Van Vactor's mug is spread all over town for the symphony and I sure wish you could be here to go. Did you know your dad's boss Breezy Wynn is business manager for the Symphony? O Brother. He and David had their pictures real chummy like in Sun. paper and I meant to send it to you and it got away from me. I sure wish you could have been here tonight. David Van Vactor was on TV conducting the Knoxville Symphony orchestra. He was wonderful as always. Just made me feel close to you, he being like a father to you. His mustache is getting a little too heavy tho."

Momma always needed money.

"That darn storage bill is worrying me crazy. The man called Monday morning with a deadline of 2 more weeks, or he'll sell our storage. I'd rather die than ask Mother and Cap for money or to let me store my worldly goods in their garage again.

"Can you spare a little lettuce? Folding kind. I'll be stony broke by Saturday. Will sure appreciate it. As soon as you can. Seems I just live from wk to wk. I've been flat on my can. It will be a month since I worked, you know, and I had been so saving with my last pay. I had paid $15 insurance for me and all you kids out of it too. Plus, your sorry Daddy! I just can't bring myself to let the insurance drop, so I keep it up each month, ever since when you were little. I can't imagine what would happen to Metropolitan insurance if it weren't for me.

"David, try to squeeze a little kale out this mo. Have had no new clothes this fall either. Write soon if not sooner. Love and a big hug.

Send Dickie and John some moola, and your old lady, as she sure is about barefoot."

I am moved to line Momma's laments as a poem.

MOMMA'S VOICE

Gay Street depresses me no end.
I think I have a hankering for Nashville tonight,
as I am so blue and bored.
Knoxville has been dead 25 years.
I had to suffer 6 weeks without a radio.
Sometimes the silence got so unbearable.
This darn room is like a prison without it.
I just feel kind of lost and no incentive to do anything.
I just go in a whirl all the time.
Meet myself going and coming.

That made me see Shelley at Lerici turning a corner on the terrace, meeting himself the evening before he drowned near the Bay of Lerici.

"I don't guess I will be going to the hospital soon as my arm isn't hurting too bad since I have taken the medicine the doc gave me. I seem to have a touch of arthritis in my arms and hands and legs and back.

"I'm not at the Maxwell House anymore. The boss wanted to play, so I told him to fly a so-called kite. So, now I am hostess in the coffee shop at the Sam Davis Hotel, named after the seventeen-year-old Rebel the Yankees hanged mainly for spying, but also for refusing to betray his comrades.

"Your old lady is now a boss and hires and fires and supervises. You know I like that, and I miss bossing you boys!

"Boss said he had to cut my salary, so we had an argument & out I went. Have several good leads on a new job.

"I answered an ad last Monday and glory! I was called into work on Tues. Southern Sewing Machine Co. as office clerk. Secretary they call it, minus the shorthand and salary too I may add. Only $30 per wk. But I can sit down most all the time to be kind to my feet and the work isn't too hard, only kind of confusing at first."

"Suddenly, I am a bookkeeper for a towing and auto repair shop at the intersection of Magnolia and Asheville Highway."

Momma told me she saw Marlon Brando in On the Waterfront. *I had recommended it to give her a sense of my own experience facing the Mafia on the Brooklyn waterfront.*

"And it was very good. My stomach is still jumping.

"I am writing this lickety split and so all the mistakes. Have 4 letters to write tonight so will cut it short. Write soon. Love, Mother."

★

FIRST CASUAL COMPANY

After Basic

While I was re-assigned to Casual Company, where soldiers await permanent assignment, I heard most often that "Regimental offices are plagued with queers." There was an atmospheric conviction that homosexuals were all over the post, throughout the Army, concentrated in Personnel and in certain companies. That Columbia, South Carolina was swarming with what the men called queers (a label the very mean-spiritedness of which had always made me squirm) disoriented me because I, having known many, wasn't aware of having met or seen any in the Army.

Minnesota Senator McCarthy attacked communists and homosexuals in the same breath. He strove to identify and demand that they be dishonorably discharged. I heard about Irving Peress, a New York dentist, a known communist. McCarthy charged the Army with promoting Peress and then, when Peress took the Fifth Amendment twice, with giving a communist an honorable discharge.

In my Manhattan days, I had heard much self-examining talk of homoerotic inclinations among artists and intellectuals and that generally people were androgynous, both male and female. I had had the impression that most homosexuals migrated into Manhattan, mainly Greenwich Village, where they were obviously habituated. I encountered many there, one of whom, Kim August, a celebrated female impersonator, Raven cultivated as a friend.

By letters and phone, I heard that two FBI agents were investigating me in Knoxville.

During one of my weekend passes, Vera told me that an agent asked her whether I liked girls, hoping to reveal hints of homosexuality that might provide a basis for a dishonorable discharge, she imagined. "Oh, he gets his share."

★

RETURN TO FORT JACKSON

On a pass, out of Fort Jackson into Columbia by bus, I visited the new museum of art in Columbia. As I walked along Gervais Street, the images from the Columbia Museum of Art vied with the images of the living among whom I walked.

Almost daily in the Army, images of paintings came to mind, or I deliberately conjured them or saw them in magazines as a vibrantly alive part of of my very being, not only as a person but as a developing young writer, a phrase offensive to my ego, but somehow apt.

On leave, at an art auction of graduate student work, after a concert of a Brahams quartet in the Art Department building, I borrowed ten dollars from Dave Van Vactor to bid on a strange nude painting of a man by a graduate student at UT, the first painting I ever bought.

Wherever I lived, at home, or in rooms elsewhere in Knoxville and in other cities, in forecastles at sea, I always taped or nailed a print of a painting or sculpture, or a powerful photograph, on the wall as an objective correlative to the terrain of my mind and imagination.

From high school until the Army, from one room, apartment, house and town and city all over the country to another, I stuck Alfred Ryder's mysterious self-portrait to a wall, the very image of the artist, as James Joyce's face was the very image of the novelist.

Movies lured me into the Strand and the Carolina on Main Street which ended at the State House Grounds.

Sketching scenes round and about uptown Columbia, I came upon the Capitol grounds. An adolescent black boy was sitting on a bench in the park-like State House grounds.

He gave me permission to sit on the bench beside him and draw him, full figure.

The Capitol Park policeman strutted toward us at a clip, yelling at the kid, "No niggers allowed on Capitol grounds!"

When I protested, he came, hand-on-holster, close to arresting me.

I wrote a poem about that episode and mailed the drawing and a copy of the poem to Mammy for safekeeping.

MONUMENTALITY

The sunny suspension of a Sunday afternoon
Holds me high in my elation for sketching
The Trinity Episcopal Church on Sumter Street.
I came upon the statued horse-high
General Wade Hampton, "Savior of South Carolina,"
in Capitol Park, in Columbia, SC.
Only the visible power of lofty iron
It must have been to aim my mind
At the drawing paper on my knee,
For civil war heroes bore me.
But a black child saw more than I
In my "sublime" subject. Public statues
Do impress some people.
He passed, tennis-shoed back, lingered,
Lovely, lithe, twint me and the statue —
"Would you like me to sketch you?"

The pigeons looked down from the general's
Forged dome, chesty, arrogant, indifferent.
What genuine patience in the child's poise,
His relaxed sprawl, unpretentious,
Upon the green bench, his eyes like poems,
His long, thin, graceful arms tranquil.
His innocent gaze caressed me with trust.

I had sketched the outline when
An officer of the state appeared.
"Okay, boy, get over on the niggers side."
Thus was my elation laid low, as the boy
Backed into his personal racial arithmetic,
At the altar of southern posterity.

★

GLENN SCOTT REARS HIS HEAD

Unknown to Fort Jackson authorities, I maintained off-hours quartered in Columbia, sharing a room above a garage with a friend.

Working, exhilarated, on the novel version of "Cassandra Singing," I thought I heard my friend coming up the steps.

A small shaven head emerged out of the ladder's opening in the floor.

"Great scot, David, it's your ol' buddy Glenn Scott come a-visiting. They finally got me, David."

Having corresponded with him only a time or two since we met at the Women's College Arts Festival in Greensboro, North Carolina where we had published our first short stories in the festival issue of the student magazine *Corradi,* I was surprised and delighted that Glenn Scott liked me well enough to look me up and come see me. In green fatigues. Seeing Glenn again — in the flesh so suddenly — was a sheer delight.

"How in the hell did you find me, Glenn?"

"Your lovely librarian on Tank Hill told me I ought to meet another writer at the fort by the name of David Madden. Your company clerk told me with a Yale accent where to track you down."

"Well, I am sure as hell glad he did."

"Hey, good fellow, come with me to the YWCA. A ladies' group invited me to talk about my novel, fresh off the press."

Glenn put plumply in my hands a book with an impressive cover, red, white, and black. A major publisher, E. P. Dutton.

Jealousy like acid reflux came up in my throat. *A Sound of Voices Dying* struck me as one of the best titles I had ever heard, so good I scarfed it right away for the title of a chapter in the novel version of "Cassandra Singing."

"Say, Glenn, mind if I read you a passage from my the novel in progress?"

"Not at all, do it. I'm curious."

"I like this part, where Lone from his cot says to Cassie lying in her bed, 'Did you hear me and Gypsy and Boyd and the Hellhounds roaring all over Harlan tonight, honey?'

'I can always tell your motorsickle from Boyd's and them. The roaring sets my bed off and I feel in my very bones the bed moving with you all, racing between ghostly fences, and horses grazing lift their faces, them lonely eyes, and stare at the blurry speed and the smoke and they stamp the frozen ground, then it commences to snow.'

'No snow yet, honey.'

'Yes, it did, yes, it did.'"

"That's ready to print, old buddy."

On the walk uptown, we talked about all the pretty girls at that Arts Festival in 1950.

"Yeah, I wish I had made love to all of them."

"I always assumed you did. *I* did. Katherine Anne Porter not included, alas."

"At least, I had a kissing companion, and I idealized Ann Hart, the tall, elegant, aristocratic-looking, aloof one from Agnes Scott College."

Talking with Glenn was easy-going, as if taking up where we left off. I liked the qualities of his soft coastal Virginia aristocratic-sounding accent. Who could have guessed that he had been a frat from Washington and Lee? We must have been a match on many points, otherwise why would he feel drawn to me?

In our eyes, all the ladies at his talk were old, too old, but suave Glenn, in his green basic training fatigues, enjoyed charming each and all.

He talked as much about literature in general as about his novel. Because I agreed with his message, I asked him to give me his lecture notes.

"The distinction is that many writers fail to become authors and many authors are not artists, creators of works of art, which is an articulated perception of the Universe. I will tell the ladies why my first book is not the work of an artist, but one of a writer, and tell them why a man writes and then aspires to the position of artist. What I mean is, giving a form to man's experiences of this universe so that it is better understood, and we have a new and vital appreciation of it."

Glenn Scott and I were happy to see a copy of *A Sound of Voices Dying* in the window of the sole bookstore in Columbia. I bought it; he inscribed it. "This copy of *A Sound of Voices Dying* is for David Madden, Brandoichio, Citoyen du Tenne, conscientiously objectionable to all mental sluggards, auteur-to-be, playwright — and very good friend. With warmest affection, Glenn."

TENNESSEE SENATOR ESTES KEFAUVER TAKES UP FOR PRIVATE MADDEN

Like my mother striving to get Dickie out of prison, I went straight to the top.

I stirred up my own security risk situation by writing to my home state senator, crime fighter Tennessee Senator Estes Kefauver, who I had watched often on TV in the Seafarers International Union hiring hall in Brooklyn in 1951 interrogate Mafia boss Don Leo Costello, asking him to help get me free of the Central Intelligence Corp's hold so I could go on serving out my time in a more productive, interesting way, maybe in Paris or Berlin.

Writing to a senator, I felt, I should engage in as high-toned rhetoric as I could, as in the first paragraph.

"Dear Senator Kefauver.

"Naturally, a man in my uncomfortable position (I may not receive a long week-end pass, a three-day pass nor my normal leave time — 10 days accrued.) is wont to seek out his familiars. I know about seven CIC holds, six of whom hold ordinary non-security jobs in the Army, and I know through them of the experiences of some more — unfortunate experiences, I assure you. Therefore, I cannot be other than extremely depressed, disconcerted, resentful, and suspicious as a result of my experiences and knowledge of the experiences of others."

And florid flourishes seemed called for in the climax.

"I need time to refine my view of the world, and the Army in this matter only serves to drive me deeper and deeper into negation. The moral of the story would *seem* to be — don't tell the truth unless it pays off in cold cash. Only *you* can invert the moral.

"May I hear from you soon? Respectfully yours, Pvt David Madden."

Getting a quick reply from Senator Kefauver lent me a sense of power.

"Dear Pvt. Madden: I just wanted you to know that I have received your letter and am looking into the matter about which you have written. As soon as I have some further news, I will get in touch with you again. Kindest regards, Sincerely, Estes Kefauver."

The rapidity of Senator Kefauver's encouraging reply that he would investigate made me feel important. For a while.

And pretty soon, Senator Kefauver sent me a copy of a reply he received from the Department of the Army, which also was at war with Senator McCarthy, promising to delve into the matter.

I wondered, was I, in a way, asking Senator Kefauver to do for me what despicable Senator Joseph McCarthy was doing for Private David Schine?

Basic Training had kept me from turning over more than only a few leaves of books, but freer time enabled me to pick up and peruse and finally finish reading a trove of books I had yearned for. Even so, the demands of Army routine forced me to read books in fits and starts.

Handling books I'd read and ones I intended eventually to read, I intoned the author's name and the title, as impressive voices spoke them in previews of movie versions of books, Max Steiner's music in the background, their being so suggestive as to make me aspire to live and write in harmony with the essence of their works.

But I read a handful of books simultaneously less and less as Ginger Van Vactor's admonition that I must finish one before starting another rang louder in my ears.

Just as from age eleven I was always writing four or five stories or scenarios simultaneously, diving into a new one as it welled up out of my unconsciousness, I was always reading from age thirteen four or five books simultaneously, absorbed in one as I was being lured to others.

Reading has always been for me far more a pure aesthetic experience than an experience in theme and meaning. Even recording the title of a book I had just read into palm-size black notebook I carried in the army, I felt various degrees of love for each author, as if each were a belated father, mother, brother, or sister.

A few days before I left the holding company at Camp Gordon, I lay on my cot in the barracks.

Inspired by my keen memory of having defended my reading of Raymond

Radiguet's *Devil in the Flesh*, in which a French teenager has an affair with an older woman, against my Knox High English teacher, Miss Ellis, who caught me reading it in class, I asked a friend of mine, a non-com, Corporal Willie Willard to take a snapshot of me, using the camera Jenny Bowling, the girl I loved very powerfully before Iva Lee, gave me for my fourteenth birthday, wearing only white boxer shorts and t-shirt, head still shorn, on my bunk, sunlight casting over me the shadow of the Quonset hut window frame, reading in conscious ostentation Radiquet's second and last novel *Count d'Orgel's Ball*, in which a highborn Creole woman is tempted during the French revolutionary era to commit adultery.

In his preface to *Devil in the Flesh*, published in 1924, Jean Cocteau said that Radiguet wrote the novel between the ages of eighteen and twenty, my own age then.

How Radiguet described that novel, which he composed in a fever in three days, appealed to me. "A romance in which it is the psychology that is romantic." Three days before he died in Paris of typhoid, Radiguet said, "I am going to be shot by the soldiers of God." Cocteau said, "Showing-off is part of his character." Radiquet was an over-reacher, like Rimbaud. I aspired to go and do likewise.

Within only a few pages of the end of *Count d' Orgel's Ball*, Willie returned. "Get up and get dressed, Madden. You and me are going out on a detail."

In a truck on a dirt road deep into a jungle, Willie told me that our CO had ordered him to drive me into the woods and beat the living shit out of "that little commie."

Why the CO disliked me to that degree, or at all, I couldn't imagine, for I did him a few favors along artistic lines.

Willie told me he had a better idea. He knew where there was a hole in the fence that surrounded the fort because he often visited his sister close by, and that's where he took me and we had us a chicken dinner with lemon meringue pie.

Days in the Army were too often andante, too seldom fortissimo.

Then papers came down ordering me to depart June 25 for Fort Jackson, to train for the ski troops on Tank Hill. Seeing myself as a moving target on snowy slopes in Korea was terrifying.

On leave, after a swift visit with Daddy in the Beverly Hills TB Sanitorium, I had just leave time enough left over to show up at the Van Vactors' house before hitch-hiking back to Fort Jackson.

Recently back from Paris, Raven was upstairs in her room talking and laughing, cavorting, with Ramona Perez, a young opera singer, one of her few girlfriends, getting dressed for dinner at the Cherokee Country Club with Ginger, and Dave, Ramona's mentor, to celebrate Ramona's acceptance at Juilliard.

As Raven stepped out of her pearly lace panties, I swooped down unseen, nabbed them, and stuffed them into my pocket.

As a private satirical gesture, a deliberately perverse, concealed protest against the Army's gung-ho mentality, I wore Raven's panties in the sack and in dark morning formations, with the considerate intention of offering them back when I returned to Knoxville as a full-time private person.

Fortune forced me back to Fort Jackson, and into the 101st Airborne Division (Air Assault), the only air assault division of the United States Army. Nicknamed the "Screaming Eagles," the 101st had consistently distinguished itself by demonstrating the highest standards of military professionalism since its activation at one minute after midnight, August 16, 1942.

July 1, or thereabout, I was assigned to M company 501st, Fort Jackson for eight weeks advanced infantry, despite the fact that I had secured a formal C physical profile for the ongoing problems with my feet.

I prepared to be very unhappy for eight weeks, to endure heat so horrible we had to take salt pills. I suffered the pain in my feet. I felt very resentful because I thought this had been done to me in retaliation for my having responded to the loyalty form the way I had. But there was a chance I get out of further training. They didn't know there that I had been given a PC physical profile at Camp Gordon. Deep depression set in.

My abiding interest in world events affected my intellect, imagination, and emotions even more up on Tank Hill.

A few days after I settled in at Fort Jackson, I was sitting on a rock under a tree on Tank Hill's highest point reading in *Time* magazine the latest report on Fidel Castro's revolutionary activities against the murderous dictator Batista, beginning to work up a desire to desert and go fight for freedom in the jungles of Cuba. I'd followed Castro's epic, canto by canto.

A soldier in civies sitting behind me asked what I was reading. He was close enough to have been reading it himself. He gave his name as Stanley Kenvin, clerk for the company next to mine.

Although we became rather constant companions, rather than friends in the best sense, he never told me much more about himself other than that he was Jewish, from New York City, and was in Princeton law school when he got drafted. That he often seemed to be keeping up a façade of some sort made me somewhat uneasy now and then.

I gazed upon the Guatemalan President Jacob Arbenz Guzman's color photograph on the cover of *Time*, a Mayan sculpture with Molotov's face carved into it behind him. A ribbon across the top left corner of that issue promised "The Oppenheimer Case. What the Loyalty Board Heard." Given my own wavering about communism, on theoretical grounds, I felt an affinity for J. Robert Oppenheimer, the world-famous atomic physicist accused of Communist affiliations.

Arbenz's rapid successes in only three years in land reforms, freedom for communists, and what I took to be improvements in the lives of the people of Guatemala, especially the Mayan natives, enthralled me. The United States was opposed to Guzman's nationalization efforts, alarmed that Czech weaponry had arrived in Guatemala on May 15, 1954, and that Arbenz himself was a communist, a member of the Revolutionary Action Party.

The CIA supported Castillo and his Army and used the threat of communism and the Cold War to accuse Guzman's regime of making alliances with Russia and with communist parties emerging in South America, threatening the security of the Western Hemisphere. Reading about President Guzman's struggles, I regarded him as a hero and imagined deserting to Guatemala to join forces with him.

I often feared I'd end up in the stockade. Facing the possibility of being sent to Alaska, I had intuitive apprehensions of the life of exiles in Siberia.

Any news of the awful situation in Panama excited my attention, turned up a great fountain of memories as a merchant seaman painting the engine room in hellish South Carolina-kind-of-heat going through the Canal.

But more than Panama, Chile came to mind, where during the period of dominance the state increased its role in the economy. In 1952, voters returned Ibáñez del Campo to office for another six years. Sad news that when 50,000 workers in Chile went on strike the government threatened menacing measures against the strikers.

My interest in France per se and knowing that events in the present elsewhere could affect the Korean conflict, and thus perhaps my own life, I followed the Battle of Dien Bien Phu between the French and the communist Vietnamese. It fell after a four- month siege led by Vietnamese nationalist Ho Chi Minh and soon the French pulled out of the region.

The events of 1954 began the United States' serious immersion in Vietnam, adding another ton of apprehension to the hydrogen cloud that hovered over us all, as if we were all halfway to hell.

"Soviet Jets Shot Down A Navy Patrol Bomber 40 Miles Off The Coast Of Siberia." Such headlines set off tremors of apprehension, not confined to me as one of those who may be sent to cold-ass Alaska to be a neighbor to Russia on guard.

Turning from an achingly clear intuition of Momma's proletarian life as

I read her letter to a sense of the romanticized life of the rich, I gently slit open another letter from Raven, this one from Paris. Blue ink on tissue-like white paper lent a certain tone to Raven's voice. As I listened, a palpable sense of Riva's personality and exotic loveliness pervaded my mind and body. Assuming that Raven was back in Knoxville, seeing her lovely face in memory, her flowing stride toward me, I was eager to tell her all about my first days at Fort Jackson.

As I read Raven's letter on my bunk on Tank Hill, I fully felt her presence, her soft white flesh splayed out on the white sheets of her enormous bed in New York, jet black hair spread across her shoulders, flowing down over her chest, almost touching her pink nipples, her black mound of Venus, aware of the odd speckle of fine, silky-like hair on the saddle of her back.

Raven's letter in the same mail call as Mammy's and Momma's latest enhanced my enjoyable sense of getting letters from three very different people, very different worlds, Mammy basically domestic, with car trips now and then to fish or visit her brother Joe Willis and his family in Florida, Momma's confined world being a rented room, from which she dragged herself to work by bus or walking, on Fridays or Saturdays escaping to dance halls. She never learned to drive a car.

I was always glad for a special reason to get a letter from Mammy because it testified to her having me on her mind, she whose dramatic storytelling techniques were the first influence on my own storytelling. Her short, simple letters struck sharply through the Army milieu. I opened her letters from the home place in a state of dramatic expectation, as if opening the front door of good ol' 206 Henegar Street.

Mammy's voice came to me as if across the cramped living room from her flowery chair by the front door, me lolling on the old, flowered davenport. Writing back to her was like talking to her across the living room.

With me, and maybe also with John and Dickie, Mammy's voice was most often sweet-tempered, but it sometimes took on a note of anticipated irritation.

Her letters were short, but her voice and face were crystal clear as I read them. Even before I opened her letters, I heard Mammy's rich voice and saw her expressive face.

Very few of my many letters home have survived. I rescued an armful from mildewed boxes out on the open back porch at Mammy's house exposed to rain and snow.

"Dear Mammy, When I wrote you yesterday, I didn't know that it would be 9 July before I could see the doctor. That's horrible enough, but this extra time can help me. The only proof I have that my physical profile was changed at

Camp Gordon is in my storage barrel in the garage. You can help me a great deal if you would get into my barrel and root for the piece of cheap white paper, probably in a folder. Somewhere on it will say either C-profile or L-3, and "temporary for 6 months" is on it too I think. It is signed by a Captain and dated sometime in May 1954. Please get the right one. Or it may be sticking out of one of my old paperback novels. Please find it as soon as you can — it may save me 8 wks of pain and depression in ski troop training. Love, David"

I was grateful to Mammy for responding quickly. The documents would prove that I wasn't fit to serve in the infantry.

"Have just found the paper. I hope it is the right one and hope you get it Sat. as I am mailing it airmail. Hope you don't have to stay on that ski troop training very long. Can I help in *any* way?"

Mammy answered my response letter affirming that I got her airmail.

"I already sent you more of those official papers you asked for. Honey, I sure am sorry you had to get messed up with the Army over that dad-blamed loyalty oath. Hope you come out O.K. and make a good soldier.

"Had a letter from John. He has Elizabeth with him, didn't say how they were living. Hope the baby's a girl and it belongs to him. What do you think?

"Oh, almost forgot it, had a nice letter from your Colonel, Infantry Commander James, and that cute picture of you. Colonel James's letter was about all the things they do for you in the Army and the clothes and food and so on. Never mentioned the trouble you got into not signing that loyalty oath. And an invitation to visit the camp which me and Cap might do some day.

"We was all here last week, just talked up a storm. Be glad you wasn't here, for you wouldn't have got a word in edge-wise. I bought John's baby some cute little clothes.

"David, your letter said you liked your applesauce cake, so I'll bake you another one day soon."

Following advice from my big brother, I got a letter from little brother advising me how to keep out of the stockade and so forth and so on.

"Hi ya Doggie; How's the Army treating you? like home I bet ha! Hows your Drill Instructor Sweet as roses or bitter than wine I bet you guys truelly love him like a father, or maybe hate him like a commie Ha!

"Give you some Military advice dont tell your Instructor that you have a brother that was in the Marines, because if you do he lible to beat your brains out he'll try to tell you the Army's the only branch of the service but dont you listen to him always say to him why didnt I listen to my little brother and join the only service the Marines (SIMPER FIDELIS — Gung Hole — Gung Hole)

"I bet you guys just like home cooking I bet, and your sacks are as soft as if you were sleeping on a foam matress.

"Well lets cut the shit and get down to busniss pal . . . David I have just sent Mom 10 dollars by western union Sunday and every pay day. I'll send her a little. . . . and you do the same as shes work for us and in return we do the same by sending money home.

"David, Lizbiths having a baby in May or maybe before and just skinhead your a uncle of two — David I didnt thing I put the prong to her that hard . . . . wow its a good thing we went back to gather again or I'd be in a mess of a hell.

"David I must be closing at this point Im going to Los Angeles with Liz she wants to see her ma and pa.

"The best of luck to you David and dont get pissed off Boot camp only last 16 weeks in the Army. (Marine is only 9 wks you should have joined the best branch instead of letting them draft you)

"So Long Doggie Be seeing you in the Funny Papers.

Your loving brother John K Madden."

★

WINN ROWE

Randy Intellectual

Separately and together, books, plays, music, paintings, and other arts were as much a part of my life as the dramatic army events. On any given day or night, walking along, eating, marching, running, daydreaming, working, reading, listening to music, talking to or listening to someone, riding in a bus or a car, music, sounds, voices, lines from poetry, fiction, plays, images from dreams, from my subconscious came to mind, so that my life at any one point was not just, or mainly, one or two actions, in a military or any other distinct ambience, but a myriad experience, from one moment to the next. One descriptive that sums it up is "myriad-mindedness."

I told Walton Rawls that Joseph Conrad lucidly articulated in his preface to *Nigger of the Narcissus* my own credo. "My task which I am trying to achieve is, by the power of the written word to make you hear, to make you feel — it is, before all, to make you see. That — and no more, and it is everything."

Among the most important writers in my life and creativity before the Army days was Thomas Wolfe. I liked the sound of the evocative titles of Wolfe's novels, *Look Homeward, Angel, Of Time and the River, The Web and the Rock, You Can't Go Home Again*, and some of his stories "Only the Dead Know Brooklyn," "Death the Proud Brother," "Dark in the Forest, Strange as Time." The fame of Thomas Wolfe's *Look Homeward, Angel* as a uniquely great achievement inspired me.

To prove to his spirit my love for him and his fiction, I risked following my two brothers into the Nashville reform school by stealing the paperback of Wolfe's stories from the racks in the neighborhood drugstore.

Rapid-fire, I reached also for nonfiction works that contributed to the intellectual life that I kept alive in my numb-skull army days, often contrasting with each other.

Vera, Walton, Brendan, Winn, and Ginger continued to stimulate my intellect.

Fear and Trembling and *The Sickness unto Death* kept coming to mind, phrases that expressed my own feelings.

"Well, you know, Ginger, what Kierkegaard says."

"No, you tell me."

"His rather positive conviction that one must first touch bottom before ascending up into the firmament of our aspirations appealed to my own basic nature."

"A few years ago, I gave you *Twelve Against the Gods: The Story of Adventure* by Bolitho. Did you ever finish it?"

"Oh, yes, ma'am. It attracted me in the early years of my agnosticism. In a vigorous, witty, irreverent style, William Bolitho, once a vagrant, a wounded WWI soldier, sketches the daring lives of twelve adventurers, Napoleon, Woodrow Wilson, Isadora Duncan, Alexander the Great, Lola Montez, Casanova, Columbus, Mohamed, among others."

"You don't have to prove anything to me, David."

And all the while, I roamed in and out of the *Holy Bible*, because the King James language, which evangelical tent preachers dramatized loudly, enthralled me when I was a kid.

My growing interest in Martin Luther made me want to know more about the church against which he rebelled, enabling me five centuries later to go to a Methodist Church in childhood.

To understand what he rebelled against, I picked up *Primer on Roman Catholicism for Protestants* and came to understand better baptism, confirmation, the Holy Eucharist, confession, penance, hell, heaven, purgatory, indulgences, miracles, mission, the seven sacraments, veneration of the Virgin Mary, charity, the power of the Pope, and the Vatican as a world power, and differences between Catholicism and Protestantism on all those subjects.

At Knox High, students and teachers often expressed concern for my soul. *The Man Nobody Knows* by Harry Emerson Fosdick was a high school graduation gift from of two of my teachers, plump, soft-spoken Miss Esther and tall aristocratically confident Mrs. Martha Mellen, who did not want me to spend eternity in hell, bless them both. That they seemed to be lesbians had intrigued me.

Ginger gave me that smile. "I'll ask her next time we dine with the Mellens."

"The who?" Dave at the fireplace was just kidding.

"The title of Alfred North Whitehead's *Adventures of Ideas* describes my experiences reading Nietzsche's *Anti-Christ* and Sartre's *Existentialism*. And George Santayana's *A Sense of Beauty: Being the Outline of an Aesthetic Theory*, and his epic novel *The Last Puritan*, a memoir in the form of a novel I started reading in Boston Public Library while waiting for a ship, but I've not yet finished it. But I will, Ginger, I will."

In the libraries in Knoxville and in cities where I worked, Washington, DC, New York City, Boston, and Mobile, I pursued my habit since high school of feverishly looking through the literary quarterlies and mass circulation magazines, imagining they would publish my stories and poems, so while in the Army I eagerly mailed off stories and awaited acceptances, dreading rejection slips.

I had had intimate contact with a few of the magazines in other ways, *Harper's Bazaar, Kenyon Review, Sewanee Review, New World Writing*, and *Botteghe Oscure*, published in Rome in Princess Caetani's castle. I had gotten a little encouragement from editors at some of those publications, so I was hopeful of joining their company.

Passionately desiring to become a high school teacher, I avidly absorbed progressive theories from education periodicals and books. In the cramped Fort Jackson service library on a steep slope below Tank Hill, I eagerly skimmed and dipped into various editions of *Education Digest*, stacking up back issues to peruse during each visit. The librarian got more attractive the closer she bent over me to transmit advice for finding books and magazines within her perfumed domain.

In that Fort Jackson library, I met Winn Rowe, a pudgy, unattractive former monk, who had refused, as I had, to sign the loyalty statement McCarthy had imposed upon the Army. Among soldiers with whom I made friends, affable and intellectually demanding Winn Rowe had the most practical effect upon my understanding of what to expect from the Army in dealing with us as security risks.

We were in separate companies. Meeting in the library, we often discussed philosophy and theology, more affably than I had done with my earlier former ex-monk friend, Brendan Liddell.

"This is not my native city," said Saint Augustine, and that's how Winn and I felt about the Army.

I liked what Winn called me — "the hovering bard."

The day he told me he had to have a serious operation, I told him I would visit him in the hospital. When I did show up, he loudly announced,

"They took my asshole out!"

When the big "they" discharged him from the hospital and the Army itself,

Winn Rowe packed up his disease-ridden anus with all his meagre worldly possessions and returned to his hometown, Grand Rapids, Michigan, where the Rowe family was prominent, and where he fully expected to die.

He wrote to me philosophically. "Suffering improves everything."

I wrote to assure Winn that I was still managing to avoid going to the stockade, though a few times I came or seemed to come so near I could smell the barbed wire, like the stinging odor of the Brasso with which we polished our brass belt buckles.

★

VERA'S COOLLY INTELLECTUAL, ROMANTIC VOICE

I wrote to Vera, eager to tell her that, "A few days ago, 15 of us were ordered to sign statements of charges for $3.90 for some sheets the supply sergeant claimed we lost, stole, or cut up, a charge so false we wondered if he didn't sell them himself to buy booze.

"He handed me a pen to sign and I very politely handed it back, stated that I'd be damned if I'd sign, and walked out amid cries of court martial threats. Footsteps began to follow me — 30 of them. The revolt was on. Well, we won, and my sergeant, who seems to like me, got fighting mad, and went to the C.O., who satisfied everyone."

Letters from family and friends simultaneously placed me in a luminous zone removed from my surroundings and conjured up the past.

The effect upon me of Vera's letters from Knoxville, Antioch College, Pittsburgh, and Cincinnati were more consistently intellectual, psychologically analytical, than any from family and friends.

"David, New York has completely possessed me. I love it immensely. This afternoon I spent in the Metropolitan Museum with Rodin's sculptures. Rodin is a master that has communicated more to me today than any other artist ever has.

"I had been there for about an hour and a half before I discovered they had 'The Age of Bronze' and 'Hand of God.' The rest of the museum went unseen after that, for I never found all those two statues had to offer. The finely buffed marble combined with the roughness and the wonderful way Rodin made the atmosphere become a part of the statue was supreme sculpture. He seemed to have gently drawn the air around the marble.

"I must stop now for New York a-waits outside. Always, Vera."

Vera often analyzed me. "Dear David, I always carry all your letters with me, and as I read some of them again, I find in the last two that you have changed a great deal. You seem a little calmer, more mature and relaxed than the intense way you were before.

"I stopped in Howard Johnson's restaurant and talked to your and Raven's actor friend Don Manfredi the other night, and I am afraid I picked a bad time. He seemed frantically busy behind the counter, but I should factor in the turrets affliction that compels him to utter gratuitous obscenities, inevitably disconcerting.

"David Van Vactor is having one of his original selections produced here in New York by the American Chamber Orchestra. I would like to hear him, but right now the financial situation is bad because I don't get my first internist paycheck from Antioch College for another week. I don't know just when I shall be home for Christmas.

"Listen, David, these past few weeks I have missed talking with you and constantly look forward to your letters and writing to you. I miss you a great deal and shall be looking forward to seeing you. Always, Vera."

"David, today is winter at Antioch as it should be with all its wonderful bareness. This morning it snowed a little as if to gently cover all the sleeping life to protect it from death. The structure of the trees is powerful and dramatic, and the structure of the line of the landscape is graceful and free. I am happy and feel free and very alive. I expected school to be dull and boring after New York and seeing old friends in Knoxville, but what a pleasant surprise it is! Dear David, you should be here to see and feel it with me.

"Being in Knoxville for those few days and seeing old friends in their same habitat was pleasant and inspiring. June Bean seemed more mature and yet unhappier in a good kind of way; Dave Holdritch seemed more confused about his love for June Brown; June Brown is more content; philosophy club and WUOT crowd are the same.

I sat in on one of C.P.'s classes, which was quite interesting as usual, and he was much friendlier to me than usual.

"I was especially happy to see you again after so long. You seemed older and quieter in a puzzling kind of way, but perhaps it was just the two cocktails. You have been so close and so far in the six-month interim since I had seen you. Many times, when I have done or thought things you might have enjoyed, I have wished you could be here to talk and share them. There were times when it seemed a shame for you to miss things that may happen only once.

"I thought how you would have enjoyed walking through the black section of Cincinnati with me the other night. Some of the people seemed like characters out of your stories, and the one about Cassie and her brother that you told me you are working on now. I watched a boy and girl necking for at least thirty minutes in a doorway, a lone man reeling across the sidewalk, young boys standing in front of a Catholic rectory that was playing jazz music upstairs, and I followed a young mother walking hurriedly down the sidewalk with a two-year-old boy who was commenting on the world around him and couldn't understand why his mother was hurrying him so."

I was slow and fitful getting into modern jazz, but Vera more than Raven led me some of the way, making me generally more aware — of Dave Brubeck, The Modern Jazz Quartet, Ahmad Jamal, Stan Kenton, Charlie Parker, Ella Fitzgerald, George Shearing, Sarah Vaughn, Bill Evans, but I already knew Miles Davis personally.

"The flakes of snow are larger and heavier now — a reminder that time too falls to the earth and melts, so I must go. Farewell. Always, Vera."

Just when I most needed a letter from her, Vera's voice spoke to me.

"Dear David, It is good to be content as you are, for your contentment is not synonymous with stagnancy, but with productivity and creativity. How nice it must be to have a calm apartment off post.

"I read in the Knoxville paper that David Madden, formerly of Knoxville and now serving with the United States Army, has submitted a play to UT's second statewide contest. "Cassandra Singing." I would like to read it or see it produced. Let me know how it is coming. How wonderful it must have been to have identified fully with your characters. It sounds as though for perhaps the first time you have begun to penetrate the depths of lives as they possess you and not you, them.

"This is the beginning of the work that could be your fullest. Your gift for accurately portraying things unknown to you shows that you have what Paul Klee, one of my favorite painters, talks of as that thing not a part of the artist or his life, but something he imagines and then transmits. This is so much more important than writing of your own experience, which is valuable only as it helps you express things that you possess that are not your own or anyone else's.

"As I look back on my trip at home, my main regret is that I did not see Raven. I thought of her every day, and late one night walking on the river along the bluff back of her house I heard laughing inside and so figured she was home, but I walked on and did not go in. Perhaps someday when she returns from Europe again, I shall get to know her better.

"Now I must major in philosophy. I cry to it to help me in the time when liberal arts is becoming chaotic and meaningless. I beg of philosophy to give order and meaning to the things I learn so I can use them to their best advantage. I implore it also to give me something I can study fully and lose myself completely in — not only a part of myself, but all. In the future it will be the firm basis for study and living.

"I plan to go to graduate school in psychology and still do counseling or psychotherapy eventually. But I fear that psychology can so easily seem full when it is still shallow.

"*Les Enfant's Terrible* was here at Antioch two weeks ago. Such impact I have never experienced in a film before. Cocteau usually makes me inquire into the world and what it is that Cocteau knows of it, but this movie made me inquire into myself and what Cocteau knew of me. It was as though Cocteau, oblivious of your volition, was pulling an intensity out of you that you yourself did not know existed within. Tell me what you remember of it from that time you and Raven saw it in New York."

Vera was becoming my teacher in some ways. Right soon came another letter from her.

"David, I appreciated your last letter very much. I was glad to hear that you are not still in the infantry. When do you expect to be going to Europe? If you do radio work, will it only be announcing, or will you learn technical stuff too?

"About your recommendation that I read *The Black Swan* by Thomas Mann, I regret that I could not find a copy anywhere in Knoxville. I always enjoy reading Thomas Mann's work even though I feel he sometimes makes his wonderful observations subservient to his main concepts, especially the elevated lonely position of the artist.

"Tell me of Chile. While you were there did you see any Indians? The reason I am curious is that I saw 'Secret of the Incas,' a very crummy movie, but with beautiful scenery and some small idea of the life of Incas there, too small. Raven's enthusiasm for Yma Sumac sings in it.

"I have been reading Ruth Benedict's *Patterns of Culture* in which she discussed several different Indian cultures, and I was amazed and pleased at the differences in their ways of coping with life. Some instances seemed to show a much better way than we in western civilization know. The calm, rational, and contented existence of some tribes make our way seem emotional and ridiculous. One tribe couldn't understand how we could make killing in war worthy of any kind of respect — it just wasn't natural. Then of course there are tribes that are quite wild, irrational, and barbarous. If I will discover any more unusual Indian tribes with a better pattern and way of living, I may just go live with them.

"Also tell me more about your beloved Dylan Thomas, or rather defend him. I have been reading some of his work more carefully than before and am quite disappointed. I much prefer your imitation of him reading his poetry aloud.

"UT Philosophy Club meets tonight, with Doctor Parsons' wife discussing segregation and some studies she has done. This seems to be an issue that is in danger of dying, as do many issues that are discussed but never acted upon.

"By the way, in my last letter my feelings about nature were also partially my feelings about you. Always, Vera."

On leave, eager to see and hold Vera, I hitch hiked to Antioch, and spent a few days there, sleeping in a dormitory.

In the dimly lit lobby of her dorm, Birch Hall, we petted as heavily as that term allows.

"Don't worry, we'll not get caught. Other girls do it."

I met her friend Arno Karlen, a writer, who wanted to be her boyfriend. Susan Cooper and Betty Berenson, a lesbian, were her best friends. Her roommate was Korean, unusual in that era, but not at Antioch. I liked Arno just fine, and the others, too.

I talked to her about Cassie and Lone and asked for her questions and comments.

"I'm happy that it is fully imagined, not based on events or people I know, except maybe a little of my daddy in Coot, and a little of Momma in Charlotte, but Cassie and Lone are totally my imagination."

"No, no, David, they, together, are you, Cassie and Lone are two aspects of you."

That plunged me into a deep silence, staring into her eyes.

A week or so later on, Vera wanted me to know how my behavior as her guest was received by her and her fellow students at Antioch.

"Dear David, as you walked away from Antioch, I called out to you to return, to stay awhile longer, but you were gone. In a week I had gotten used to having you around and you had become natural there. For a few days every boy sitting alone in the Tea Room that I waited on was you. Each person that came out of the library stacks was you, and in each class discussion your ideas seemed to be voiced.

"You made quite an impression on many Antiochians. Charlotte said that she hoped you would come to Antioch because you had a certain liveliness that they needed here. Sue Hill had nearly the same sentiments, and several others thought you added a lot to the reduction of apathy. Sue Cooper liked you because you liked her and could run in the glen with her.

"Whenever you can, wherever I am, do come again to see me. I feel as though I know you better each time I see you and feel closer to you each time.

Vera's next internship sent her into Irene Kaufmann Settlement House set in what I remembered as the strangling smoke of Pittsburgh.

"To You.

"The city is clear this morning, so everyday life in Pittsburgh is closer to livable. The hills, though covered with houses, are barren. A church steeple does not rise cleanly and purely to the sky because it too is stunted and dirty. As I walked past a drug store this morning there was a window full of colored Easter chickens. The live chickens walked among the dead ones and knew no difference. Do the dead always lie among the living? And this is Pittsburgh on my first morning here. No, it is not very pretty, and yet something about it has encased me, and free breathing is difficult, and not just from the dense smog.

"After two days I am settled in my new job, better than Cincinnati, the best one I have had. Pittsburgh is about the friendliest town I have been in, even in the slums where I live."

The more of her letters I read, the more lucidly I heard her voice, like cool water.

"I have been in Knoxville for three days' time off. This time I got to see Raven and she invited me to that grand house. We got along quite well, but she went through a little scene after drinking too much. Her father was arguing with David Wilcox, Collin's father — "

Collin had been sensually wonderful in Black Chiffon *at Carousel.*

" — and this upset Raven since she thought he was getting too excited. She yelled at him, and then he got angry, pounded his fist on the table, and pulled Raven out of the room. She left, and I found her a few minutes later stumbling barefooted over the rocks by the river. We walked along the river, while she cried and complained about the way her father treated her.

"Finally, she went into talking about how the spiritual was the only thing she wanted, and yet she kept ending up with the physical, which never completely satisfied her.

"She kept talking about how much she felt that you understood all about her, more than anyone else in the world. She said she loved you because you understood her. I am telling you all this, because you already know more about what is happening to her.

"At first, I thought she was being a little too dramatic, and the more she talked, the more sincerely desperate she was and more almost pitiful. She seems to know what she wants to be, how to act and think in all situations, and yet she seems continually disappointed when she cannot carry this through all the time. Do you think she will never find the calm she seems to seek?"

More about Pittsburgh in her next letter.

"All the hills I see are filled with ugly (of course, as Victor Hugo said, nothing really is ugly) houses, the rivers bordered by steel mills that flame at night, and the milky way galaxy is on the nearest hill at night instead of in the sky. To get out with the people in the city it becomes more beautiful, but from the inside looking out, the struggle to respond to the nature around the city, the struggle for individuality in architecture and never finding it, and all other struggles are frustrated.

"It is nearly noon, and so I must go to work. Count not the term of days remaining in the army but count the fullness of each day you live. (Obvious influence of reading too much in the oriental line.) Always, Vera."

★

WAYNE ROGERS

A Young Artist Teaches Me

In the Fort Jackson Service Club, I met a young artist, Wayne Rogers, a quiet fellow, whose comments on my drawings inspired me to change.

"You always outline your faces with a continuous hard black line. Try softening and breaking the line."

On four or five occasions, I told him about my experiences creating and listening to works of art.

"My high school teacher never bothered to tell me such as that. Out of Miss Virginia Parker's face, its severity enhanced by the constant shaking of her head, what we were told was the St. Vitus Dance, came her ghostly severe voice commanding us all to go to the Audigier Gallery at UT and write a report on the Everett Ellsworth Lowry Memorial Exhibition.

"I had nurtured a mindless contempt of modern art, but seeing in real life the actual paintings of Picasso, Matisse, Braque, Mondrian, and twenty other modern artists wiped the superior sneer off my face, letting me in for a conversion experience like St. Paul's on the road to Damascus.

"I went abstract in my own work. My short-tempered, mean-faced, hateful-talking, laser-eyed old art teacher, Virginia Parker refused to allow my paintings — ironically, far too wildly, weirdly modernistic — to be considered for a scholarship in an exhibit at UT. But the artist who was one of the judges told me my drawings were superior to the winner, my classmate.

"My drawings in colored ink using variations on pointillism led my UT teacher, Mr. Cox, to urge me not to get stuck in that style. My realistic drawings and paintings were bizarre. I especially liked doing two drawings of a plump nude woman wearing curlers, sitting on a kitchen chair, one leg up, cutting her toenails."

"Sounds like a cartoonish variation on a combination of the awkward postures of Degas and Balthus."

"Does? Yeah. I reckon."

"In New York, desperate for the painted image, I paid a visit to my favorite Museum of Modern Art painting, Pavel Tchelitchew's *Hide and Seek*, wondrously strange, unique images of infant faces emerging out of trees that sprout faces as leaves, a young girl prominently facing, maybe embracing the tree.

"As I was leaving, I came upon the bizarre sight of Salvador Dali and his wife Gala contemplating an indoor exhibit of an antique black taxi getting rained on. It may have inspired an image I imagined of a man coming out onto the sidewalk who sees his childhood love carrying a small grandfather clock along 53rd Street coming toward him, passing him, oblivious. When I wrote a story about it, I called it 'Hurry Up, Please, It's Time,' a line in — "

"T. S. Eliot's *The Wasteland*."

"One of my best portraits was of a patient in a wheelchair, an old man, the summer I was 15, recovering in Fort Sanders' Hospital from that surgery on both my feet to correct insipient clawfoot deformity.

"When I was aboard a ship, in the army, on post in the library and off post in various places, including rooms I rented, I often drew portraits, sometimes for a fee, working from photographs of girlfriends or of soldiers from life. On a ship to Savannah, I drew the man who introduced me to Segovia holding my own Stella guitar that I had bought in Galveston but never really learned to play.

"Portrait of the Artist Listening to James Joyce Reading 'Anna Livia' from *Finnegans Wake*" in my room in Boston on St. Botolph, "the Street of Broken Dreams," is one of the few self-portraits I have drawn.

"Stored during my army ordeal in a barrel of my stuff, among barrels that Momma stuffed her things into, in Mammy's garage, is a photograph from *Life* of *Modigliani*, whose "Nu Couché au coussin Bleu" is one of the finest examples in art's universal gallery of reclining nudes."

"Good. If true."

"Picasso was, of course, special. 'A Woman in White.'"

"And his circus folks, especially Harlequin?"

"Hell, yes."

"And I drew from photographs in magazines, especially photography magazines. A man stands beside his horse, running his hand along its belly.

Head view of an existential young woman reflected in a window covered with rain drops in Jean-Paul Sartre's Paris.

"Influenced perhaps by Giacometti's sculpture, I drew very skinny men and women, usually nude, long hair flowing, or in awkward postures."

"David, I am amazed you can remember in such detail."

"I am afflicted with a terrible nostalgia. . . . I drew a few abstracts, and characters in movies or books, Arjuna and Khrisna, for instance, and characters in my own stories, focusing on scenes from 'Cassandra Singing.'"

"May I read it?"

"Yeah, sure, I'd like you to, but not until Cassie and her brother get closer to being living and breathing human beings."

"My Field First got me off KP to draw a few nudes. His response was that they didn't look like real women."

"Not only did I draw dirty pictures in basic in the firing range target tunnels for the cadre but that serious sketch of the black boy on the Capitol grounds bench, and sketches of the men, Bill asleep, a soldier wearing horn-rimmed glasses, and Stanley Kenvin, in pencil and in ink on actual drawing paper, from life, some aware, some not, and for money, portraits from photographs for a fee. A pretty girl, someone's wife.

"And I drew in various styles for my own pleasure. Even architectural images. Towers, those where Joyce and Yeats lived, and the one Robinson Jeffers built with his own hands.

"Comes to mind Raven asking Dave, 'Daddy, do you remember that time you took me to take a look at Jeffers' tower that time we made that disastrous trip to Carmel?'

"Frank Lloyd Wright sorts of houses, and my ideal houses I promised Iva Lee, enhanced streetcars or silos."

Wait, you actually saw Jeffers' tower?"

"Yeah, I've always been attracted to towers. The love of my life and I planned to live in a silo and, well, also considered converting an abandoned streetcar into a place to live."

"Do you like the opposite, graveyards?"

"Yeah, I've explored a lot. Wrote a story about a soldier who befriends a young girl whose father is superintendent, and they live inside the cemetery and so when he has to report to go overseas, she locks him in the fanciest tomb and visits him until he dies, then visits his bones."

"Macabre, Mr. Poe."

"I cut the raven out of the final draft.

"On various kinds of paper, I drew pictures front and back, mostly imaginary faces of women and men, profiles usually, but also frontals, fewer full figures — a nude, holding a peach, her head turned aside, faceless — a few cartoon characters, only a few drawings from life. I drew faces sometimes on the paper where I had written poems and fiction sketches and short stories — Coot, Cassie's drunken Daddy, and his hounds, and Cassie in bed, Lone on his motor'sickle."

Wayne taught me how to soften and sometimes break the main outlines of cheeks, jaws, lips. I was grateful.

But my hard lines led him to recommend me to his boss at training aids studio to be assigned to draw for training manuals. The Training Arts commander hired me. So, I drew training posters, and signs, like my Uncle Phil who had German prisoners working for him in his military sign shop.

I drew an image of a drunken soldier at a bus stop leaning against a telephone pole smoking a cigar. "The eyes of Augusta are upon you." Two soldiers talking in a train station as a man in a trench coat pretends to read a newspaper, listening. "The enemy is always listening." A soldier with a bayonet in his heart. "Somebody talked."

My own enemy was attentively listening. "Your drawings are very effective, Madden," the commander told me, "but sorry to tell you, I got a call from the CIC. They're afraid maybe you'll sabotage the training postures."

But Wayne told me that I really got fired because my skill drawing realistically was not good enough.

"Technique in all the arts is, you already know, everything."

I never saw Wayne again.

Again, all my friends in the holding company were shipped out while I was placed in another holding company where I pulled KP five times in less than two weeks. Other days I wasted pulling labor details with men being held back for various reasons.

My very identity dimmed off and on, sudden stabs, taking my breath, I went weak in the knees. Sadness was a dull ringing, creating zones of vacancy.

The psychological ambience of my military days was what one might imagine if one knew one would die soon. Missing Iva Lee was like having a lingering sickness, often about to vomit, expecting no relief, a sudden ache, sometimes a stabbing pain.

All events, real or imagined, positive or negative, had a nimbus of Iva Lee-lack. Even as I read and as I imagined and wrote stories, poems, and plays, she was a constant hovering presence.

On a scorching hot and humid afternoon, I lay on my cot under the canvas tent the Army called a cabin in a coma of nostalgia for Iva Lee. Into the repository of my imagination, I reached for photographs, taken all over Knoxville, all taken with the camera Jenny Bowling gave me for my birthday.

Aching, I let images of the six years of our love flicker by.

I see Iva Lee

On an excursion boat on the Tennessee River, offering views of Knoxville, she is wearing a starched white dress with red ribbon trim around her neck and where the puffed sleeves embrace her upper arms, and a ribbon in her hair. For the photograph, she leans back and rests her arms along the railing, her hands dangling delicately, her head slightly tilted back, her lips parted in a smile her brown eyes enhance, her hair darker in twilight, the paddle wheel in the background churning the Tennessee River, the girders of the Gay Street Bridge, across which we often walked, in silhouette over her shoulder.

Having ridden the streetcar across the river to Island Home in South Knoxville, we are sitting on a derelict wooden dock, and then we walk in the woods and make love in the jungle of bushes as fishermen in motorboats speed by and small aircraft took off from a little air strip.

I listen to her come up the stairs and feel her naked crawling into bed with me, as I pretend to be asleep, then suddenly turn and tightly embrace her as she giggles a little, then settles into a snug embrace.

The sight of her standing, animated, among her four best girlfriends on the sidewalk and in the halls at Christenberry Junior High and later at Knox High.

Secretly, we meet in the various theaters all over Knoxville and in my house or in friends' apartments on various streets and parts of town and in Dave's grand study and in Daddy's hot room in a slummy house that had once been a grand house of a grand lady in the sagging past.

Seeing her come out of the restroom in the huge, very tall Methodist Church by the river, wearing the blue velvety dress I had just bought her and posing for the camera Jenny had given me.

Watching her in a game dribble and shoot baskets on the Knox High court and twirl and twist on the football field as a majorette as I boiled in a fury that she was showing herself off to boys and men.

Watching her practice ballet on the floor above where I worked delivering eyeglasses to various optometrists.

Suddenly there she is, coming to comfort me in the hospital after Dr. Inge transplanted the bones in both my feet.

Using the camera Jenny had given me, I snap a shot of Iva Lee and Jenny standing in the middle of Walnut Street as they, the two great loves of my life, who had become good friends, turn toward me smiling, holding on to each other, as their facial expressions suggest that they shared an attitude about me.

Sitting hip to hip with her in the sanctuary of Oakwood Methodist Church where, solitary, I had prayed to God that I might find such a girl as she.

The day the clerk typist school company disbanded, a friend told me that Captain Buckner, the director, with whom I had voluntarily discussed my concepts of religion, government, etc., interrogated three of my co-workers and a corporal under whom we worked. I stopped by to see him. He wanted to know if I had ridiculed religion or talked sympathetically of communism. The three later voluntarily assured me that they had answered in the negative.

And from some unnamed person, my CO was informed that "Madden spends all his spare time spreading Red propaganda." No rumor or direct lie could be more absurd, as any of the men who know me could testify. "I am not a communist nor do I agree or 'sympathize' with the communist party, either here *or* in Russia."

My sergeant informed me that the Central Intelligence Corps had information about my situation to offer and that an officer was on the way over. He never arrived, but three days later he informed the sergeant that my case was closed. All obvious indications led to the contrary.

Now I am at a new holding company, same regiment. Every day I pull details. However, I am treated as the rest and have no complaints about the company nor the cadre. They wanted me as a clerk in the orderly room but that was forbidden by S-2, which handles the processing of intelligence and tactical information for the commander.

Since Junior High, using the professional format, I had had long experience in writing radio plays, adaptations and originals, five of which I broadcast over WKGN, located on the top floor of the Park National Bank building.

Mr. Gentry, the city superintendent of schools, who liked me for my literary talent and lofty ambition, used political pull to secure for me my own show on WKGN, when I was a junior in Knox High.

Then Mr. Bowman, the owner, liked my voice, so he hired me as a late-night announcer and disc jockey for a country music program called "The Nightwatchman," until I made a stab at educating Knoxville by playing Tchaikovsky's "Romeo and Juliet Overture," faking a call-in request from Iva Lee, known far and wide as my sweetheart.

At WUOT, the UT public radio station, where Vera had worked as music librarian, I had recorded poetry, the great ones and my own, and my short story "Seven Frozen Starlings," for broadcast while I was at sea between quarters.

Raven, John Cullum, and I also recorded the opera libretto I wrote for

Dave Van Vactor, a modern adaptation of Euripides' *Medea*, inspired somewhat by Robinson Jeffers' version.

I applied for and was offered various jobs on post based on my qualifications, but the Central Intelligence Corps blocked each of them, my sergeant told me. On Police the Area detail, bent over to stab a cigarillo butt, I noticed a sign that declared the site of a radio station. I had not thought of that.

I returned that evening and caught the captain in charge just as he was leaving. I tried to impress him with my announcing experience and a sample of how my voice would sound on the air.

"I will contact your company commander tomorrow. I need you."

I returned a few days later expecting to go on the air. "I was all set to put you on the air, Madden, but the CIC called me, said you are a Red, said you might broadcast subversive ideas in code, so what could I do?"

Out of my subconscious, voices from people and books welled up, even when I was forced to march.

Voices had always captivated me, in radio plays, such as "The Shadow Knows," and movies, especially Bogart speaking, and family members, especially Mammy telling stories, so I was attentive to the quality and variety of voices. As I read stories and letters, I distinctly listened to the voices.

I had always imitated voices coming at me from the radio and the movie screen, and poets speaking to me on Caedmon and Library of Congress recordings. "One could do worse than be a swinger of birches," intoned Madden-Frost.

Raven told our friends that I was a great mimic, as good as her American Academy of Dramatic Arts acting school friend John Cassavetes' compulsive, manic imitation of Jerry Lewis, which I had heard a time or two at parties in New York across from the Red House on West 85th Street where I had a tiny apartment.

Across the street, one of Raven's friends gave a party honoring the black folk singer, Josh White.

"Sing 'I Gave my Love a Cherry.'"

He looked down at me where I sat at his feet. "Later. First, here's one for you Southern boys."

He moved me deeply with his soft, resonant voice, singing "Strange Fruit."

"Southern trees bear a strange fruit
Blood on the leaves and blood at the root
Black bodies swingin' in the Southern breeze
Strange fruit hangin' from the poplar trees"

Raven urged me to go outside and comfort Mendel, whose Hebrew name meant "Comfort," because she was suicidal. The odd way she looked at me, her blue eyes framed by blonde hair, her aura ethereal, I loved her from afar. She pressed against the stone railing of Riverside Park Drive, mournful, while I coaxed her back into the party.

I enjoyed the sometimes-jolting juxtaposition of getting letters from Raven and Vera and my friends and teachers to letters from Momma and Mammy and John and Dickie, but Uncle Phil never wrote to me.

Vera's distinctive voice was very different from Raven's in its effect upon me, both voices conjuring up images of Knoxville, New York, and beyond.

I conjured images of Vera's house at 1416 Forest Avenue — at the other end of which I once lived as a babe in arms, a block away from the house where James Agee was born — the wall beside it close up and as if from an aerial view of Knoxville.

Along with her story, Vera's letters told my own story, past and present, and prefigured my future somewhat, and her perspectives on my life, her ongoing comments on my sensibility, affected the evolution of it and stimulated my creative energy.

Within the confinement of the Army, my mind functioned within the milieu of the intellectual lives of my friends, especially Vera's. Her lyrical, intellectual letters showed me aspects of myself before and during the army era. And I was falling in love with her by stages, interesting to observe.

As I read her letters, while I was still in basic training, I heard Vera's voice.

"March 26 midnight 1954.

"Dear David, I'm writing to you tonight in total darkness. I have a terrible headache, and it is a lot easier to write in the dark. Also, it gives me an odd sensation to move about in darkness and to type with my fingers waiting for the carriage bell. . . . I have just returned from Philosophy Club. The meeting was quite good, and we discussed Islam. That there were several interesting foreign students made it more engaging.

"From your letters it sounds as though you are trying to outdo the Army in trying to command them. It makes you sound like a sergeant in private's stripes. Don't try to reform the Army too fast.

"So far, I have found C. P. Lee's essay writing course more stimulating than Dr. Daniel's poetry class, but perhaps it will get better when we move on to someone other than Gerard Manly Hopkins. I can understand why C. P. would advise you against the course, given your interest in creative writing. It is far too analytical and interested in form of presentation for the public. We have all kinds of dull housewives and accountants in that class.

"Today I appreciated C.P. more than ever before. We communicated today, for the first time. I am going to have to write my paper over in this class, the one on Rilke. Today he tore it apart in class, and I was extremely pleased.

"I was most pleased though when I found out C. P. had gotten my ideas perfectly and had felt the very things I had intended in my paper. He had even sensed the words in which I had trouble expressing my ideas. I have never had a teacher before who was so sensitive or capable of reading between the lines. I wonder frequently where he got his extraordinary insight into people — he who is such a cynic. It is strange that he lacks his usual cynicism about people he likes — Proust, Rilke, Camus, and others.

"I was quite pleased with the cute picture of you. It looks as though you have really been regimented. You looked like a UT engineering major that had taken too many home ec or ag courses. I was pleased with your words in your last letter — such little gems as 'holey arguments' and especially a seeming unintentional one like your getting 'quiet lonely.'

"You mentioned that the Army was consuming your physical self for twenty-four hours, what about your mental or spiritual self?

"Are you doing any writing now, or anything creative? I haven't been taking any psychology courses so it will be a long time before I can psychoanalyze you. However, I am reading Freud too, *An Introduction to Psychoanalysis*. And I am NOT READING *Nightwood* for even the third time damnit. As she is a known Lesbian, do not get the wrong idea about me from that."

On leave, I invited Vera for a walk on rough ground along the north bank of the Tennessee River, her step so confident that I was aware that taking her hand for safety reasons would be irrelevant.

A week or so later, after she had returned to Antioch College, I got a letter from her.

"You can't tell a person by his reading matter. Even you have been known to read some crumbs. I do not think Djuna Barnes is a crumb. She writes with great intensity and feeling. She has insights and ideas that seem to be unique with herself. People who see only the homosexual angle miss the real questions. I think she is just unusually responsive to the intensity and torment around her.

"Do write again soon, for I always enjoy hearing from you. Always, Vera. P.S. Charming green inkblot in your last letter. I saw a flying green horse in it. . . ."

Feeling that she was moving closer to me, I was eager to read Vera's next letter.

"Dear David, I was glad to hear that the Army is not as bad as you had expected.

"Our teachers ply me with queries about your fate, as when you came and went as a seaman. Professor Daniel asked if you knew a Pvt. Schine (or something like that) who is at Camp Gordon. He was one of Senator McCarthy's men, and Dr. Daniel thought you might have tangled with him already.

"I saw Raven the other night at a play at Carousel and she mentioned you were taking Army life as 'a big laugh,' as she is fond of saying. She was in a little different mood, kind of gay and loud, but still very enjoyable. It seems she is going to do the dance from *Carmen* again at the next Symphony concert. She said that it was real sexy and no one would approve.

"The play at Carousel was *Summer and Smoke*. It was very well done. I think it was the most complicated and expertly done play that Carousel has produced. But Knoxville audiences didn't take to Tennessee Williams too well, much as they reacted to your play 'Call Herman In To Supper.' Nine people left in the middle, the night I was there. C.P. talked about it in class and recommended that all his students go and hoped that they would be above being shocked by it as many were.

"Did you see this month's *Mademoiselle*? There is a story by your friend Doris Betts, who won their 1953 Fiction Contest. That probably helped her in getting *Gentle Insurrection* published, which is a combination of short stories. She seems to have outdone the boy you praised. Glenn Scott?"

Jealous that she had published her first novel before mine, and that it had won the very first Putnam University of North Carolina Prize Contest, judged by James Street, Marjorie Kinnan Rawlings, and Pearl S. Buck, I checked Doris' *The Gentle Insurrection and Other Stories* out of the post library. Doris had been my first editor. Editor of *Coraddi*, the student literary journal at Women's College of the University of North Carolina, she had published my uncanny imitation of my hero Thomas Wolfe's style, "Imprisoned Light." Two of the stories in Doris' collection were first published in that magazine, and two in *Mademoiselle*, the editor of which had come down for the arts festival at Women's College, where I met Doris.

"As things look now, next quarter will be my last at UT for a while. I have been accepted at Antioch, a bohemian college in Yellow Springs, Ohio for next fall.

"I have been reading an interesting Spanish writer (in English), Miguel de Unamuno. Have you ever heard of him or read anything? He is a novelist, psychologist, poet, and philosopher and is considered the Dostoyevsky of Spain, though quite different. I think you would like him. He was greatly influenced by Nietzsche. He has something of the same depth of insight into people that Rilke has, though not quite the gentleness.

"Saturday, I went to the film series at Knox College to see the Swedish film, *Torment*, by Ingmar Berman and thought it was quite good. The plot was one you would have liked, for it was about a strange kind of growing pains. . . . a beautiful study of the pangs of European youth. I feel that this kind of sensitivity is more prevalent in Europe than in America. It seemed odd to be walking to Knoxville College without you, and I missed all the interesting comments you would have made on the movie.

"More than once I have missed you. . . . Though you are far away, I feel strangely close to you; perhaps it is because there are plenty of vivid memories.

"Well, I must stop this disjointed letter now, because it is getting late. I shall be looking forward to hearing from you soon, David. Always, Vera.

"PS. I see our Knoxville a little more in detail when I realize that if I go away next year, I will not see spring come to Knoxville as I have for the past nineteen years. It is kind of like trying to impress a friend's features in your mind before the friend leaves forever."

Even as I was steeped in melancholy over Iva Lee, I wooed Vera with verse, compulsion infusing it with allusions to Iva Lee.

In the tranquil pools of evening,
The ethereal respiration of night
Draws together its billion parts.
The tenderness of twilight tailors
The pale radiance to fit me
As I lie upon an Army bunk,
And by the grace of that terrible thing denied the ape,
I stroll thru the two groves of my love
Amid the paradox of my passion — ecstasy and despair!
Dreams I dared not leave unguarded,
Standing like antique furniture from
Another time, a different love,
In a shroud of dust one impulsive breath
Could make stark and terrible.
In the balmy rooms littered with corpses of agony,
New York, Boston, Ogunquit, Tal Tal
Rose like beautiful monsters in the azure pain of memory —
Under the mist-knitted trees of those groves
Like ghosts strong men of intellect deny and mock.

In the gloom of those mistakes, I waited
For the lie that would allow the kindness
One doesn't deny a cripple in a hurricane.
Nothing appeared in that patience grove, despair —
But it and its sister — ecstasy.
You are wearing them — strange flowers in your hair.
I thought you came to mock with your clinical stare
To probe like a disembodied universal conscience

The fallow terrain of my disturbed self-deception.
Demure and white-handed you set your Egyptian stare
Upon my brow and said,
"Lost and silly, the path lies un-weeded now."

You did not take my hand but left to me
decision's horror and challenge. Staggered
by that faint promise of love, I,
swathed in ecstasy and despair, rearranged
The acts of my unbeliever's prayers
And harvested the two groves in the palms of my damp hands.
Dreams such as these, I, lying on an Army cot,
Wait for, as a grove, suspended in the bleak womb of drought,
Waits for the sound of rain.

"David, so, humbly, and sadly I read your beautiful poem about me with its complex expression which almost simply carried me with it. I longed to be the rain that could quell the drought over the grove, but sadly I realized the cloud contained only one small drop of water and try as it might, that small drop could not stop the drought or even be felt on the grove."

Henry James' sensibility and style, the length and rhythm of his sentences, so delighted me that I sometimes imitated him in the prose sketches in which I indulged myself. Dressed up in his style, how would Vera and I look?

"She was much taller than he. Few people failed to notice immediately. Usually, he was aware of it and some of his public mannerisms were attuned to the note of social discord it struck. Had this been the only aspect of their appearance as a couple of which he suffered awareness, the mental discomfort would have been less than it actually was. Not only did her slender stature dwarf him, but about her there adhered an air of self-reliance and of little concern for the petty prejudices of others, and observed beside this, that his obvious preoccupation with their vertical and behavioral incongruity only aggravated the irritation that always engrossed him when they appeared in public. But he knew, as nearly all their acquaintances knew, that while she was of course totally innocent of her height, that aura of aloofness was even less an invention of hers calculated to humiliate him in the eyes of men and women."

Reading Vera's letters, so full of lyrical feeling and intellectually so wide ranging, made me love her more and more.

"David, it is one of those miserably hot spring Knoxville days that is only a forecast of more miserable days to come. I am sure it must be even worse where you are.

"You should have been here to go on the walk I took this afternoon. . . .

I sat in a field and watched two fool birds splattering around in a muddy puddle. The idea of thinking muddy water could either clean or cool them. Then I thought of the idea of me two summers ago thinking swimming in the muddy puddle of the Tennessee River with you, thinking that could cool us off.

"We read W. B. Yeats' 'Wild Swans of Coole' in Dr. Daniel's modern poetry class, and the one you love to recite, 'Leda and the Swan.'

"And now spring has taken possession of our hometown. I have become convinced that fall is a far better season. There is almost something vulgar in spring. It seems as though spring is a season at its most extreme. Fool birds singing outside the window every morning. Fool people playing tennis, sitting on the lawn, completely unable to concentrate on anything, and lonely people with a new kind of loneliness.

"Then there are people who are only happy in the 'spring.' What kind of superficial happiness is this that depends on such erratic external forces as the weather or seasons? Thus ends the casebook of a sentimentalist turned cynic. I just go on trying to appreciate this damnable season that everyone is so in love with.

"The other day I went out to Eastern State Mental Hospital with Dr. Milton's psychology class. It was good to be back with the insane. They are so wonderful in complete lack of insight. One girl out there thought nothing was wrong with her, and she only begged to go home. She is so typical of all mental patients who long to go home. They seem to constantly seek something without knowing what. Their hallucinations are rarely completely satisfying for them.

"The thing that makes working with them so interesting and rewarding is that no matter how diverse or violent they are, being gentle with them and caring what happens to them makes a real difference. If you listen long enough they will pour out the most fantastic things you have ever heard. My wish for you, dear David, is that you will be able someday to work with them.

"Really it is the only place where I can feel most completely free. I can completely lose myself in them. They ask nothing of me, and hence I will give them all I can. They don't care about me in so far as it affects them. Occasionally they will ask about me to try to see what *they* ought to do. It is wonderful to completely lose myself in someone else.

"While we're on a both psychological and personal matter I want to offer some kind of explanation for this letter and generally the kind I write, however dull. It is almost impossible for me to talk out things, but I can write things out completely uninhibitedly. Occasionally I try to carry this over into conversation, with you and a handful of others, but as yet I have been unsuccessful.

An example of its therapeutic effect is this ongoing talk of my 'gender.' Writing to you about it and time itself has gotten me to the place where now it bothers me no longer. It was very good for you to bring it up as you did by the river, for when I think of something myself and realize a fault, I won't bother to do anything about it until someone else notices it, thus making me realize it is now time. So please, have no regrets about bringing up that question, for it helped me and I am sure it has had no traumatic effects.

"On your fervent recommendation, I have been reading a few of Dylan Thomas's poems, but have no definite opinion, yet. My opinion of your imitation of how he reads his poetry aloud is, however, definitely that you are a master mimic.

"David, I haven't honored your request for photographs of me because I just don't have any pictures of me that I can find.

"Your interesting ink blot had a very three-dimensional effect. It looked like a young deer and then a lady in a bonnet.

"Some people are trying to start a chapter of the NAACP. (I am presuming you know what that stands for here at U.T.) We are working in connection with Knox College. The group here kind of lacks life. It seems like something you would be interested in, and we could certainly use your liveliness. These people all believe it very strongly, but not actively. I don't know quite what to do with them. It promises to reek of being a subversive organization, though even several of the English department are in it.

"By the way, C.P. was in a wreck and has been sporting a black eye for several days now. Before that he had wrecked his old car and had to buy a new one. That is about all of the Knoxville news I can rake up.

"Are you doing any writing at all in the Army? Is Cassandra becoming more and more real, at least in your wild imagination?

"I hope being in the Army won't prove to be two years of creative aridity for you. Your growth seems so important to your writing that I hate to see you give it up even for a little while.

"In what ways are you outdoing Pvt. Schine these days? I think it is time these McCarthy hearings were over. This total waste of time. If only they could do something about him, but he is so immune to everything since he is a senator that it seems impossible to do anything. Despicable Ray Jenkins, pride of Tennessee, is not doing much to help. It was kind of an insult to him — well deserved — to be chosen for not having any opinions on the matter. I suppose he was too busy getting criminals out of penalties around here to pay attention to national matters.

"Now it is raining quietly and coolly, and midnight has just come so I must stop this chaotic letter, and so I say. . . . Good morning.

Vera.

"PS I want to say simply and without explanation (I'm sure you need none) that your last letter meant more to me than any other."

From Knoxville came Vera's lucid, somewhat alarmed voice.

"David, I hardly know what to say. Your letter came as only a partial surprise — no shock or insult. I heard you that night by the river, and I knew why you talked rapidly and almost as though you didn't know what you were saying.

"But David, I made no visible reaction because I didn't know what you expected of me or what I felt enough to react at all. I thought about it quite a bit and then figured that you weren't sure of yourself or of me and hence I was afraid to say anything more.

"Now as you ask me for a reaction, I am more sure that you are uncertain of yourself. I felt as though you wanted me to help you and I feel that you must be sure of yourself and so I didn't help you formulate any definite ideas. There were times when I felt helpless and like a fool because I wanted to get you to say what you were thinking but I couldn't.

"As for my reaction to you, about which you expressed some doubts, it has always been good. I have always looked forward to seeing you as a time of enjoyment, new insights, and a time to free myself from myself. With you I have felt like a child listening to a storyteller as you talked. You have an imagination that makes life new and exciting, and yet also infinitely simple. The foreign movie series at the black college, our walks, and talking with you have always been times filled with new understanding. You helped me to notice things I had not noticed and to realize more than was easily seen. You have had the ability to make your life and your struggles my life and my struggles, and this was a new and rich experience for me. Through these and many other experiences my feelings for you have grown deeper.

"I think that you have potentialities that perhaps you will never touch and many you will fulfill. I don't want to lose contact with you because I know that you will mature and fulfill them all. I also know that your maturation will go on all through your life, which is something highly unusual.

"But David . . . love? For me there is a psychological problem in my liking anyone developing into love. There were too many times when it was refused, and I withdrew to keep from being hurt again. This was a long time ago and never happens now. In fact, I have long since sublimated it into a love for all people — almost altruism. But this way is too safe, this is bad, for I want to love individuals but cannot get excited about anyone. I have made a conscious effort to get interested but with only partial success, even when response is favorable. As a result, I am considered overly independent or emotionally cold. So, love to me is merely a deepening growing affection I have for many people, but I can't say that. That is not exactly what I mean but I can't say it.

"Perhaps I mean that I have a growing liking for you that has possibilities but an ability to love someone is at the moment lacking. This is an inadequacy that I am hoping to grow out of. . . . and so, all I ask of you is patience. Please don't feel that there is anything about you that displeases me. I realize all this is frightfully vague and perhaps meaningless and clarifies nothing, but it is hard for me to write.

"I immensely appreciated your letter and everything you said in it. I have read it many times and it always makes me feel very close to you. The poem I also liked. It showed an ability on your part to see below the surface of the things around you. Your sensitivity is something I am always very pleased to see.

"I went in and talked to C.P., who is quite a contrast to Dr. Daniel, for about an hour the other day, and we spent half of the time talking about you. He said he was very sorry he had missed you when you were here. He should be back from Mexico Sunday.

"I must go to work at WUOT now and shelve some of those Gregorian Chants you used to tease me about. One of the last paying hours I shall spend there before I go to Antioch. Always, Vera."

I became exquisitely eager for Vera's next letter, hoping for expressions of love, but never for a moment did I expect her to overshadow my memories of Iva Lee.

"It is two in the am in Knoxville, and WBBM Chicago is being played quite loudly. Ironically enough they are playing Ravel's "Pavane for a Dead Princess," which reminds me of you, since as we listened to it together you seemed to like it as well as I did. It helps make writing to you a very enjoyable and yet almost melancholy experience.

"Last night I had the strangest dream about you. My one short book of Freud was not enough to help me interpret it. I was working in the library, and we were quite busy, but strangely enough the only customers were very old ladies, half of which were dressed in black; the other half, in white. I kept having to get books for them and couldn't stop a minute. I saw you outside the window smiling. I kept trying to get through work so I could talk to you, but I never did, so I merely imagined talking to you and that seemed to suffice for the real thing.

"You know, David, your love has meant more to me than you will ever realize — almost more than anyone else's feeling for me has. Perhaps it is because you give it so freely and unafraid of the consequences. You demand almost nothing of me, and this is so very greatly appreciated. I want very much not to hurt you, and yet there are times when I think perhaps the kindest thing I could have done would have been to completely withdraw while you were still uncertain. But, not knowing my own feelings well enough, I did not."

For a moment, I was surprised to realize that Vera was the first girl I loved totally without jealousy.

"That night at the Van Vactor's when you kissed me, you gave it more meaningfulness and sincerity than I realized could exist. It made me feel very humble and almost ashamed of my inadequacy. For some reason I felt quite sad.

"After hearing you and C.P. talk so much about Carson McCullers, I have gotten her pocketbook of stories entitled *Seven*. I was immensely impressed. She has such a vital vision presented in such a simple way. Never have I found anyone who gave their endings such impact. She leads you to a climax where you feel most writers would solve the problem by a beautiful death, but not her.

"Never have I heard you so vehemently and emotionally rave against the Army. It certainly seems to have gotten worse than when you started. Ours is the country and Army noted for justice, but it doesn't sound as though you are getting your share.

"There are two ways in which people stand up for principles. One makes his fellow men notice the man who is standing up, and the other one makes the men noticing the principle standing up. Which are you in your fight with Senator McCarthy?"

I imagined a subtle accusation. Jealousy out, but paranoia still alive and well.

"Many times, I have wondered if one social system, even communism carried out according to Marx, which would be the most Christian practice possible, can solve all the problems you seem to think it will. I believe a certain amount of struggle is good for man, but society must not create unnecessary ones. It takes more than a social and political system like communism or even democracy. The system seems fairly irrelevant once all the people are fully educated to find their fulfillment and greatest creativity. Once they know what they are doing, they can find the right road for them. Education, of the best and ideal kind, could solve the problems of the world best.

"Frequently I think of your writing at this stage and your aim at publication."

Another possible criticism?

"You know how I feel about that, but Rilke expresses my sentiments so much simpler and more accurately. Read his *Letters to a Young Poet*. Rilke and I disagree on a few points, but the general tone is complete. 'You must change your life' is a killer. You'll find it in 'Apollo.'

"I have read your last letter over many times and especially enjoy your poems. Did you not once say that poetry was too restraining?

"It is nearly time for sunrise and so, Good Morning! Always, Vera"

Vera's voice so embodied her as a vibrant person that it came to me like palpable presence that embraced me.

"A week ago today I was in Columbia for about an hour, and then a few days later spent five hours of the night there sleeping. But David, how does one find anyone at Fort Jackson? I could not remember your number or division — nothing but your name. None of my relatives knew how you found anyone there by phone. It was strange the way I began to think more and more about you as we neared Columbia, so I was very sorry I could not phone you.

"How many times have I read your last letter? I could not count them unless I counted every moment there was a small thought of you, and I went back to the letter to find you. Sure enough there in your beautiful and clear expression, I found you very much alive.

"There was the usual pang of humility and sadness as I packed all your letters with my books for Antioch again. They are right on top of *Great Essays* and *A Pocket World Atlas*.

"I have just about finished *The Heart Is a Lonely Hunter*. Thanks to your fervent recommendation, I had also read *Reflections in a Golden Eye*, *Member of the Wedding*, and *The Ballad of the Sad Cafe*. Now I can find no more. Surely Carson McCullers has written more than this. What are some more?

"It does not seem at all ironic that you should be so interested in reading Pietro di Donato's *Christ in Concrete*. You seem to want to do something that Christ would have liked very much. Many Christians seem to want to do nothing but imitate him, and you would prefer to become more individual and more creative in your own way, which should be more to His liking. Also, Christ was the first communist, which I am sure you have told your fellow soldiers and made them squirm.

"I agree with you, David, that as your play 'Idealists' rather overdramatizes the concept that economics are in all aspects of civilization, but also education, culture, and religion too are in all aspects of all civilizations; so any government built solely on the economic structure would be almost as bad as none. I also think that struggle is vital to human existence. Perhaps under the ideal that if people are placed correctly, they will lead their struggle to doing their work well according to their ability and struggle to improve. I believe though that with a certain, though small as possible, amount of struggle to find their place, they will become more capable and better able to pursue their ambitions. This is one place communism falls down to me, and ideal democracy with the freedom to search and find what you are searching for with all the pitfalls is better and more to my liking. Communism still seems too ideal, and the elimination of class struggle impossible. Always, Vera"

"David, It has been a very hard and fast six weeks that have just gone by — never have I done so much in so short a time. Outside of taking such courses as Economics, Social Psychology, Math, Physical Science, Canoeing, and Personality Study, which is a course in self-analysis and the one you got the form from. I did very much appreciate your help by answering one of them. The answers other people gave about me were quite different.

"I am immensely pleased with the unique 'culture' of Antioch and the classes. We have plenty of active social and political groups here, which I am sure you would like. There are the Young Progressives of America, Students for Democratic Action, Civil Liberties Union, Minority Group Relations Committee, Pacifist Study Group, and various others.

"Also, there are concerts frequently, and the record library is the most extensive I have seen. Josh White, whose singing I remember your playing for me, and Andre Segovia are common everyday words around here. They are as popular with Antiochians as Marilyn Monroe is supposedly with men.

"Do you know when Raven will be back from Paris? I thought I might see her sometime if she is in New York between now and Christmas.

"Your stories and poems and letters always affect me like a breath taken in a moment of action. The freshness and simplicity your writing has is quite unusual. It still seems quite pliable with no excessively demanding style to tie you down.

"Also, to receive your letter at a time when there are no ties of real importance or other stimulation was very comforting. I had looked each day hoping to hear from you, and when I did, it made everything much more worthwhile. Many times, here on the campus I think of you and wish very much you were here to help improve many of the things wrong.

"Occasionally there is too much apathy about the students around an individual. Also, there is too much conformity to non-conformity, which seems to be the worst kind of conformity.

"David, do forgive me for this short chaotic letter."

Taking a letter from Vera from the indifferent hand of the mail clerk, who never looks at any of us, I stepped away, literally a spring in my step in my combat boots. Describing New York as she saw it revived and vivified memories of my times there, coming and going.

"David, the confusion and chaos of this greatly organized city! I wish so much that you were here to help me understand it and really live in it."

Vera's letters made me fervently wish I could be there with her, actually, as she drew me into her own experiences and insights.

I wrote to her. "Not until I read Thomas Mann's bildungsroman *The Magic Mountain* — about a young man's intellectual development, did I realize that the Army had been my own magic mountain. Hans Castorp, the protagonist, is imprisoned by tuberculosis in a sanitorium full of people who stimulate his emotions, imagination, and intellect."

At the Van Vactors' traditional New Year's Eve party, Vera and I passionately visited the maid's nook in the basement, where I had tasted her mouth for the first time.

Ginger blessed me out for taking the liberty of sneaking into the maid's room in the basement. "The evidence was clear."

"March 26, 1954. Midnight

"I have been thinking quite a bit about our talk that night by the river. I wonder how many other people have gotten the same impression about me that you had. I have wondered if perhaps there could be more to it than I had realized. I was quite sure that I had no such tendencies, but now I wonder. Perhaps it was not too good that you made me conscious of such a possibility.

"No danger about boys making passes, because I just reek with queerness. Originally, I purposefully cultivated such a cold attitude for the purpose of avoiding being molested when I went out walking alone.

"Raven's dance as Carmen was not very sexy at the concert. Then I saw Raven the other night at a play at Carousel Theater and we reminisced about the roles you played there."

I got a pass to Myrtle Beach for "Rest & Recreation." I took up with Bill Davis and another soldier, and we took up with twin girls who asked to be with us. But nothing came of it, so to speak. We were fearful of tough Latino kids called "Pachucos." The old steward on my first ship called me that. Also, "mericone," queer. I took photographs, including other soldiers round about us.

I took a bus to Union, South Carolina, hoping to encounter Vera, who said she'd be there for her cousin's wedding, and rented a room and read.

"Sunday as I walked alone in the woods near my aunt's house in Union, SC just eighty miles from you, I thought a great deal of you. You seemed almost embodied there. I am with you.

"I imagine you as a nine-year-old boy rolling and throwing the Knoxville News Sentinel."

I was gratefully aware of the way Vera had of weaving memories and thoughts about me in illuminating ways throughout her philosophical musings.

"Is Riva the bisexual painter you told me about? That picture you carry in your wallet of her with the Van Vactors in Spain wearing a beret made a somewhat puzzling impression on me. Raven took the photo? Do write more about her.

"These past few weeks I have more than ever missed talking with you and constantly look forward to your letters and writing to you. I miss you a great deal and shall be looking forward to seeing you. Always, Vera."

I was always alert to her insights about who I was in her eyes, as contrasted to Raven and others. At the Van Vactors' one evening, not with a pointed finger, but with a piercing look, Vera declared, "You, David, are a possessed demon."

"I often re-read Poe's 'Alone,' which increasingly suits my temperament and evolving predicament, before and during the Army ordeal."

In my radio voice, I intoned

> The mystery which binds me still.
> From the Thunder and the storm,
> And the cloud that took the form
> (when the rest of Heaven was blue)
> Of a demon in my view.

"Beginning with Poe, I've always responded to the bizarre. In Virginia Woolf's *Orlando*, the male hero lives 500 years, changing from a young man into a woman. Woolf's style seemed ungodly fine.

"A line from Coleridge's 'Kubla Khan' describes my mind. 'Weave a circle round him thrice, for he hath drunk the milk of paradise.' And 'In Xanadu did Kubla Khan a stately pleasure dome decree.' The army became for me an exotic country called Xanadu in which I endeavored to decree an intellectual and artistic pleasure dome."

David Madden as a merchant seaman.
Photograph shortly after joining the Army.

David Madden as a merchant seaman. Photograph shortly after joining the Army.

Madden's comrades in basic training. Photo by David Madden.

Dickie Madden,
my big brother.

My little brother,
John Madden in
Marine uniform.

The author sculpting Buddha from clay in the Service Club Art Studio.

Photo of a young woman in motorcycle gear alongside a drawing done by Madden and labeled as Cassandra.

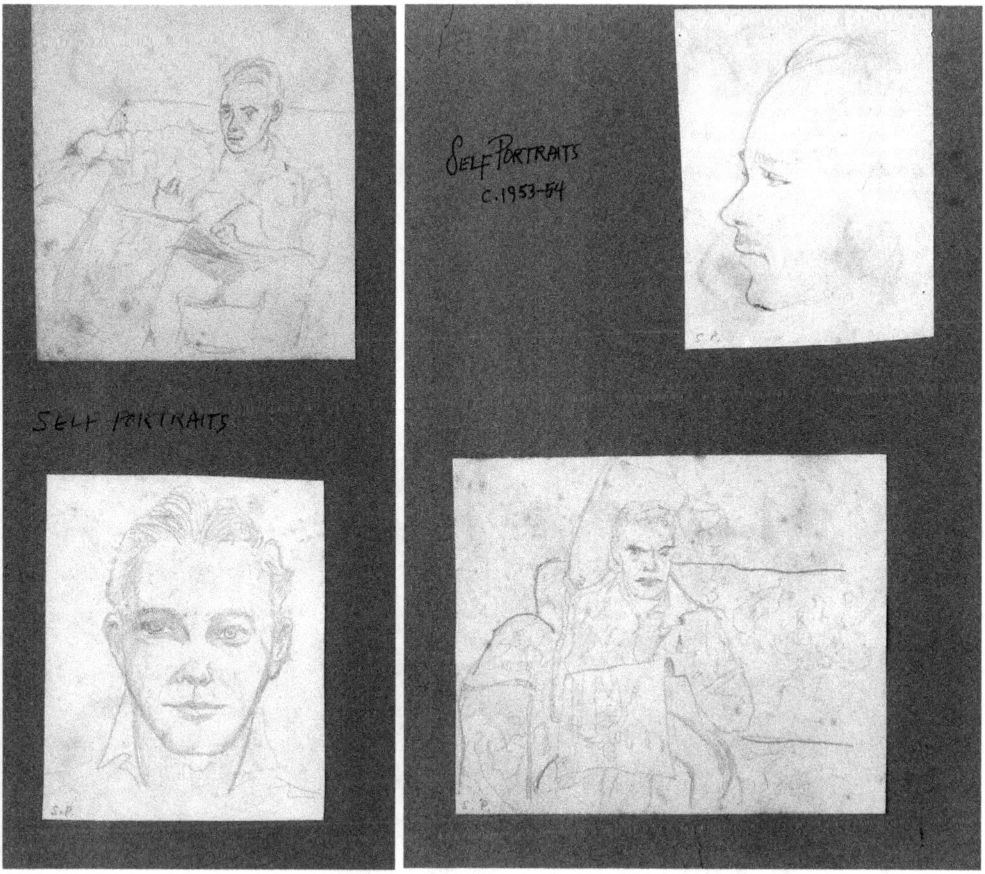

Self-portraits, 1952–1954.

Vera.

Adrien Van Vactor,
aka Raven Harwood.

Hope Savage.

David Van Vactor, my mentor, composer, conductor, and Adrien's father.

MISS HOVEY'S FICTION WRITING CORRESPONDENCE COURSE

Miss Hovey's fiction writing course, coming out of the University of Iowa, struck me as basically very good, and I thought that anyone could have learned a great deal from her lucid commentaries, especially as they were embedded in ongoing responses from C. P. Lee, my first creative writing teacher, from Walton Rawls, and from a not-so literate soldier I nabbed as captive listener in the Post library.

"Miss Hovey, I need this course because here in the Army one tends to become repulsed into near creative sterility.

"I enclose 'The Fall of the House of Pearl,' the only writing I have with me, because it just came back from *Discovery*, rejected by editor-novelist Vance Bourjaily, who greeted me at the door in his jock-shorts when I submitted the story in person at his apartment in Manhattan soon before the Army collared me. In a scrawled note, he declared that my story was 'too much indebted to Truman Capote.' Although I knew about Capote and had a copy of *Other Voices, Other Rooms* on my shelf in Knoxville, I hadn't yet gotten around to reading him. A few years ago, I was also accused of craven imitation of Tennessee Williams when my play was performed. I had never heard of Tennessee Williams."

Still working on my American History correspondence course from the University of Tennessee with Professor Stanley J. Folmsbee, I was excited to open the first lesson for a fiction writing correspondence course with Miss Alma Hovey.

The creative writing syllabus, like clerk typist school, gave commands, but quietly.

The two books Miss Hovey assigned were *The Pocket Book of Short Stories,* edited by M. Edmund Speare, which 'round about 1947 had already been my first experience with most of the famous American, English, and Continental classic writers, and *Story Writing,* Edith Ronald Mirrielee's then famous textbook, with a laudatory preface by John Steinbeck.

Miss Mirrielee got tough in the first few pages of her book. "You are, that is, the very worst variety of amateur, the one who knows not but knows not that he knows not." Well, maybe so, maybe not so.

The first book on writing that I had read was W. Somerset Maugham's *The Summing Up*, which included the repeatable phrase, "Aim at lucidity, simplicity and euphony."

When I was fifteen, seeing the need, I wrote a program for broadcast on radio on the techniques of writing fiction.

As my first lesson, Miss Alma Hovey instructed me to write my autobiography. I imagined impressing her with the story of my life, in 12 pages or less.

Unimpressed, but concerned about the sordidness of my life story, Miss Hovey annotated "The Fall of the House of Pearl" and later my play "The Great Wings Still Beating," prompting my counter reply.

Miss Hovey's next assignment was in two parts.

"From a story of your choice, copy a description of a character." I chose "A Passion in the Desert" by Honoré de Balzac, one of my most favorite stories. Miss Hovey's commanding voice struck a note heard often on the drill field. "Copy a scene of dialog that evokes a sense of who the speakers are." I chose "The Killers" by Ernest Hemingway, another great favorite.

She usually inked her comments internally, snugly.

["That is typical Hemingway dialogue. Have you noticed any change in later Hemingway fiction — The Old Man and the Sea, *for example?"]*

Create your own description of a person, then revise it.

"Some people insisted that she was nine feet tall. Perhaps because she was Texan. Though she seemed to have no control over her white arms, *[Age class? What did she do with her arms?]* her small hands were magnetically expressive. Her ankles were like four large *[A quadruped?]* mauve agates — curiously had a sexiness. Now her buttocks were famous in the Village, for truly they were marvelous! Believe me. But while there was nothing to her hair, *[Bald?]* Charltas' black eyes were pools of oil. She not only wore braces, but she lisped and stuttered.

[It is not easy to see Charlta. The underlined details interpret instead of picturing, and though interpretation may be very effective, in this case is does not hold the description together nor let a reader gain a distinct impression.]

Hovey: Create a scene in a story you have outlined but have not yet written.

I imagined a scene that captured the conflict between Iva Lee (Arabel) and her mother, implying that she is going to meet me (Noel) against her mother's sharp objection.

"Arabel, where are you going?" asked her mother, looking up from the sewing machine, stopping, pretending to look for a new needle.

"Out."

"Out where?"

"Well, I don't know where. Anywhere but here."

"Well, you needn't act so all-fired smart about it!"

"I'm *not* acting smart," Arabel said, wearily.

"Don't you tell me you ain't acting smart, young lady. Don't you think I know if my own daughter is acting smart or not? Ain't I your mother?"

"There's no denying it," said Arabel, immediately regretful she had said it.

Mrs. Traven rose from behind the sewing machine, pointing the long, thin, closed scissors into the air, flashes of reflected light dancing along the hot blades. *[Vivid.]*

"Now you listen to me, you little no count bitch! Don't you ever talk to your mother like that ever again! You'll wind up in the reform school yet. By thunder, I'm at the end of my rope!"

Incensed by the contagious violence her mother had so sharply stitched into the hot, quiet room, Arabel uncontrollably *[not needed]* shouted, "That's where you should be!" flinched, turned and ran frantically out of the house, her mother's words darting after her like needles. *[You carry out the figurative comparison with sewing skillfully.]*

"Come back here! You come straight back into this house! You hear me? Arabel! Little bitch, little bitch!" There her voice broke like gray thread had moments before, between the snappy fingers. "Little whore . . . O, my baby. Baby . . . Arabel . . . honey . . ."

[In this bit of dialogue, you achieve a unified effect. The speeches and the incidental description build together to show character and situation.]

Miss Hovey told me to describe a setting for a story.

I felt a need to seize the occasion to re-create Tilly's Pond from the three years I lived on Cedar Street before I went to Christenberry Junior High.

"Old, cranky Mr. Tilly worked all day every day on his pond between Cedar Street and an alley where we had lived briefly to improve the six-tiered marble terrace around the pond he had dug himself and chased me, Dickie, John, and our friends away, or paid us a few nickels to do a trivial chore or two. But daring Dickie would sneak onto the little raft made of planks attached to barrels and float upon the pond or sneak when Mr. Tilly wasn't close by into the houseboat the old man had transported from the Tennessee River, inside of which he kept a Charlie McCarthy dummy. Only Dickie was allowed, now and then, into the houseboat, while we wondered how he persuaded him."

Across from my house, Buddy McDaniel and I crawled through the sewer pipe under Cedar Street, under the jungle where we most often played, and came out high above on Ailor Street. From up there, the sight of my house gave me a strange feeling, as if it had a reality apart from my own life, like seeing my mother suddenly at a distance walking on Gay Street on a crowded sidewalk.

After Buddy and I had crawled awhile through another drainage pipe in the jungle across the street from Mr. Tilly's Pond, our ritual pattern was to hide in the jungle to spy on Amara, the voluptuous refugee from Italy, as she walked stately by after work in C. B. Atkins Furniture Mill, who turned one time and looked us right in the eye and smiled."

I surrendered to a compulsion to write a completely imagined short story, moved by desegregation and racial discrimination, and vaguely under the influence of James Joyce's short story "Clay" from *Dubliners*.

Miss Hovey asked for the theme.

"I never articulate a theme before plunging deeply into writing a story. But this may do: How common people, when placed in social contexts contrary to their nature, in which all their old values are questioned, and absorbed into a body of vague morality, will give vent to strong sexual impulses that have survived from primitive times. How it is only the weak made strong by experience who triumph over their desires, the imaginative person who can find a lesson in the misfortune of others and then seek a way out for themselves. Does that do it?"

I felt good about the opening paragraph of "Gristle," about a black woman's bitter love affair.

"She woke that morning from a dream of him: in his black shirt, cream colored trousers, brim-down pearl-gray hat, and his shiny black shoes. She lay a little longer than usual before getting up and going down the hall to take her shower, remembering him and what their love had been. But that was a time long ago and she so seldom really thought of him, that by the time she'd gotten out of bed and finished her shower, taking a little longer with the frayed rough towel, and drank her coffee by the cold window, she was no longer thinking of him, though a vague feeling remained. She was thinking of how she might afford a pair of pink lace doilies to go on the mantel."

Miss Hovey gave me a reasonable reason why my scene with Arabel and her mother offended her on behalf of readers in general.

"Dear Mr. Madden:

"If you must write about degradation and degeneracy, I must insist that you learn how to do it less crudely and clumsily. Repetitions of profanity and obscenity grow very tiresome when they become more monotonous than nauseating.

"It is difficult to understand how a young man with your wide reading and skill in some kinds of writing can have been so blind to artistic effect as to write as you did in this sketch. Good taste and a realization that restraint and suggestion are far more powerful than repeated expositions of indecency will, I hope, prevent a repetition of this kind of writing. Consider Somerset Maugham's "Rain." See how Sadie Thompson is drawn, how the tragedy of the story is achieved. And perhaps you know Salinger's "Pretty Mouth and Green My Eyes," another example of just enough, not too much. Of course, learning to write is learning how much of anything is enough."

I enjoyed very much Miss Hovey's responses to my lessons.

"Dear Miss Hovey, you referred in your note on my biographical sketch to the element of abnormality in my play "The Great Wings Still Beating."

"Frankly, I have sometimes found abnormality (whatever that is) as interesting as normality. You suggest then that I write about real people I know. I know a number of people who're not normal by orthodox standards and they manage to seem quite real to me and somewhat more readily understandable and often more interesting than the so-called normal people I grew up among, attended university classes with, went to sea with, and am now soldiering with.

"I have encountered as many mental cases, eccentrics, misfits, perverts, etc. in those areas of life where normal people congregate as I have in the bistros and saloons of Greenwich Village or among the intellectuals of Knoxville. After all, so much of that kind of behavior which we are expected to believe is normal is given to us in capsule form via TV, radio, movies, and that hideous institution most powerfully in America — mass advertising; and few intelligent persons not seeking a false sense of mental security will identify themselves with those stereotypical traits.

"But I know what you mean, what you were thinking. There is, I believe, a stage through which every young writer is expected to pass or get stuck in — that one in which his stories seem over-populated with intellectual homosexuals, lesbians, nymphomaniacs, paranoids, and other 'mixed up kids.' *[The important thing is to grow out of this stage, isn't it?]* I must admit that I consciously have sown my own oats in that obdurate terrain. I *still* write about odd people."

I imagined Professor Hovey understanding my creative temperament more fully if I explained the force of the bizarre in my imagination. Mainly the lingering impact of the Harry Clarke illustrations long before I really delved into Edgar Allan Poe's stories and poems. His profoundly bizarre vision took hold of me and has never let me go.

"I think *all* people are extremely bizarre! How can I be expected to write about *normal, real* people when I think I would have a difficult time finding one specimen? *[Surely not all people are abnormal. Some are merely eccentric; many are individualistic whose interest lies in their not being types.]*

"Perhaps you can understand me better when I say that I have no desire whatsoever to write for or sell a story to *Saturday Evening Post, Colliers* or any other pseudo-normal-subject-matter-periodical.

"When I was fifteen, I had an agent in New York, Sydney Saunders, who represented Raymond Chandler. He sold exclusively to the slicks. During my first trip to New York city, his assistant, Jo Stewart, said to me, after a series of failures to get my stuff accepted, 'David, I don't think you'll ever be able to write the kind of s — t that I have to sell. And that's a compliment.' I have always taken it as such."

"In May of 1953, Jo had said to me, 'The last three stories you submitted are too grim and your characters too unpleasant. They appear too shadowy and obscure. Do, David, try to write a story about pleasant people that has reader identification, so I can sell them for you. And David, watch your spelling!"

"I think you've read Thomas Mann's short story 'Tonio Kroger,' Miss Hovey, in which he sets forth the idea that all artists, deep in their souls, yearn above all to be normal, average, accepted into society. I think he infers that all artists are somewhat abnormal, and if he does, I agree. *[But few writers are Thomas Mann or Dostoyevsky.]*

"It may be normal behavior for a man like Raymond Chandler to sit down at his typewriter and in a matter of a few weeks write out what amounts to a large check. But is it normal behavior for a man like Dostoyevsky to labor long, insufferable hours, his body racked with disease and weariness, on a book called *The Idiot*? Not by any stretch of any normal person's imagination. I'll admit that the inner feelings which prompted him to write such morose stuff derived from that basic compulsion which also results in folk tales, many of which express anything but normal sentiments.

"And let us not ignore the Bible. But doesn't abnormality evolve from normality? Obviously. *[But is abnormality obviously normality too? But why quibble about words when you really understand them?]*

"You suggest that these lessons will start me as an 'amateur' (hateful word), in the right direction. *[Let me say then that I hope they will help you to continue to develop skill in your writing.]* I like to think that all these years I have been writing that I have been moving in *some* direction, and it would bring me infinite remorse to know that it has been the wrong one. *[Usually, gains are not made in straight unbroken lines, but by some degree of trial and error.]*

Is any man ever sure of himself? Was Thomas Wolfe sure after all the sweat with his beloved editor Maxwell Perkins, effort that, it is said, killed both men? And was Flaubert after all those years of striving for the impossible goal of perfection — the perfect word — ever free of frustration? Yet his achievement is truly remarkable.

"If I were sure of myself, I don't think I would 'need' to write. I am sure of only two things — which is that I 'need' to write, that I 'must' write."

Eager to begin the next complete short story, I asked Miss Hovey which of the three scenarios I had enclosed, "Rosanna," "Thad Miller in Atlas," and "Cassandra Singing," she would choose, expecting her to choose "Rosanna," a tale set in Tal Tal, Chile, seven thousand feet up in the Andes Mountains, that I had imagined at sea, just after leaving that little Andean desert town.

"Dear Mr. Madden: If you know enough about life in the Chilean village to make the story ring true, I hope you will choose to write "Rosanna" first, as I imagine it will develop into a fine story. The focus of your second plan for a story, "Cassandra Singing," I am not sure of. What is it about? I can find three possible themes, but I can't tell which is the major theme. 'Cassandra Singing' will need cutting and shrinking to keep it from seeming repetitive."

"Thank you for your complimentary letter about my comment on your lesson.

"I think we understand each other now. And you will remember, I hope, that you are not writing *only* for the reform school graduates you referred to. Also, I hope that you can read of and meet people on a somewhat higher level than those you knew as a boy and realize that they, too, have been material for literature, that they are not always weak or insincere.
Sincerely, Alma B. Hovey."

I surrendered to a strong urge to plunge into "Cassandra Singing."

But persistent nostalgia for Tal Tal, Chile compelled me to set "Cassandra Singing" aside for three days while I wrote in green ink an acceptable first draft of "Rosanna."

"Dear Miss Hovey, please read this story very carefully, not that I think you wouldn't, but I have tried to work into the fabric a very complex symbolic association and repetition of ideas in different contexts. Please be severe where needed and comment as exhaustively as you are inclined. Now, as

Fitzgerald said in *The Crack-up*, 'Draw your chair up close to the edge of the precipice and I'll tell you a story.' D. M."

Possibly for its mechanical errors, Alma gave "Rosanna" a B, and some very useful revision suggestions that I drew upon, as in these first three paragraphs.

"It had been three days since the boy died. The corpse was poorly embalmed and could no longer resist the terrific heat. But in less than an hour, less time than it would take the child's mother to drain the cask of cheap Chilean wine, Rosanna would hear Moro's old blue nag's sluggish, iron hoofs clacking, and the creaking of his hearse in the cobbled courtyard. Then long hours would pass in her heart before she heard the rasp of pitched sand upon the small wooden casket, lined with the hide of a mountain lion.

"Thinking of her pale, drunken mistress, her sickly playmate of many years ago, Rosanna felt a perverse compassion pervade her mind and body as one shudders with the sudden brief chill one gets in the noon heat that drops down like a pall from the arid Andes.

"Before the dawn the pale light lay vaporous upon the pallid roof-tops, and cocks bugling into the chill misty air sent a ripple of sound into the massive silence that bore down upon the rough and unverdurous terrain. The uncomprehendable, ponderous, immutable hugeness and height of the barren Andes of Northern Chile rose tremendous and visibly staggering before Carlos as he stepped out of the house with the uncertainty of the body still numbed with sleep's narcotic effect. Not after three weeks and now as he gazed dazedly out across the sandy stretches, beyond the railroad tracks lying in a womb of mist like something in a Dali painting and up at the magnificent obduracy of the mountains, he thought, not after months longer will I be able to stand there in the morning light and look at them without a feeling of looking upon something hardly real but too massive and blood-jumping to be otherwise.

"Rosanna told herself, 'If I forget everything else about her, I think I will always remember the way her mouth moved when she talked about the things she loved. She did not make of her hands two batons as some Chileans do when they conduct a concerted conversation, but her eyes waltzed when the things of which she spoke were things she loved and wanted you to love too.'

Miss Hovey wrote, "In giving this story a high grade, I am considering its strength perhaps more than its weakness. It is not yet evenly fine and strong in expression, but you have attempted a difficult story and have gained more in writing it than you might have in perfecting an easier and less significant narrative."

I almost daily pursued three schooling activities simultaneously. US History, the lessons never returned, the creative writing correspondence course, and how to become an accurate company clerk.

Passing the supply room door, seeing the mail clerk fiddling with mail, I hoped I'd get my American history correspondence course lesson back from Dr. J. Wesley Hoffmann in the University of Tennessee history department with another A.

One of Miss Hovey's lessons focused on the effective use of repetition in "Haircut" by Ring Lardner. I quoted and cited repetitions of the idea that Jim Kendall loves a joke, whatever its consequences. The list excludes those jokes without harmful effect. Then I cited repetitions of the idea that Paul Dickson has enough mentality to understand revenge.

In "Paul's Case" by Willa Cather, I found indications of the passage of time. [*This lesson will be worthwhile only if it points up for you the need of implications and indications of passing of time when you write your own stories.*]

I added a passage of my own that expresses action.

"The horsemen rode through the night, swiftly through the moving mist, crashing in speed through waves of moonlight, diluted in the trees, flaying the air with their balancing arms as they swerved under and between low branches on the narrow trail, up and down, and long distances along level fields. [*Here the parallelism is not quite beside or across complete.*] The horses' legs stood up amazingly to the running pace; only their flared nostrils, their flanks with a sea-risen look in the queer morning moon's-glow were evidence of the terrific going, and not one cried in anguish nor faltered in the gullies nor the jumps over fallen trees. But two miles outside Harlinsville, one of them suddenly went down crashing to earth, screaming and raking smoke of anguish into the chill morning air, its bit-cut mouth bleeding into the frost-webbed pine needles."

[*A very vivid scene, strengthened by vigorous verbs.*]

Miss or Mrs. — I never discovered which — Alma Hovey's first letter had started me off wondering how she looked, a wide and deep range of likelihoods. Early on, she was an old maid, thin lipped, her voice a steely whisper, brown eyes behind steel-rimmed spectacles, her hair yanked back tightly into a perfect bun, she was incongruously busty, always in a gray sweater, her shoes shined a lustrous brown.

Midway in our somewhat telepathic relationship, I saw, as I read her letters, envisioning her reading mine, and my fiction, or saw her in my fitful or focused reveries, she as a pretty lady, blond pompadoured hair, eyes like Balzac's "The Girl with the Green Eyes," flaring nostrils, lustrous lips, a smoky voice like a film noir movie actress, wearing sibilant sounding ballet slippers and dresses of Harlequinesque colors.

Reaching up to take the letter that the mail clerk handed down from his perch, I hoped for some C. P Lee intellectual simulation, and there was C. P. Lee. A full sense of C. P. Lee swept through my consciousness as I slit open his letter with my thumb. Eager to know what C. P. thought of "Rossana," I had risked sending him the original handwritten copy.

"My dear David, I answer at once your charming letter.

"About 'Rosanna.' Frankly, I do not like it as much as your other stories, and I hasten to tell you why. It is surface. That is, you are *interested* in the surface of the story more than the interior. One feels that you did work on the symbolism, that it was planned rather than spontaneous.

"And, too, there is no feeling that you feel what you are writing, in depth, except for the picturesque detail. The whores, the dust, the heat, the physical details are excellent, but there is no patch in this in which one senses your emotional involvement, and the projection of it, as in 'Seven Frozen Starlings,' that wonderful first story of yours I read about little hare-lipped Rosemary, despite that damned 'moon-blasted cobwebs' image.

"I feel that you should not try foreign scenes; a good story, like an iceberg, is nine-tenths under water, and you cannot, I suspect, sense the Baroness yet. Or ever.

"Back from a wonderful trip, I now face Knoxville. Leaving Thursday, and I shall probably live in my cabin on Chilhowee Mountain during October, while I hunt for an apartment. I have finally given up the apartment over the florist shop by the railroad tracks where you first visited me, appearing three steps down from the threshold, holding aloft, as one would a gift of the gods, a foot high stack of your stories — in somewhat readable longhand."

On one trip, C. P. took me further up the mountain to meet unattractive, constant talking Professor Barnacle, folklorist, folk song expert. He thought I would like to listen to her talk about folk songs and such. Yes, I did. She was living in sin with a rough-hewn mountain man. Walking back down, we came upon him as he was returning home with items he got bartering with mountain blackberries down in Maryville where Miss Barnacle taught at the college.

C. P. told me that he had heard from Robert Daniel, reporting that he and the family were all having a lovely time. "Quoth he: 'There's no telling what famous foreigner will turn up with the next batch of tourists. Steinbeck was here in the fall, and Humphrey Bogart and his Lauren Bacall are expected to arrive who knows when."

On leave, when I showed up in the doorway of his office, C. P. was into a mild fit of scratching his eczema. "Well, Robert and I were wondering whether you had perished."

"No, merely surviving. My imagination, though, is slowly giving birth to Cassie and Lone."

The English accent he had adopted when he was a Rhodes Scholar enhanced his commentary that day on "Rosanna." "This is peasant Rosanna's story in focus, while it is, of course, a story of the Baroness too. Doubtless you want the Baroness to lie like a captive, languid fish on her bed, as strange to us as she was to Rosanna, transformed from the little girl of their childhood to this bizarre, titled woman. OK. And effective, too, but if that is it, then we do not see the Baroness through Rosanna's mind, though we see her through Rosanna's *eyes*. There is a difference. One needs Rosanna's helpless inability to solve the enigma of another human, known in two disconnected aspects, in order to feel *ourselves* involved. That is the real technical defect: the reader cannot feel for Rosanna, and so does not feel what she must feel as she walks behind the hearse. Remember, we can all be an outcast, harelip or otherwise, scorned by others, dreaming our dreams.

"Although your style often misfired, the first story of yours that I read, 'Seven Frozen Starlings,' involved us in Rosemary's story. Now, this can too, but it doesn't yet. You must make us feel that we are akin to Rosanna, that we see but cannot understand. Why? Why? Why do other people behave this way? And then, alas, why do we? This may not be your story as you see it, but it may help clarify in your mind what you want me to feel, through whom you want me to feel it.

"Robert's address for the nonce is 3 Odos 25 Martiou, Philothei, Athens. Be assured that he would warmly welcome words from you."

For "Cassandra Singing," Miss Hovey instructed me to get to know my characters by telling about the past lives of Cassie and Lone's parents, beginning with the father.

To test the effectiveness of their backgrounds, I asked a back-woods fellow dozing at the next table in the Post library whether he was a southerner. His having replied, "Yeah," I asked him to let me read my narrative summary aloud to him in a library whisper for his responses. Bewildered, he nodded.

"Calvin 'Coot' McDaniel was born and raised on a farm in the Great Smoky Mountains in Cades Cove Community. All his ancestors back to 1750 had lived there and very few had made a treasonous migration from to the city, mainly Knoxville, folks being quite satisfied in this pastoral setting and the way of life that had, due to ethnocentric pride, changed little through the years. But by 1920, the McDaniel family itself had been reduced to Coot and his father and a brother wounded by gas attack in WWI.

"Say, soldier, tell me why so far you want your story to be as boring as two shackled prisoners trying to play jack rocks?'

"It's the historical context, man."

"Kotex or no Kotex, it's boresome."

"Stick around for the good parts.

"So, that year, Coot met Charlotte at a square dance fifty miles from Cade's Cove in Knoxville. Every weekend for a year, Coot hitched a ride into Knoxville to court Charlotte, a waitress in the Gold Sun Café in Market Square. Then they secretly got married, and Coot left the farm, disowned by his proud father who presented him with two shotgun shells to save until city life got him down and he found it necessary to leave it and the rest of the world. Coot never got over the influence of his father and his severe Calvinism, and he reminded Charlotte of that every day of their marriage.

"Coot went to work on the section gang of the Southern railroad and Charlotte in the Cherokee Knitting Mill. Lone was born, raised in relative lower-middle class comfort. Cassandra was born three years later. Coot was planning and saving to buy a farm near Cade's Cove, but his foreman offered to sell him a farm cheap on the outskirts of Lonsdale beside an abandoned rock quarry on Sharp's Ridge just outside Knoxville, so he bought it and worked it, and invited his father to come see how well he was doing. He wouldn't come, but Coot's sickly brother came, and stayed a while, and died in the house of typhoid.

"Coot took to drinking — "

"I knew it, I knew it, sure as the world." The hay-seed fellow picked his teeth.

" — and more often went on long hunting trips into Black Oak Hills, ignoring his wife whom he loved, rejecting his seventeen-year-old son Lone, who didn't like farming or hunting.

"Meanwhile, fourteen-year-old Cassie, through whose mind the story is filtered, looking like her older brother Lone in her features and build, was growing up, an anemic, tall, skinny girl, frequently ill from the long-lingering effects of rheumatic fever. Coot had a gruff affection for her, Charlotte was merely dutiful, and Lone gave her hot and cold affection. Coot finally returned to working on the railroad, and the farm deteriorated.

"When they were younger, Cassie and Lone, who also had had but recovered from rheumatic fever, shared the same bed, and played games and sang together. When she had periods of better health, she was full of explosive vitality. But when she was ill, Lone avoided her. She sang folk ballads and played Lone's guitar, which he had abandoned when he took up motorcycling. When she was very little, she had learned the ballads from workers and hobos on the railroad below the house and had never forgotten them.

"Coot became moodier and treated Charlotte very badly, while she sought refuge in the Holy Roller Church revivals at the bottom of the hill and in her great attention to Lone. Coot hated Lone and Lone hated his father. Cassie feared Coot and admired her brother's energy and adventures — he was her hero."

"Excuse my snoring, but I kain't hep it."

"Here the story begins, the background coming to light in Cassie's reverie, and in dialog in scenes.

"Confined to bed, Cassie reads the *National Geographics* that the former owner of the farm had left littered in the attic, and daydreams and sings.

"Coot, 48, has been laid off the railroad, never having bothered to learn to do anything but farm a little and lay and repair track and ties. Every morning Coot takes his seven hounds into the hills to hunt small game, seldom bathes, drinks, very seldom speaks to anyone but Cassie, who listens, usually with her back turned on him.

"Out of school, working in the textile factory with his mother, Lone had bought a motorcycle with money saved from his job, which he despises. After work he rides all night with a gang, the Hellhounds, as their respected leader. Former leader of the gang, still a member, Blackie Weaver, is his only friend."

"Look out! Look out!" By now, my listener was under the pleasure dome of storytelling.

"Cassie alone is aware that, beyond ordinary familial discord, something dark and tragic is evolving to destroy them all. She feels it, rather than thinks it, expresses it in the folk songs she chooses and the songs she improvises. Enhancing the effect of the songs, she tries to tell Lone about what she feels, but he laughs at her and can talk only of how wonderful it is to ride fast into the wind, forgetting everything. She yearns to be like him, healthy, carefree, strong, popular among the boys (not that she likes boys sexually yet).

"She better watch out!"

"From her window in the mornings, Cassie sees Coot go off to hunt and come back at dusk when Charlotte goes down the hill, across the swinging bridge, down the road to the revival meetings. Through her window, Cassie can see and hear the singing in the church.

"She watches Lone ride off on his motorcycle and come in late at night in a fury of speed and sound. She suspects his goings-on with girls, especially Gypsy, in roadhouses and tourist courts on the highway below.

"His friend Blackie, 19, the leader Lone beat up and replaced, shows up in her room now and then and teases her and tells her she is pretty and that all she needs is a man to love her. Once she told that to Lone, and when he came in later with cuts on his knuckles and face, she was both frightened and fascinated.

"One morning Cassie awakens from a frequent nightmare: Coot had sicced his hounds upon Lone and Cassie's face was one of them and her mother's another and her grandfather's another, and Coot was the huge tree outside her window.

When she awakens, Coot is calling the dogs out of the run-down barn, and Charlotte is making coffee in the kitchen before going to work, and Lone, fully dressed in jeans and leather riding jacket, lies asleep on his cot in the bedroom he still shares with Cassie.

"Charlotte brings the *Knoxville Journal* to Lone, wakes him, stands drinking coffee at the window, casually asks how Cassie is feeling. Cassie is noticing the X mark made with a finger in the dust on Lone's boot, thinking Gyspy had made it as a yes to sex with Lone, probably in a tourist court.

"Lone gets up, hints, as he does every morning, that he may not go to work again at the factory. Coot is heard going off into the woods, which Cassie and Lone call 'the Jungle,' the hounds yelping.

"Lone and Momma are talking in the kitchen. Cassie senses an ominous silence. Then Lone runs through the house and out the front door, Momma running after, calling him back, sounding terrified.

"Lone goes to Cade's Cove to look for his grandfather to meet him for the first time. He wrecks his motorcycle and dies.

"Hey, man, what's you want to do that to him for?"

"After Lone's funeral, Cassie lies down on Lone's cot, hugging his boots against her only good dress, and Charlotte is sitting at the kitchen table drinking a cup of coffee, staring into space. Cassie remembers leaving her in there fully dressed up, silly old hat on, her worn pocketbook on the table, pale, glaze eyed.

"Cassie learns from Charlotte some of what follows and imagines the rest. Lone had kissed his mother passionately in the kitchen and he had seen his father coming toward the house from the barn. Coot had stopped and looked and turned slowly into the barn.

"Coot's dogs lying around him, he sat down and thought of how he had not wanted to come to the city where his wife had lived, had wanted to farm with his father in the Smokies, who had resisted threats to buy his land for the Smoky National Park. For years he saved money to move to the outskirts and farm and work too, hoping his son could do most of the farming. Lone *had* done that until he rebelled and went motorcycling. Now nothing at all is any good anymore. Coot looks at the dead rabbit in his lap, puts it, still warm, in his shirt next to his body and shoots himself.

"Now Cassie remembers hearing Charlotte's scream when told Lone had been killed in a motorcycle accident, seeing her running out the front door, awkward, unreal, then hearing the shot, feeling disgusted, assuming that Coot was killing rabbits again.

"Gran'paw does not attend the funerals of Coot and Lone. He had always rejected his son for moving away, letting a woman rule him, deserting their heritage, becoming a moonshine-runner, a railroader, a dead-beat drunk. But Lone had won him over and had often gone up into the mountains to visit him, had raced there in ice and snow that morning, and skidded off into a ravine.

"Cassie thinks of how Lone looked like her when he lay in his coffin, and remembers that as kids both were always sick, in the same big brass bed, he coming out of it because Coot made him get out and exercise, derided him, called him sissy, estranging Charlotte. Then Coot was kind to Cassie, but she rejected his rare fatherly caresses.

"Cassie puts on Lone's boots and goes to sleep.

"She goes to work in Kress'. With her first salary, she gets Lone's cycle pulled out of the ravine and put in the shop. Charlotte wanted to burn his cycle clothes, but Cass hides them in the woods.

"Cass comes in from work, very tired and ill — fired for being too weak. But she has enough money to get the motorcycle out of the shop if she can steal some from Charlotte's pay. As she lies on her bed thinking, hearing the singing and preaching at the Holy Roller Church where Momma has gone, she smells something in the room, finds a bottle of medicine with mold like a mane of hair under the bed.

"She takes Charlotte's scissors into the woods, strips down naked, cuts her long blond hair and buries it, feels great freedom, looks at herself in her pocket mirror, tears her dress off, puts on Lone's clothes, and runs wildly to the crest of the ridge.

"She becomes queen of Lone's old gang of motorcyclists, the Hellhounds, who hang out in front of a theater in Lonsdale, terrorize the people, ride up Sharp's Ridge, and over cars on planks in the railroad workers' parking lot. When the foreman calls her a lesbian, the Hellhounds maul him.

"Cassie and Blackie leave the others, go for a moonlight ride on the railroad tracks, then they lie in a deserted boxcar while he sings to her, and she sings ballads, and cries, remembering singing to Lone. Blackie makes an X mark on her boot, tries to seduce her. She runs away.

"As she is riding very fast, she feels more fully what being Lone was like. She gets excited, goes to Blackie's house and calls him out — they ride to a tourist court. He starts again to make love to her, and she resists, repulsed because she realizes he is trying to pretend he is Lone, knowing that she *herself* has been trying to be Lone.

"Blackie gets furious, tries to rape her, calls her a freak, she runs out, gets on her 'cycle, can't operate it, too weak, lapse of memory.

"Blackie lovingly takes her home.

"In bed that night, she hears Momma praying, goes to her, begs to know from Charlotte why Coot shot himself. Momma tells about her life with Coot and begs forgiveness. Cass tells her she'll never ride again, will become a ballad singer. Lying in her bed, she feels clean, well, and herself. Free.

"Okay, Buddy, you can stop squirming now."

He raised his right hand, as if swearing in. "Ask me, I'd do it up as a novel. Who the hell goes t'see plays?"

Miss Hovey's comment was "Don't you need the scope of a novel for this story?"

So, the one act needed to be a three-act play, and the short story needed to be a novel. Yes, I saw that. I had been working on the play and the short story simultaneously. From eleven years old, I had written a good many long novel and movie scenarios. I thought this one might well become my first published novel.

One of Miss Hovey's creative writing lessons required a dramatic scene of action. I imagined this one would help me handle the pace of the narrative of Cassie and Lone's story.

"Hugging the guitar, Cassie watched Lone pull on a boot and then the other. She always felt him leaving even before he set off toward the door to their bedroom. As he pulled on his black leather jacket, she felt how she supposed it felt to him, felt thumb and forefinger grip the bill of the cap and pull down, tight. The sibilance of his boot-shod feet on the bare floor set her finger to strumming the strings of the guitar, her heart beating faster, and her heavy breathing burst into singing, 'Hangman, Hangman, slack your rope a while. . . .'

"Lone out of sight of the house now, she went with him to the waiting motorcycle, swung onto the seat behind him, hugged him around his leathered waist. Cassie and her brother as one, they zoomed in pure speed and sound down the hill, onto the swinging bridge, onto the highway, the coal truck, missing them. She imagined everybody, every place, every action Lone and the Hellhounds would roar into, and imagined Lone lying down on his cot, telling her everything, everything, threading through his pauses her descriptions of what she had imagined.

"Woebegone. Woe. Woe. . . ."

Miss Hovey's comment was, "Once again you have created a very vivid scene, strengthened by those vigorous verbs that seem to come naturally to you. With an English teacher's habit, I correct spelling errors with the faint hope that you won't continue to make the same mistakes."

Many stories went unfinished as I responded to another image or sound welling up out of my unconscious, but the memory of those characters and imagining their lives continued to be vivid.

Miss Hovey began to assign me to analyze stories in *The Pocketbook of Short Stories,* setting in faster motion my inclination toward writing literary criticism, which my old Knox High friend Walton Rawls had encouraged me to pursue. Miss Hovey bolstered my confidence by telling me that my commentaries on the assigned stories were excellent.

I had read Willa Cather's "Paul's Case" before at two different stages in my life when Paul's life and mine converged. He is one of my favorite characters — a more bitter, a psychotic version of Holden Caulfield in J. D. Salinger's *Catcher in the Rye.* I know of few other short story characters so fully and convincingly brought to life.

"Paul in his negative reactions to such things as 'the grimy zinc tub, the cracked mirror, the dripping spigots,' Cordelia Street, his father at the head of the stairs — is turned inward to himself, where he creates an impossible world; but when he steals the money and tries to buy that world and a place in it, he is not really altering circumstances. He is adding the last fatal strokes to a self-portrait of destruction, an act predetermined by the rebellious pattern of his behavior as set in motion all his life by environmental demands.

"His lies, his contempt for his teachers, the naïve reverence for a painted, unreal world, created and sustained by people who are themselves, many of them, too sophisticated to be enchanted by their own magic, constitute a kind of adjustment to the circumstances against which he struggles, although it is also a removal from them or denial of them; but the fugitive trek to New York is the climax to a cumulative process of personal disintegration.

"Paul's every lie, every pang of nausea, every action is a heroic defiance and a rejection of the dismal squalor of his physical surroundings and their causal mental manifestations into petty thoughts and puny, unattractive aspirations. He had in him fine qualities struggling to emerge, but the undertow of society kept them down, and not until it had transformed them into anti-social traits that were strong enough to rise defiant."

Next, Alma Hovey assigned a lesson in reading as a writer alert to technique. Reading Katherine Mansfield steeped me in an experience in style that I had already begun to learn from Henry James and James Joyce, having avoided Wolfe's style soon after my imitative "Imprisoned Light." I understood the obvious and the subtler differences in the ornate style of Thomas Wolfe and the simple but suggestive style of Ernest Hemingway.

"Miss Hovey, I thought you might be interested in the way in which I correct my writing as I go, so I did not recopy the lesson."

Miss Hovey responded by saying, "It is a pleasure to read your discerning comments on these passages. You do this kind of writing very well, indeed. A.B.H."

And so, the passion Miss Hovey encouraged resulted in six more such brief analyses.

"Miss Hovey, I'm still at work on revising 'Rossana.' Temporary lapse — thus I'm sending this lesson early."

"Although you admire completeness in brevity as in 'The Killers,' you still work on a large scale in planning your stories. I remember that you do cut and shape when you write a story, but I still wish you could subject yourself to the discipline of a more restricted theme and plot. A. B. H."

In C. P. Lee's Cherokee Mountain cabin just before going into the Army, I had imagined images of a first draft of "A Human-Interest Death." Set in my hometown Knoxville, it was the story of Edward, an ordinary, quiet man married to Reba, an enormous, vulgar, domineering woman, whose best friend is Myrna, a "half-wit" young woman next door. On a Sunday excursion into the Smokies, Reba gets out of the car to empty her bladder in the pitch dark and shoves her voluminous rear-end backward — over a cliff.

"Edward befriends the 'half-wit girl' Myrna, who one evening fires her brother's rifle straight up into the air. The falling bullet hits and kills Lucy, Edward's lovely five-year-old girl. I returned to the story, finished it, and sent it in to Miss Hovey.

Aesthetically, what I liked most about it was the symmetry between the accidental death of Reba and the accidental death of Lucy, and Myrna's role as friend to Reba and Edward, and the irony of Myrna's innocent firing of the rifle that kills Lucy.

Alma Hovey saw a bright future for me in fiction.

"Mr. Madden, 'A Human-Interest Death,' I shall remember, I think, for the characterization of Edward — a weak, rather helpless man; 'more sinned against than sinning.' The irony of his situation reaches its climax in his memories and reflections, making him forget the child who should have been put to bed before the honeysuckle and his mother's rocking chair started the train of thoughts, alternatively bitter and triumphant, which filled his mind on that summer night.

"You have learned to shape your material more selectively to short story form, but probably the novel will be your choice for much of your writing.

With its broader canvas, it is better suited to your literary temperament, as we begin to see in "Cassandra Singing." But this work in the short story has improved your narrative style, and it may help you, too, in construction of a novel– in shaping each chapter to its special purpose, neatly and firmly.

"When I read reviews of your first published novel, I shall say to myself, 'Oh, yes, I remember David Madden. The stories he wrote had something about them, whatever their faults, that I did not forget.'

"If you prefer not to revise 'Rosanna' you may send another story. Whatever happened to that bizarre young girl Cassandra? Sincerely, Alma B." Now she was signing her first name. Listening to her voice in print, I tried again to see her in the flesh.

Eager to hear his somewhat aristocratic, lucidly intellectual voice analyzing my fiction as he often did in Knox High School study hall, I was glad mail call produced a letter from Walton Rawls.

"Having worked my way through three Harvard-worthy essays it is only now that I am able to examine 'Rosanna' critically. I will read it again with blue pencil in competition with Miss Hovey's professional red and your ghastly green. Allow a few observations to suffice meanwhile.

"I must say that the story falls short of its possibilities though it has exceedingly good parts. I won't say that your sentences are too long (one of the longest ones is one of the best) but that there is poor relation between the clauses. One can go back and find the connection, true, but the fact is that one *must* avoid alienating the reader. Faulkner gets away with his long sentences because they flow clause into clause and the attentive reader is rarely troubled by connection. The structure or the word combinations must never call attention to themselves.

"I didn't have the trouble following the '*story*' that Miss Hovey had, but I was continually kept at a distance by the writing — and this is not a good effect to achieve in this kind of story.

"I think that the primary trouble is ambiguity of point of view. This is obviously an omniscient narrator who spends most of his time in Rosanna's mind and occasionally moves into others'. I think this is a bad choice. It makes the story lack a tone, or at least makes it ambiguous. Rosanna seems to me the person to tell the story!

"Restrict the point of view *entirely* to her consciousness but keep the same language. Faulkner often gives highly articulate language (interiorly) to naturally inarticulate characters, and most effectively. You can still keep the third person narration for omniscient type comments or scenery, and also run Rosanna's story in third. An example of this is my boy-horse-girl story, which is on its way to your criticism — and praise.

"Confine a third person narration to one consciousness. If you take care with your language you'll produce an unbroken tone, which is necessary in any kind of emotion story. This is another difficulty with your story, i.e., sometimes your language is so striking that it detracts from what you're trying to say. Miss Hovey was dimly aware of this, too. Nevertheless, my comments later on will be more extensive and to the point!

"I'm God's horniest bastard right now, and something has got to be done. I think I'll go to Montreal this weekend. Is Raven back in New York? I'd like to run down and see her. Read John Hawkes' *The Cannibal* — best novel I've ever read! I met him this fall. I think I'll go ahead and get back to your story now. Your pal, Walton."

Miss Hovey and Walton Rawls hovering, I revised 'Rosanna.'

Miss Hovey's response was extremely encouraging.

"Dear Mr. Madden, it is a long time since I read the final version of the story, but I remember it well enough to recognize the improvement you have made in the revision. It is better in construction, and better in expression, too.

"You may remember my saying that although your critical style was excellent, your narrative writing was rough and ragged. Now I am happy to tell you that your narrative style, although not always evenly good, is approaching the level of your critical writing.

"If your story should be rejected, lay it aside for a time, then revise again, and try it once more, or several times."

The now frail hand-written manuscript of "Rosanna" in hand, as I had read in-coming comments from my friends, my own reactions of self-praise and shame enhanced the effects of their analyses.

Vera knew me even better than Miss Hovey, C. P., or Walton, and now she came on as a critic I could very much trust. "I have just finished reading your Chilean story for the second time. I have not yet read C. P.'s and your Iowa correspondence teacher's criticisms. I have just one plea; for simplicity and clarity. You have made obscure a wonderful idea and one full of rich symbolism, symbolism that should flow naturally and with a clarity that would be missed by no one who read it.

"I was not completely sure of the conflict within Rosanna and what the change in her was. Her realization would probably have come as the spontaneous consummation of many smaller realizations that I did not see clearly. I was not sure whether you were saying that those in servitude and menial positions we can respect without realizing that they do not serve virtuously but become in a position of servitude that demands they lie to themselves and others as to what they are (as Rosanna to the villagers who respected her and yet she deceived them by playing the role of the Baroness where the

Baroness herself should have been, and where Rosanna found it necessary to take the blows intended for her mistress and yet which she herself deserved); or whether you were saying that the leader or mistress who keeps her subjects always in a lower position or one of degradation finds that even that cannot be demanded of them. Just what was your message?"

Oh, well, I should have foreseen that Vera the social worker might misread Rosanna's story — one motivated by simple love, with an ironic effect that some readers might not perceive.

"Generally, I thought this story was more mature than many of your others and had more objectivity, and yet you retained your almost instinctive insight into many things that you yourself may not have felt. This is one thing that you will never grow out of and should give your writing a firm basis on which to grow.

"If it is all right with you, I shall wait until the next letter to return your story as I would like to read it over again and let a roommate or two read it."

Although I was not qualified to perform as a US Postmaster, I was put to work in the regimental headquarters and service company post office.

Within a week, an order came down to the Company Commander from Counterintelligence Corps. 'We are informed that you have Private Madden in your company mailroom. Get him out of there. He's a red.'

Next, the company commander figured putting me in charge of the orderly room would not get the CIC on his ass or mine. "They said okay but told me to keep a close eye on what you put on that bulletin board."

What I put on it earned the monthly award for the most attractive and informative bulletin board of any orderly room at Fort Jackson.

One bright morning, a court martial was scheduled to be conducted in my orderly room. "Sorry, Colonel, I just now mopped the orderly room. You all'll have to wait till it dries."

With vague gestures of reluctance, the Colonel obeyed me, his entourage following.

Eager to hear the latest news about Senator McCarthy and his cohorts Roy Cohn and Private David Schine, I walked into the company dayroom, my finger saving my place in *A Little Treasury of Modern Poetry*, e. e. cummings' "I Sing of Olaf" still ringing in my brain chamber, Olaf "does almost ceaselessly repeat/ there is some shit I will not eat.'" Senator Joseph McCarthy was conducting his hearings into Communists in the Army. I wanted to find out the latest on Roy Cohn, who was charged with taking audacious steps to ensure preferential treatment for Private Schine and signing McCarthy's name without his knowledge on a request for Schine to have access to the Senators' baths.

That Cohn and Schine were very close had come out in investigations. In one instance, they chose not to work out of the Senate offices, but to rent nearby office space and share bills. Dayroom commentators suspected they were "queer" and threw McCarthy into the mix. I sat among the men, interested, but often delving into *A Little Treasury of Modern Poetry*.

But the sight of a fat giant fixedly reading *Reader's Digest* distracted me. Mildly feeling duty-bound to defend the frontiers of literary culture, I attacked the superficiality and sentimentality of *Reader's Digest*, arguing with the fellow, Tom, who warded off my attack with such affable sweet reasonableness I surrendered.

Turned out Tom was a Baptist preacher, who languished in the purgatory of the holding company with me because a taxi driver forced his Christian wife to commit fellatio, putting her in the hospital, traumatized, and the rapist's trial was about to come up.

Tom and I frequently said or did the wrong thing, so to speak, qualifying us to solve problems on shit details. Cleaning out the grease pit, I heard my old boss at Dixie Vim filling station telling me to get all that "shit and corruption" out of a holding tank, and the chief engineer in the harbor at Tal Tal, Chile ordering me to go down into a tank up to my chin in oily water and scoop the sludge off the bottom before he would allow me to go ashore.

Preacher Tom was persecuted, as had been my wiper mate Jack, an Argentinian, derisively called Peron, on my voyage to Chile. But Tom was as jolly as Falstaff, always grinning, pseudo-angelic, sardonic. Seeing that it bugged the mess sergeant, he sang hymns and acted slaphappy. Knowing he would end up there anyhow, he begged to clean the grease pit, deliberately flummoxing the sergeant.

"Why in the hell do you want to clean the grease pit?"

"I wish to learn a trade, sir. Please, I beg of you, sir, make me clean the grease pit! Make cleaning the grease pit my own province."

Kneeling at the altar of grease, he prayed there, sang there, and meditated there. "Jesus said, I am the light of the world," Tom reminded us. As an agnostic, I liked Jesus and liked hearing Jesus say that — and much more.

By contrast, short, squat, rotund Episcopalian Father Frye was coldly formal. He bragged that he had inveigled a respectable job working for the chaplain. A shit detail, as it turned out. I saw him in his element when I visited the chaplain at the chapel to beg his help to get me off getting assigned to the grease pit detail so often. Cadre often held Father Frye up as a behavioral good example to Tom and me.

Tom was not so much a Baptist that he would refuse to listen patiently to my reading to him a passage I had written on Nietzsche.

"Nietzsche may have been mad when he wrote *The Anti-Christ*, but if so, what sublime, pearl-pure madness to offer the world, and how wonderful, how valuable a madness which so lucidly articulated that other madness of which it raved. Can this madness have survived on the patronage of atheists alone or has its fascination posed a diabolical attraction for men whose will is Christian, to love, pity, and show charity? That, or can it be for all men who believe or have once, in the tenets of Christianity, of any religion, a stark unavoidable, long sought, recaptured affirmation of the natural in man which religiosity has perverted? But religiosity has never destroyed those victimized aspects of mankind's nature, rather merely subdued them to a state of nominal activity; perverted and crippled, they have survived and shall someday revolt and set man back on the natural course. Call man superman then if you please or just man as he *should have been*."

Brendan Liddell sent me a detailed progress report on his life as an ex-monk Jet pilot, which struck me as even drearier than my own base-line existence.

"Dear Brendan,

"By some great stroke of luck, I was taken out of advanced infantry training after only three days in the field and am now typing this in the typing class of Clerk Typists' school.

'The whole set up is very desirable, and the training is not without interest. In 8 wks. we graduate and will be shipped out to just about anywhere. Of course, I hope it's either Paris or New York so I can be near Raven in either place as she needs me very much and I need her for — among other things — intellectual stimulation.

"Another Knoxville friend, Lee Winfrey, a newspaper writer in Miami, just breezed through on his way to Camp Gordon for boot camp."

★

MY CREATIVE LIFE IN CLERK TYPIST SCHOOL

A document stated the purpose of Clerk Typist School quite simply: To learn to type Army business.

Exercises in training to type well went like this:

"Some Apache hunted buffalo before they had horses, but now they could go into the plains, where the buffalo were more common. On foot the hunters had been lucky where they could steal close enough to a buffalo herd to shoot one of the stragglers. The frighted herd would run, leaving the dead or wounded a mile behind. On horseback, the Apache would ride right into the herd, shooting even the giant bulls."

After typing such as that, I meshed my creative and intellectual sensibilities into the cold, mechanical military mind-set, by taking advantage of breaks and of finishing assignments early to create and enter at will into wildly imagined passages, a great flood of writing in all genres.

While enjoying the irony of being able to conjure and sustain a creative life in the army, I also enjoyed the irony of pursuing and sustaining an intellectual life in the army. Even as I wrote lyrical stories and a variety of poems, the intellectual stimulus of history, past, current, and as forecast, enthralled me.

Often during clerk typist class breaks, I set down in type the philosophical thinking I was doing as I read books and the daily news and observed human behavior in the Army. I continued to plunge into psychological and philosophical works, some of which made an immediate strong impression, others gradually.

I fell quite readily into all rhetorical exercises, eager to try all types of styles, as in this formal piece on communism, in which, since I was being investigated as a communist, I tried to articulate what I might know about the communist philosophy for my own comprehension.

"It is the States' responsibility to educate as well as to rule. Unless, in the phase of the dictatorship of the proletariat, the governed are educated in the philosophy and the pragmatic application of communism, the State cannot expect from them behavior true communists should exhibit.

"One schooled from the nursery up in the fundamental concepts, ethics and proper mode of behavior that are characteristic of communism, will better appreciate, sympathize and work with the communist program for creating out of the cancerous capitalist chaos the world community of effort and possession predicted by Marx and begun by Lenin and, however brutally, furthered by Stalin.

"The ignorant, due to the centuries of suppression under the Czars, a thing not easily rectified, are not fit to take a *direct* hand in government. Among these people who we have not yet been able to free from ignorance, there moves the spirit of a crude wisdom, which we must not ignore. The fine points of communism they may not comprehend, but fear, hunger, cold and death they know better than most and any way out, promised or in sight, appeals to them. The communists make promises to these, the unfortunate children of the world, gain their support and allegiance, but the delay between departure and destination is quite far in consequence of our own lack of knowledge in some areas of the problem, so tales of American cars parked in the yards of factory workers, bathtubs-abundant, television, etc, are enticing to our future citizens of the world and we in the midst of acquiring such things for all everywhere in the world, not just here at home, cannot too well cope with the ensuing discontent. We cannot communicate to their sense of logic nor touch their sense of sacrifice — they have been forced to sacrifice too long.

"But if from birth on they were educated to believe in the ultimate achievement of the ends toward which we communists work night and day all over the world, such decadent luxuries would have no such demoralizing appeal.

"In the meantime, while this great program of education goes on, expands, improves, becomes more conscious and keener its nature, function and purpose, turning out model communist youths with fresh, revitalizing outlooks and attitudes, the elders now unversed in our ways and aims, must be handled with propaganda aimed at undervaluing the false attractions of the Western World, and ignorance of such things had better be the alternative to unresponsible exposure. The problem here is how to prevent the demoralizing effect of the gossip and uninformed instruction of the elders upon the rising generation. Plato too faced this problem, but his solution is not altogether practical in these times and in these world situations. If son must be taught to show contempt for thc ignorance too long embedded in the minds of the father, then education must accept that added task; undesirable though it may be, its necessity is irreproachable.

"Because of the ridiculous but humanly understandable resistance that faces our movement in the world, we are forced to direct our communal effort to munitions, to the war-economy that is so deplorable in any country. But education will not be seconded. We must send teachers into the deepest places of the tundras, the forests, and even toward Siberia. We must learn more about the nature of education and become more aware of our purposes in the elements that go into shaping the education of the young communist."

Responding to an impulse to engage again in the realm of nonfiction rhetoric, I rapidly described the moment in my seventh year when I experienced a major epiphany, and wrote in the memoir mode:

"Walking home from school was different in the Fall. The trees were yellow and red and orange and brown and green and full or skinny and tall, looking black and dead or as though tired from the Spring of erupting exuberance and the summer of languid extravagance. A time of vegetable contrast, a time of ghostly evenings with gutter fires and the strong acrid smell of dead leaves burning, grey smoke pluming the charred brown heaps, and a time of walking in the chill of the morning mist and in the solid chill of the lavender evenings, a time to feel differently all the strange and the familiar things one encountered, to wonder about all the things one has always pondered, the great and the small things with the melancholy of Fall and all its sounds, smells, and sights touching, marking all the thoughts and feelings as it marked the leaves and the grass and the hillsides and the faraway Smoky Mountains. He was a witness to the death of trees and flowers and fruit and grass and the vivid colors of summer. But the sadness he felt was not for those things because he knew that come Spring they would again as always in all the millions of years the world had lived shed that pallor of death and blaze into life and he knew without words that the sadness, so sweet and yet so bitter, was due to his own mortality, due to the wintry fact that when he dies, perhaps even in the very embrace of summer, it would be forever. Thinking of God and His promise of life after death offered him no solace."

As a high school youth hot with revolutionary ideas, I once wrote an essay intended to win in a contest called "I Speak for Democracy," sponsored by the American Legion, that I had lost to Walton Rawls, my best friend. It began — "I advocate a total revolution!" It has not come and I, poor petty Hamlet that I am, have toward its incitement offered but little.

And in the post library, I continued to satisfy the intellectual urge, each stroke of my green-inked pen somewhat orgiastic.

"Introduction to Random Speculations Upon Present and Future History

"History, because it is cubistic, teaches too little and too much. Understanding, interpreting history is the task for a gargantuan intellect that has yet to see the light of day, with thanks to Spengler, Taine, and Toynbee for trying. History is not a circus for fortune-tellers." And so on.

Reluctantly leaving my thoughts behind, I joined the march in the blazing sun back to the company area. After chow, marching back to class, I was eager to pick up where I left off in what I considered to be my contribution to the intellectual history of the Western World.

"The first lesson is this: Remembering Marx's exhaustive research and his final explications, one can realize the urgency for absolute caution, for undeniably there are faults in his conclusions detrimental to his basic contentions." And more. Then the conclusion.

"If the would-be historian feels passionately about what he sees in the myriad historical record can he not be excused for his exclamatory asides? In this light, regard my excesses of esprit and with patience abide my errors of reasoning, though for them I owe an apology to myself alone."

My interest in psychology pervaded much of my writing of nonfiction.

"No philosopher is published today who does not prophesy abysmal doom or at least reproach this modern era for its self-inflicted blindness to external falseness or self-incurred deafness to the internal rumblings of a spiritual, intellectual, moral and emotional empty stomach. If optimism rings in the dullness of this twilight of reason and self-awareness, it is the idiot swathed in the rags of Christianity jumping up and down on the rotten rope in the bat-swarming belfry.

"We need to hear Nietzsche on every street corner in every city and town to preach the anti-Christ, the anti-fear, the anti-ethnocentric. But wishful thinking on our part only seems to inspire the boneheads to further degradation of man.

"Is it any wonder that man is empty, hollow, riddled with the tubercular germs described by Mr. Rollo May, Mr. Erich Fromm, Mr. David Riesman, Mr. T. S. Eliot? It surprises no one, least of all you and me. But what of our proposed remedies? Are they straws extended to men sinking in quicksand or are they signs that read: 'Do not go gladly into that dark night.' The mirror reflecting society shows the death mask of a creature determined to fulfill the primitive death wish. What irony! Just when man reaches his technological heights, the primitive compulsion toward self-destruction erupts, explodes at Hiroshima, Eniwetok, and Bikini.

"What is this creature I see standing on the smoking horizon with the way of angry bulls of a frightened, galloping herd, burning nations at his back?"

Again, and again, I plunged into the short, brief space between finishing one exercise in Clerk Typist School and the one upcoming.

"When the desire to write comes most passionately after reading from the thoughts of great men, such as Nietzsche — this is artificial respiration of the intellect. But when a man is drowning in a quagmire of anxiety, artificial respiration is merciful. Still, the finest that comes from a man's mind to appear on paper should arise through his own exertion of intellectual will as removed for a time from the influence of heroes."

I often plunged from a single phrase or sentence that arose suddenly to consciousness into prose sketches and poems. I never had writer's block. I almost never pre-imagined what I wrote. The impulse itself to write rapidly produced a start. In an unbroken spirit of defiance, I made good use of the time between prompts from my amiable typing instructor.

Still there is time — or is there? — to 'disturb the universe.'
Do I dare, or do I care, or would I better fare
going hog-wild to-- where? Where
can one go to escape one's youthful dreams of revolution?
In abject destitution, one must remain, half mad,
half sane, and endure, brow-deep in social manure,
the lack of action, of courage, the stale taste of rage
left to spoil, and contemplate in smugness sedate
the festering boil, diabolically grinning, symbolically
sinning, with the silver needle poised to stick,
with the delicate finger before the dike.

"Nowhere in the world can the artist find his Euripides cave today. Ironic that Euripides could exile himself to a cave so near what was bustling life, the world to him — Athens — when he had a vast unexplored world into which he could go without fear of discovery and molestation. The modern solitary spirit cannot find peace and solitude even in the most remote place without fear of something like an atom bomb experiment suddenly one day, without warning, casting its shadow over the page he is reading or the page he is writing in his study."

The physical contexts for the various things I wrote were the large squad tent in which I slept, the mess-hall, the roads on which I marched to the wooden framed building where they had set out to train me to become a company clerk, the classroom, to which I marched to arrive at 8 am, from which I marched for lunch, and marched again to arrive at 1 to 5 pm to get taught, from which I marched to arrive at the company area for formation before supper. Hot sun to and from, hot classroom. Waiting for the cadre to reach us to march us back to the company area, we lay in dark shade under the porch.

Inspirations came swiftly. "At last they are leaving me alone. Everyday that's the way it has been — nurses, doctors, visitors with pull coming in at odd hours and visitors at the proscribed hours — then a long lull. Just myself and the room, and rarely these winter days, sunlight on the floor broken, coming through gleaming-clean venetian blinds. This time alone is precious to me. Restlessness fills me up like a reservoir. But it is also a time to think, and my bed grows larger and larger and becomes a white desert like a sheet of typing paper. My mind begins to write — like a pencil that needs sharpening.

"I remember everything, to the last detail, even the very print of Charlta's dress that first night when my strange emotions reared up as bluntly as a black whale thrusting its massive and startling bulk suddenly up from the hoary deep. I have not even forgotten the peculiar blonde curl behind Helen's ear — Helen, that unpredictable little hellion. I was thankful for the details. They helped to obscure the sheer horror of the events leading up to that inevitable, climactic night. Someone is opening the door.

"Ah, Ann. Now you shall know my story — from the first sordid incident to the last. Sit there, look at me with love and forbearance and listen to the silence of my spiritual agony."

I confess. I don't remember whether I wrote the following passage or whether I copied it, perhaps with changes, out of Aldous Huxley's *Point Counter Point*, or . . . whatever.

"He stood in one spot on the soft, dew damp ground and slowly turned around like a man following a lovely woman's circuitous walk. The trees stood in pools of frosty morning mist, rimmed in golden lace of hard, penetrating, but heatless light, each group of trees seemingly separated by a veil of mist from the lake. Come dawn, dark is done."

My memory of Henry James' sensibility and style had become readily accessible.

"Costigan stopped talking. He knew it was no longer any use to argue. They were going to do it in spite of his advice. What galled him more than their disobedience was the fact that they insisted upon his advice as everything but what it was, as petty nagging or domestic filibustering. He would tolerate the persistent distortion of his every word and act until his gentle nature could no longer endure the damage to his pride.

"Perhaps Margo and Verna were right, but the future still had not been revealed. At any rate his understanding of the workings of the minds of those creatures who inhabited his house informed him that not one of them would admit error. Was he capable of doing so? he asked himself, with a faint feeling of horror. In looking so deep into the hearts of others, was he ignoring some urgent signal of distress from the seat of his own heart? He directed these questions more inwardly and concluded that he was not aware enough of his own desires, of his personality, of that *I*, that *me* to which he, like so many other people, was always referring, and this realization filled him with a loathsome shame, and he could not bring himself to judge Verna and Margo because there was too much to judge within himself."

And I readily called forth an aura of Poe's sensibility.

"Her long mauve gown hanging limply around her exhausted body, she came into the room like a figure from the images in a dead man's mind."

In the fictional memoir mode, words let me see myself as Noel and, sadly, Iva Lee as Arabel, Jenny as Madelaine, still my beloved of the year before Iva Lee, hovering below the threshold of consciousness. And Harry as Ralph.

"Noel stepped outside the hall-door. The sun struck him. Dazed pleasantly, he stood on the small landing looking out over the school yard, the moving heads of the kids going home or standing in loitering groups under the mimosa trees now in full bloom.

"Alan Ladd still one of his heroes, he was trying a new stance — a nonchalant lean to the right, the right arm hanging casually, the hand almost below his knees, the hand holding his black notebooks with Arabel's name scrawled on it. He was looking for her and for Madeline at the same time, hoping they were already looking at him, standing there in that manner in his tan leather jacket, his black corduroy trousers rolled up to expose his uncle's army combat boots. Harry had worn them yesterday. He was getting to where he acted like he owned them, and when he wore them, the way he walked, they seemed a part of him, and Noel putting them on later felt as though he were wearing Harry's boots.

"Noel looked around, slowly holding his head up, just so, putting on one expression after another, not satisfied with any of them, self-conscious, but enjoying the self-inflicted effect. His hands caressed the deck of cards in his jacket pocket, and he wished Harry would come on so they could start trudging up steep Harvey Hill and play blackjack for pennies as they walked, dealing sideways.

"He imagined himself and Harry passing Madeline, Helen, Ruby, and Norma, dealing the cards, ignoring them, then suddenly acknowledging them and laughing as they pretended stuck-upped-ness.

"He saw familiar faces, calling to some, slyly ignoring others, shifting from one foot in the new stance to another, reverting now and then to that old abandoned false mannerism of wiggling his fingers rhythmically.

"Then he saw Arabel coming along the walk with five other girls, none of whom he trusted or had any liking for, few of whom he knew to any real degree. She wore a very gay summer dress — red skirt, white blouse with red ribbons around the neck and the bulbed short sleeves. Around her head she wore the red ribbon he had urged upon her, and her lipstick had paled from the day's wearing and gave her mouth a wistful aura. Her small slender feet were sandaled, and she walked like a junior high school girl athlete.

"He felt the sight of her in his chest and was surprised that seeing her could shake him. Moments later he caught sight of Madeline and the rest of the girls walking up the hill and Ralph in his blue and white jacket was walking with them.

"He stepped down from the porch and walked quickly along under the isle of mimosa trees and up the back toward the sidewalk where Arabel and the girls had slowed their walk."

Memory of Iva Lee too lucid, I stopped.

Out of the prevailing aura of all the girls and women I had loved, I felt impelled to create fictional women in their midst.

"I went into my room and, exhausted, sat down on the edge of my bed. The door to Charlta's room stood open. I saw her change of underwear lying like a flag over the edge of her bed. Somehow this familiar sight excited in me a slowly accelerated sensuality. I went into her room and took the panties up in my hands and felt the soft material, ran it between my fingers. Then, thoughtlessly I raised it to my nostrils and inhaled. It awoke in me memories, unbearable nostalgia, of odors of her body as it had been when she was seventeen and I was a young rebellious student of law. It was an intense emotion without imagery, yet definitely associated with the bliss of that lost time, that forever gone time of innocent unfettered lovemaking in which the most excellent happiness is attained, however sad its brief duration. And below in my mind, thoughts and images of Charlta moving about her room across the hall were straining thru this reminiscence. Suddenly I had a picture in my mind of Charlta standing in her room clad only in her panties, just as years — how long — ago I had stood in the same room with Laura, and she wore only the red panties I had brought her from New York. As with a reflex I brought the panties to my face again and buried my perplexing images there."

Now and then, as Henry James sneaked into the length and rhythm of my sentences, I suppose Noel Coward's dialog hovered in the wings.

"It's just that lately you seem isolated from me, Paul — almost insular."

"Don't be silly."

"Please, Paul, you know how I despise that odious phrase. It says beyond nothing."

"Quite the contrary, my dear. It sums you up perfectly when you're in these — goddamn it! — silly moods."

"Oh! Paul, let's just shut up and sit quietly if we can't keep from alienating each other."

"All right, we won't speak another word until dinner. At which time I shall turn to you with an expression of tender appeal and ask, Darling, please pass the salt."

"You're intolerable."

"My dear, no one is intolerable — in the final analysis." Here his tone of voice was bait-like, and how well she knew it. She decided to nibble at the morsel.

"What do you mean?"

I kept hearing male and female voices, listening to what they were saying and might say.

"Darling, hadn't you ought to phone the — "

"Certainly not. Let them sit there and wonder why I — "

"Really, darling."

"Don't really darling me, Nora. Isn't it quite apparent I am definitely decided?"

"But of course, dear. And I have no intention of dissuading you."

"Very intelligent of you, for as you must see, I can't be moved."

"At least let's not quarrel. If we're to give up all we've won here, there is no use in crowning our defeat with dissent in the ranks."

"Defeat? Jumping the gun, aren't you? Does that omnipotent mind of yours already have the news of my defeat?"

I didn't leave Hemingway out of the ritual.

"The next morning when we opened the windows the trucks were waiting in the road. It was too dark to see the men in the cabs clearly, but Bixby said he thought they must be Russians by the jerky way they smoked their cigarettes, the red tips of which we saw moving in the bad morning light. Even in this cold climate, Bixby said, Chinese don't smoke with movements like that. But we could have saved our powers of induction. As soon as the sun appeared they opened the door and led us out under the gun. We were pushed into the trucks. It seemed as though the guards wanted to get their hands on each of us. We heard a cock crow and felt the truck begin to move."

Still trembling, I turned to the task of typing mechanically.

During the next break, I envisioned another scene.

"As he crossed the frost-knitted grass and entered the house from the kitchen door, his whole awareness was in the premonition that something terrifying was going to happen, that his life lived respectfully forty years now was hanging over the precipice, and most exhausting was the realization that he couldn't force himself to turn around and get back into the car and drive fast, away, somewhere — perhaps to the only person who would help him, Ann. But what he was doing, the mere act, was so simple, so routine, a thing he had done thousands of times, a natural diurnal occurrence — "

Called to return to the teaching experience, I sometimes had to stop in the middle of a sentence, and often did not return to imagine a finish.

I never wrote in the tent among other soldiers, but sometimes when I found the day room empty or quiet enough.

"Noel did not go out of the house until after three days had passed. When he moved in, he had brought enough food and wine to last. On the fourth morning as he lay in bed his mind turned the situation slowly around, as in the dusty window of a jewelry shop one often sees some dazzling gem revolving upon a purple velveted disk. Perhaps, he thought, it had not been wise to stay inside, making it appear as though I were hiding or did not wish to associate with the villagers. Though he had not been lonely in the dark, hot rooms, but rather content and relaxed with his second-hand books, purposely losing himself in the labyrinthine convolutions of their immense profundity, often he had stopped reading and looked out through the half-open shutters at the village of Tal Tal below and out at the hull-shaped manure boats out in the bay, and felt a keen yearning to go out and walk down the rocky hill and go into the village streets to speak with the people in a language of which he had only a limited knowledge.

"After pondering so for beyond an hour, he got up and put on his clothes and cooked a Grecian breakfast and set out for the village, feeling very much like Carlo Levi in his experiences with the Italian peasants in the village of Eboli during his exile. That Noel's position was more irksome in many respects altered his sensations little."

I had seen Ginger Vactor in her sunlit room, lying on her chaise-lounge, and often saw her there in my imagination, like a character in an impressionistic novel by Virginia Woolf.

"Since four o'clock Ginger had tried to stay awake, had tried simply to do that which she had intended when first she lay down upon the chaise-lounge as almost every evening she had done for a number of years. If one slept, being so tired and exhausted, awakening as one must at six-thirty to call Davie in to supper and to go in and awaken Dave from his usual afternoon nap, would be too tortuous to be worthwhile. But how pleasant just to lie down, birds chirping outside in the complexity of vines and blossoms, and wait for a whiff of breeze to happen in. Never did it seem other than peculiar at this time of afternoon and in this relaxed state, how the furniture and the other objects in the room, and their mass, form and space relationships took on such unreal and unnatural appearances, so that she felt quite removed to another world, fascinatingly strange and familiar all at once.

"Ginger's mind had come to be befuddling. Her body relaxed and released its local tensions by sections and sections, by degrees, until it quite ceased to exist, and her throbbing feet and her hot neck alone remained demanding of her consciousness. But when the fading and the dizziness and the lulling sensation crept into her unresisting mind, nothing but her wandering, capricious, wild, scandalous sometimes frighteningly unnatural thoughts could register anywhere in the conscious being of her existence."

Another.

"Monica wore a tan camel-hair overcoat. Ann told me Monica had stolen it from a cheerleader at a high school football game. I could see her doing it. In my mind I went over the incident imaginatively. Somehow this excited me, and to watch her standing there against the cool green of the cement wall, the long folds of the hairy coat hanging to her small, bony ankles, a cigarette held meditatively in her mouth, was almost unbearably sensual."

And another.

"One can't ever get away from oneself any more than from others. Deep inside us we carry this realization all our lives, but suddenly one day when we are alone and thus our perception is keen, we come into a room and there before us is the evidence of this fact, at once terrible and fascinating, and, if one can extend the experience, illuminating. So that evening after awakening from my evening nap on the living room divan and trudging up the staircase just when the sun renders it strange yet too familiar, I came into the bedroom and suddenly stopped startled and vaguely afraid at what I saw. The faint impression of a figure showed wrinkled on the pale blue spread."

Reading Sara Teasdale, Elinor Wylie, and Edna St. Vincent Millay again for a while, though with residual disdain, probably inspired this poem.

CELLISANDI

On the hill nothing moving,
Nothing moved on the hill.
Then like jeweled smoke

The yellow manes and the grey eyes
Of a thousand horses rose up on the horizon.
And we were very afraid.

I shall come in from the sea
And my skin shall be of fine salt,
While you, Cellisandi, shall lie waiting,
Deep burrowed in silk and lotus.

My great cracked hands
Shall unloose your manifold robes
And your pink thighs shall smile
At the awkwardness of my blunt fingers.

You shall come in from the sea,
Your shoulders draped in seaweed,
But I, Kulandi, shall lie sleeping,
Deep slumbered in silk and lotus.

Your great ponderous feet
Shall shake the walls and wake me,
And my pink thighs shall lock
Before the sting of your cracked fingers.

Out of nowhere, the most overpopulated place in the universe, came this.

In a long black alley
A little white dog
Stood on his hind legs,
His pink tongue pulsing,
His tail like a feather beating the foul air,
his eyes expecting something
from a tall emptiness where no master stood.

Mindful maybe of James Agee's "Knoxville 1915," I wrote:

In the black belly of the whale of despair,
I sometimes lie and think of Knoxville:
Come winter or summer I could not care
For anything so much as sunlight on the sill,
Or lying back in the hot tall grass,
I loved the jungle beside my house,
And lonely and dreaming as the years pass,
My heart into beauty crept like a mouse.
Gay Street in the evening sun was hurtful,
So lovely in its ugliness, so acrid in its glow,

And my cold hand in hers, so beautiful
Was the city's cruel touch and go.
Distant lands and ways may ever call
But my last night shall on Knoxville fall.

Even lovers lying in the grass,
Rooted in the subsoil of love,
Have no light mind for the moon,
In the silence, in the fields of love.

For too few the moon is a looking glass,
In which to see one's heart hung high,
The ruins of time on that globe hewn,
Or hope to hear infinity under its burden sigh.

The hypnosis of the moon is a simple cure,
For lummoxes, brutes, and each miscast mind.
But too long stuffed with ignorance-manure,
They who never search will never find.

And the moon each night will stare,
Unaware who loves its reach or denies.
And being ageless it will not care,
But avert its glance when someone cries.

Robinson Jeffers' bleak vision of the world affected my own now and then. I longed to visit his tower at Carmel someday.

Men of a sick world!
Create your Gods in your own image,
And let the mountains and the sea remain.
Deform minds of children
But do not wreck the golden fields,
Let them live.
Worship nothingness and kill for it,
Turn your eyes from the good of man
As man, as self-savior.
Let Folly too live on,
But go softly by the golden fields.
The rain will wash your tracks away.
Bombardier stay your hand
When a river in clover fills your eye.
Bomb cities.
Come winter snow will fall,
Come spring snow will melt,

Just the same.
If you must make battlefields of beauty
And feed the grass with blood,
Do one final act of Love, if you can,
Leave one green place in which a child may stand.

A MODEST PROPOSAL

Leaders of this sick sphere
One second in the chaos lend an ear!
Go ahead,
Continue creating God in your own image,
Always be led
By this monstrous logic
To wars by him you justify.
But do not ask me also to die.
Oh, no, Senator, Rotarian, Legionnaire,
To be born is not to follow
The crowds' roar.
Deform the minds of children,
And order youths to perish,
But do not referend
That I deny what I cherish.
Bomb places
But do not wreck the golden fields.
Hate faces
But do not destroy the natural yields.
Let mountains stand and rivers
Go as they will.
The golden fields, let them live,
And go on killing in the name of your God.
Though you march across the golden fields,
The rain will make of your tracks
Eternal sod.
Bombardier, when rivers and flowers fill your eye,
Stay your rod.
Bomb cities — that's the place for bombs and God.
For winter snow will fall
Though no one live at all.
In summer the sun will burn intensely,
And the world shall be silent, immensely.
Flowers, strange ones, bloom in fields of shame,
And no one living to give them name.
If you must make of beauty a battlefield,

And feed the grass with blood,
Gesture one final act of love,
If you can:
Leave one green space of land,
Where the last lonely child may stand.

I returned often to A. E. Housman, who feared remembering a moving line of poetry while shaving his throat.

Under the raining trees,
Along the rivers' edge
Where flowers hide the bees
And birds sing in wild hedge,
Summer days of years ago,
Moments spent in lover's awe,
Entreat me again to know
The ecstasy of a lover's call.
When evening creeps into the wood
I stop amid my evening chores,
And think of the lack of brotherhood,
Between statesmen, priests and whores.

For such times as these so grim,
Men need the arms of love for comfort,
Before the light of love grows dim —
And loveless fools reach the last resort.
We swam across the river,
In the cool evening light.
We rose with a shiver,
In the cool evening light.

On a hill, in a field
We lay down to rest.
The darkness a shield,
We lay down to rest.

We talked for awhile
And looked at the ground.
She gave me a smile
And looked at the ground.

In the spiritual presence of Vera, I wrote.

I knew I loved you months ago,
Or even a year, I don't know.
But my heart was laden with rue
Until last night — I kissed you!

To hold your hand in ancient India,
To kiss your hair in a temple's shadow.
To run with you through the Black Woods,
Lying down breathless under the huge trees.
To climb the rocks of Normandy in winters' cold,
And wear wooden shoes down Netherland streets,
And sing Italian songs with you, my darling.

Always (or all my life) feeling the ache, wide as a barren landscape, of the loss of Iva Lee.

When in the labyrinth of old ages' despair,
In the hollow heart of the figged shape,
I behold my life laid bare across a dimming sky,
Let me say, my dear, that it all wasn't bad,
That the futility brought a working anger,
And the mocking mistakes bred a small greatness.

I hope I was right to feel that the revision, conducted in tranquility, was better than the draft.

When in the labyrinth of old ages' despair,
In the hollow heart of that figged shape, that lair,
Where bitter veins roaring anger have become.

I was not, I don't think, humorless, but few of my poems were chucklers.

I may go away and never return,
Run like hell and never look back,
But with fear and time I soon will learn
That my heart belongs in Hackensack.

Old Mindy Lewis wasn't very old
When they lowered him in the ground,
Still had many stories he hadn't told
When they lowered him without a sound.

He was the village character, yes,
And always carried a walking cane,
But the thing you'd never guess
Was that he died without any pain.

I often delighted myself and friends imitating the voices of poets from the Caedmon and the Library of Congress recordings, especially Dylan Thomas's sonorous, performative voice reading "Fern Hill."

While the composer Virgil Thomson was visiting Dave, Ginger turned to me. "Do Dylan Thomas for Virgil, David."

"'Oh, as I was young and easy in the mercy of his means, Time held me green and dying,

Though I sang in my chains like the sea.'"

Virgil Thomson shivered appreciatively. "I simply must set Dylan to music."

Thomas's poems have influenced my own. I often just missed meeting Thomas in Greenwich Village at the San Remo Bar and White Horse Tavern. Reading in his *Collected Poems* was a soaring pleasure, and when alone I often intoned his wonderful first lines.

"Do not go gentle into that good night"
"Light breaks where no sun shines"
"The force that through the green fuse drives the flower"
"And death shall have no dominion"
"In my craft or sullen art."

An exploratory drive in Stanley Kenvin's car one Sunday evening inspired another of the many poems I wrote while "in the line of Duty."

Through the sun's late October chill
We sped along the tapeworm
Of time and travel, divided between
Going and coming, arrival and departure.
My friend the wheelman
And I hovering in light
Between sleep and the open eye.
Suddenly the dividing broke
And wide awake, I saw
Three buzzards around a dog,
And but for the shell in which we sped
Would three more sky high have seen.

They looked up at us as we passed
Like grave robbers curious of the living.
In black with sleek grey hoods
Their eyes were like human eyes,
Asking, "What are you doing here?"

We slowed and stopped and turned around.
They looked like priests around an altar,
Two halting their feast, one still tearing.
It stood still after the others flew away reluctantly.
Then we too close, he joined the mob's better judgment.

The dog, white and brown, was half gone.
From the tip of his tail to the spear of his chest,
The bones were picked clean — methodically,

Not like a mob at all.
The dog's eyes were open,
His face was calm and serene in death,
As though nothing was happening.

Like generals they perched on dead limbs
Of a tall dead tree and looked down upon us,
Patient, waiting for us to admit
Our breach of etiquette.
And after they flew away,
Respectful of our shame,
We confessed to each other.

Again, I was always open to the brother-sister theme, and the dark lure of incest as I was imagining it developing it between Cassie and Lone.

Prowling through the Fort Jackson's post library's poetry section, I was delighted to come across Robinson Jeffers' *Roan Stallion, Tamar and Other Poems*. Tamar, incredibly beautiful, was raped by her half-brother and abandoned.

A potent lure for me was the image of Jeffers' face, truly a poet's, the sound of his voice on a Library of Congress recording, and his pervasive pessimism, though I only half-heartedly shared it. Like James Joyce's ancient tower in Dublin, Jeffers' tower of stone, which he built with his own hands hauling stones from the coastline in Carmel, California, appealed to me.

The collection included *Tower Beyond Tragedy*. Slain Agamemnon speaks through the body of Cassandra, a brilliant concept, as Clytemnestra offers Cassandra's naked body to the citizens.

One of my favorite Jeffers poems, "Cassandra," was not in his book. My favorite phrase:

"to men
And gods disgusting — you and I, Cassandra."

My life in the army was an immersion in language — of many kinds. My pure damn love of language, the very sound and rhythm of it, for its own sake, apart from love of art for art's sake, opened me up to bizarre, absurd, nonsensical stream of consciousness, automatic writing, about which I knew little, none of which I had read as strange as what rose with very little coaching from my unconscious. Only James Joyce's *Finnegans Wake*, Gertrude Stein, e e cummings, and Dylan Thomas' most obscure poems were compatible.

I had written my freshman English research paper on Gertrude Stein. During a break in typing class, I plunged into a piece in one of Stein's several styles.

"They weren't ready for it. Nor was he. When he died he nor they were ready for it. But he died and they buried him, unready and all. When they found him, they lost him and when they buried him, they had a grave among them and gravely they regarded it and unready for it they were dismayed. For he went down under not being ready and gravely regarding life so that he as well as they were unready and grave, though he left a grave among them to trouble their stare and hide their moon and snuff their sun. And they were one in their unreadiness to admit it had happened, that it had happened which was never to have been allowed, especially since no one, not even he, was ready for the death and the grave and the startling of their stars, the paralysis of their moon and the obscuring of their sun. But he unlike they did not suffer celestial calamity, rather he inherited the stars cold to them, the moon frozen to them and the sun unkind to them. By the very fact of his being dead he became heir to this, him and a part, a part of that as well apart from them, they who were so very, very unready when it happened."

And more flattery by imitation to Gertrude Stein.

"The big brown cow couldn't understand how anyone big could sound so unkind when walking or lying down in the blowing grass. No one explained. He complained and went on being brown in the loud town. Regarded too brown by the loud town, lying down and standing up, he was cast out without a sound, kind or unkind. This worried him. They hurried him as he ran brown and wondering away from the town so loud so unkind. And the stars lit his plight as he ran through the brown night into another town, devoid of fright. Quietly and alone he walking brown, chewed the blowing grass lying down."

I was veering toward automatic writing.

"They were all in the living room living. The party was exploding like a Catherine Wheel over the cadavers of less festive evenings in this living room where dying too took time from the lives living in its dying a little each dead evening in the living room, with folded hands, fortressed ears, harnessed tongues, shrugged shoulders, perspiring buttocks and twitching hearts. But all that those minor — " Not finished.

Before I heard the instructor's call to return to the exercises, I raced through fragments of absurd writings.

The hairy woman ducked the daisies in blue feathers
didn't ask if flies were dancing on her elbows
she just rode willow whips through all kinds of weathers,
and received foreign guests in diapers through her nose.

"I saw you waltzing in the sphere of a scorpion's tear and when I called to you from my pocket in the ear of an orange gnat, you answered with a hymn of silence only we stretched like mercury across a pain of space, could understand. How many rains ago, how many million snows since silence so sent us into a humming embrace beyond all sound? As you flew away in the smoke of a rose's burning cry, I remembered all you were winters, summers ago when I did not know you any better than I know the keys of the locked houses under a whore's yellow tongue, when the chattering veins scream at midnight in the blanketed tundra of despair in a madwoman's hair."

Reading this one aloud persuaded me that it *sounded* boundlessly beautiful, if not sublime.

"The legion of dandy doddle busboys lead the weary way toward ostracization. Nobody in the troop had brought along his bottle of curried grass. It was indeed a matter for the ambassador of neurotic who handled all cases of dullness in the seams of old men's trousers and counted the raindrops in yellow commodes left out in the open fields."

Perhaps this ultimate example was partially inspired by James Joyce's *Finnegans Wake.*

sorta singing silly siblings sauntered sagaciously south
singing senile sentries suspected sex segregated.
babbling babies buried billions
born bastards began bellering blantantly.
absent Andrew arranged apples appendixes
appropo abstinence altarwise
and alibied alaster allubial annapastos.
Read ruddy my luddy or sand qual line
Let answer in sin ull losters woe
We Daddy dubellers set siblings kine
Or supernumeral sorta shanty-wisen doe.
Aft lukerswine ach ibling so
Ichinwield url kuster supra vo.
Ansqua inserbo il kitchin jui
Beberatoler mine kinder sue.

The Red Cross enabled me to go to Knoxville to see Daddy.

He was supposed to be in the veteran's hospital, housed in an old mansion on Kingston Pike, once home of a very wealthy man and used in the Civil War. But he had been transferred to Bellevue Sanatorium for folks with tuberculosis. I visited him there.

A month later, June 26, 1954, on Bellevue T. B. Sanatorium stationary, Daddy wrote a telegraphically short letter.

"Dear David. Well I guess you think I am a heel for not answering your long letter. I was sure glad to get it though. I am O.K. now, I hope. Was glad to get the poem — explain please.

"I am not at the same address. I hope I didn't miss you again for I was at the Belle View Sanatorium at the time of last letter. Son I will sure write a letter soon. Lot of Luck. Love, Dad."

Then came Daddy's voice in the second of only three letters he wrote to me while I was in the army.

"Well I have been back in the sanatorium a few weeks now and must say I don't feel so hot. I have been sick most of the time, David. I guess it was a good thing I came on down here for they found out I had a bad liver. It is 30 percent damaged so I can't take the Antabuse treatment, but I won't need that now. I know my drinking days are over if I expect to live much longer. I hope you got back OK. David, I don't think there is much use writing me down here for I expect to go home Tuesday. I will have to take treatments from a Doc there at Knoxville or go to Johnson City V.A. Hos. So, son write me at Southern Athletic Company. Well Bud I just wanted to let you know the score. Write me soon. Love, Dad."

The Red Cross wrote to inform me that Daddy was in the Veterans Hospital in Johnson City, Tennessee, and in the same mail call, I was surprised to get a postcard from him.

"I received your nice letter. Was glad to hear from you again. David, I am back in Knoxville for a while then I am going to Johnson City V.A. Hos. My liver is in a bad shape. I have quit drinking for sure now. Son, I will let you know when I go. So for now this is all. Love, Dad."

December 1954, incongruously, on Southern Athletic Company, Inc. stationery, came a scrawled letter short as a telegram, so drunken I could make out only a stray word. "Dear" page 1, and "over," page 2, "Bud" and "Love" and "Dad," only a little less distorted than a Rorschach test, and "write a gain" twice, the first unreadable.

★

"WHAT? YOU REFUSE TO SIGN A GODDAMN STATEMENT OF CHARGES?"

In the Army, quite naturally, Kafka's name came up often right and left. Having read "Metamorphosis," I read "In the Penal Colony," my most haunting Kafka experience, about an ingenious apparatus equipped with a needle that writes at an excruciatingly slow rate the name of the prisoner's crime over his entire body.

An officer explains to a stranger, an Explorer, how the machine works. "This prisoner, for instance, will have written on his body: HONOR THY SUPERIORS!"

So, one afternoon, I had good reason, as it turned out, to shout to Sergeant Brasbee, "Somebody stole my cartridge belt."

Under his blue cadre helmet liner that made him look like an anemic turkey with a bowl on its head, Field First Sergeant Brasbee smiled. "You are out of u-nee-form, Madden."

"Well, that's why I'm reporting somebody stole my cartridge belt, 'cause I know it's 'gainst regulations to be out of uniform.'"

Brasbee gimleted his eyes, pooched his thin lips tightly, swung around to face the troops in formation. "Men! Madden claims one you's a mullafuckin' thief!" The least offensive approach I could have expected.

"Ah, shit fire, Madden!" somebody yelled from the ranks. "Knock it off! This sun's boilin' hot!"

"I need some chow, bad, man, bad!"

Executing a smart about face, Brasbee looked down at me again. I began to cool in the shade his skinny shadow made.

"You *will* sign a state-mint of charges, soldier."

"You ordered us to stack arms, Sergeant." Noticing the men shifting sullenly in the sand, I stepped out of the shade Brasbee cast and squinted against the glare of the sun. "You posted no guard. So, the way they taught me the military code in basic, it's your responsibility either to track down my cartridge belt — "

"It ain't *your* cartridge belt, soldier. It's government e-shoo. Just like you are."

" — or pay for a new one yourself."

"*Me*?" Bent at the waist, tapping his chest, he was almost as short as I am. "*Me*?"

"And I'm not a government issue."

"In formation, soldier!" When somebody crossed, contradicted, or questioned Brasbee, his thin voice quivered hysterically as if on a trilling operatic high note. I always half-expected his deadpan facial expression to crack into a grin, finally admitting he was putting on an act. Brasbee pivoted to face Stinnet, the Black cadre who usually marched us in to lunch. "Move 'em out, Corporal!"

Stinnet was straight-faced, too, but a deliberate comic, his mouth always hanging open in a put on, slack-jawed, half-assed grin. He had a trick of breaking a long marching silence suddenly with a cadence call just enough off to force us to shift to hit it right.

Back in the company area, as the men ran screaming like a hundred new species of pampas birds and animals toward the mess hall to get close to the food they would have to gag down, I went into our tent-roofed cabin and chose a book to read in the chow-line appropriate to the present situation — *Generation of Vipers* by Philip Wylie.

"Hey, Madden," said Puckett, a freckled redhead from Alabama, from down the line, "Brasso's really out to *get* your ass *this* time!"

Brasbee's fanaticism on the subject of buckle-polishing had earned him the nickname 'Brasso.'

The dominant odor, from first days to last, was the odor of *Brasso*, from a distance faintly suggestive of one ingredient of the toxic effluvium of Knoxville chemical plants.

In the mess hall, Rastelli asked, "Why not just take somebody else's belt at the afternoon formation?" I liked Rastelli, a friendly, amused New Orleans Italian who had become a student of my encounters with the Army.

"I don't like stealing," I said, for the benefit of all listeners at the table.

I had given up stealing that time the cops rounded up Dickie, Freddie Weaver, Buddy Smith, and me for raiding an abandoned grocery store. Caught, we all four, including Dickie, became versions of Huck Finn when the cops threatened to ship us off to the reform school in Nashville.

They finally let us go when Buddy Smith asked, "Can I take my marbles with me?" and they all laughed as if a boring day had been rescued.

On the way home, Dickie ducked into a little Jewish store and came out with one pocket bulging.

That near arrest was the occasion on which I promised Jesus and myself that I would never steal again.

"It's not exactly stealing, Madden. Half the company's been doing exactly that for two weeks."

"I know." I had watched the process daily, disgusted, ever since the first man wandered around asking if anybody had seen a stray cartridge belt.

"He can't do that *now*, 'cause he's already reported it stolen." Puckett sneered violently. "If you'd just kept your mouth shut like everybody else and gone ahead and taken one when we fell in, you wouldn't have any problem."

"The problem started when the first man took his buddy's belt." I sensed that deep down they respected the concept of the buddy system even more than I did.

"You don't think it was anybody in the company the first time, do you?" McFarland was a skinny, buck-toothed blond from Jackson, Mississippi. I liked him, but not Puckett. "We were all in uniform when we marched out of the company area."

"While we were in the building, somebody must have snuck up on the porch — " Puckett imitated the action. " — and slipped it off the blamed hook."

"Right. Then the victim should have reported it, because it was Brasbee's fault for not posting a guard."

"But that's too much trouble, Madden. What the hell's a little ol' cartridge belt?"

"It's not the damn cartridge belt that counts, MacFarlane. What bothers me is that at every formation, twice a day for about two weeks, a new man becomes a thief."

"You callin' me a thief?" Puckett got a foot taller.

"Hell, I used to be — when I was little — stole a lot of stuff. Almost got sent to reform school. Both my brothers are in prison, right now. I send them money out of my measly paycheck."

"How come you to quit?"

"Got saved. On sawdust in a revival tent."

"You don't talk Christian to me." Baggett, who had been mesmerized by a Sheila of the Jungle comic book.

"I'm not. I'm an agnostic, by god."

"An ag who?"

"A person who doesn't know whether there's a god or not."

"What the hell. . . . Well, you believe in Jesus Christ, don't you?"'

"I like him, but I don't believe he was the Son of God, born of the virgin May, and will come again."

"What?" Baggett strangled the funny book. "You don't believe in no motherfucking Christ?"

"No, but maybe your example will persuade me."

"I hope Brasso gets your ass court-martialed."

"He'll play hell!"

I was sitting by Jesse, a Black fellow from Alabama who slept on the bunk next to mine, when Brasbee walked by carrying his tray. "The sergeant said he'd open up supply five minutes early so's you can sign that state-mint of charges."

When I didn't reply, he dumped his garbage and strutted out.

At five to one by my gold-plated, radium-dialed Elgin wristwatch, that I bought when I was an usher at the Bijou when I was twelve years old, I saw Sergeant Marcos, a handsome but surly young Greek with curly black hair, climb the steep steps of the supply building that sat on a rise above the tents in the shade of three tall pines.

As we stood in formation five minutes later, waiting for Master Sergeant Garrett to receive the roll report from Brasbee, I saw Marcos standing half in the shadow of the cool supply room and half on the bright top step, looking down at me where I stood in the sand under the 102-degree sun.

"All present 'counted for, surp!" Sergeant Hobart Rudd was a big, tough, heavy red-faced fellow just back from combat in Korea, who hated my guts double when he learned we were related in a half-assed way, nephew through my step-grandfather-in-law Cap Rudd of the Oak Ridge fire department, a man he disliked anyway, because the chief had risen in the world on a third-grade education, higher than Hobart, who was a fifth-grade graduate, and maybe like Cap's sons and daughters resented his decades-long affair with Mammy until his sick wife finally died. And my two years of college stuck in Rudd's craw like week-old cornbread.

"Sergeant," said Field Sergeant Brasbee, "you got a man in your platoon's out of uniform" — in a tone as if he had told him that ten times before but was only patiently reminding him again.

Sergeant Rudd did an about-face and walked among us. "I God," he said, looking down the squad line at me as I looked straight ahead. "I might a knowed i'd be you, Madden! Whur's your gotdamn cartridge belt?"

"Somebody stole it, Sergeant."

"Why didn't you report it?"

"I did, but Sergeant Brasbee said —"

"Well, go sign a statemint of charges for another one. On the damned double!"

"Can't, Sergeant," I said, suspecting that he was only pretending not to have heard about the missing belt at chow. "Wasn't my fault."

"Yours ain't to reason why," quoth Rudd. "You just do or die. Alfred Lord Tennyson, shithook!"

"Let's have the report, Sergeant," said Master Sergeant Garrett, a fat balding man who looked up when he spoke.

Field First Brasbee twisted off an about-face, rendered a salute, and yelled, "All present and accounted for, surp!"

Brasbee stepped up behind me, saying, "Madden, when you fall out this afternoon, I want you to jerk one of those fuckin' cartridge belts off the hook."

"If somebody was to add one while I'm inside," I said, "that would solve everybody's problems."

Not until I'd marched off to take up the rear did he figure that one out.

"You better shape up or ship out, soldier!" yelled Brasbee, lamely. "I got your name, Madden!"

"Madden, get in formation!" Unlike Stinnet, Corporal Keats had no sense of humor, and called cadence in strict military fashion.

Before returning to school, we had the week's indoctrination session in a building on a high sandy hill.

Corporal Keats, a short, lithe, handsome fellow with a swooping blond pompadour like Alan Ladd's, marched us out of the area. With Sargeant Rudd, Keats had just returned from Korea. While the platoons passed by me, as I stood at attention, waiting to take up the rear, I savored a few moments of separateness and freedom.

After Sergeant Keats had delivered us to Clerk Typist School and had trounced down the eroded hillside and started off across the field among bunches of tall, tough grass, he reminded me of Alan Ladd, riding away at the end of *Shane*.

"Come back, Shane!" I called. "Come back!"

Just as he turned, the laughter of the men reached him.

"Who said that?" he yelled, looking through heat waves up the slope at us.

"Brandon de Wilde," said Jesse, who had seen *Shane* with me on post the Saturday before, my second time.

"Better shape up!"

When he had gone too far to be likely to turn back and march us up and down in the sun to teach us a lesson, I yelled, and all the others joined in, "Come back, Shane! Shaaaane, come back!" imitating little Brandon de Wilde, and it made him dancing and stomping mad.

When we came out an hour later, it was Stinnet who emerged from under the building raised on exposed brick pillars, where he'd dozed in the shade, to march us over to the afternoon session of Clerk Typist School.

"Hut, tew, threet, hoor, Madden keep in step! Hut, tew, threet, hoor, Madden keep in step!"

As we fell in after school was out, Brasbee screeched, "Madden, you are out of un-i-form!"

"You didn't have any luck tracking down my cartridge belt, Sarge?"

"I ain't tracking down snake shit, soldier. Now, you got two minutes to break formation when we get back to the company area and sign a damn statement of charges and get issued a by god new cartridge belt and fall back in formation for re-treat. If I have to report you out of uniform at re-treat, your ass belongs to me, Madden. Two minutes!"

"That's two minutes wasted, Sergeant."

"You still claim one of your buddies is a mullifuckin' thief?"

"Whether he fucks his mother is a private matter." I hated that expression.

"All right, by god! 'Ten-hut!" Brasbee waited a minute. "All right, men, Ali Baba says one of you forty thieves rogued his cartridge belt. Now we're gonna stand here at attention in the blazing ass sun until the one that done it fesses up."

Sergeants Brasbee and Stinnet loped over and sat on the porch steps out of the sun and fixed us in a double stare.

In the three months that I had tangled assholes with the Army in various situations, I had never caused others to suffer for my own causes. And I had never really hated comical Sergeant Brasbee until now, as I stood there in the sun, feeling the hostility of the men sizzle around me. They began to grumble and some of them shot whispered demands and threats to me to sign. Silently, I recited Lord Byron's "I stood among them, but not of them," and A. E. Housman's "The laws of God, the laws of Man, he may keep them who will and can." And Robert Frost's "I have miles to go before I sleep."

All around me in the blistering sun the men stood rigidly at attention, their minds working in the same way others had worked in basic when we were ordered to report to the company commander to sign that loyalty oath that Senator Joseph McCarthy had somehow forced upon the Army.

Every few minutes, Brasbee stood up on the steps and yelled, "All right, the pig-hopper that done it better confess or ever' swinging dick *will* stand here till the dew falls."

But after ten minutes, he must have worried about our not showing up for retreat, because he stepped down and yelled, "Okay, move 'em out, Sergeant! On the double!"

When we hit tent city, Brasbee slowed us down to a march and Stinnet opened us up in song. "If I die on a Russian Front, wrap me up in a Russian cunt! Sound off, one, two! Sound off, one, two, three, four. . . . One, two!"

As I stepped off the blacktop, bringing up the rear, and marched between the two pines that bordered the sandy entrance to the company area, Sergeant Major Garrett violently pushed open the orderly room door and jabbed his fists into his fat hips. What he hated worse than listening to us sing cadence was to see us come in late.

Rudd and the other platoon sergeants stepped out from under the narrow eaves of the tent-sided cabins and jumped down the short bank to the parade ground.

Breathless from the brisk march, drenched in sweat, we watched Company Commander Lieutenant Glass, a tall slender Black man from Arkansas, step out of the orderly room, looking sharp, crisp, cool.

I liked Lieutenant Glass's walk, his sudden white smile. I imagined that when the cartridge belt incident came to his attention, he would resolve it justly. I refused to use the men's nickname for him, "Oily-tongue" — assigned because he often mispronounced words such as "Souse Carolinas." The prejudice against Lt. Glass reminded me of my fo'castle mate Peron, the scapegoat on the LP St. Clair oil tanker.

As the squad leaders made a head count and the platoon sergeants and Field First Brasbee made their reports to each other up the chain of command (the one the young chaplain had assured us went right on up to God) I thought maybe Brasbee and the other cadre would keep the incident from Lieutenant Glass and that they would keep trying to wear me down.

But Lieutenant Glass's sharp eye noticed me, and in a clear, civilized voice, he said, "Sergeant Major, there is a man out of u-nee-form."

Sergeant Major Garrett did an about-face. "Man out of uniform!" he yelled, as if such behavior from me were inevitable.

The other sergeants didn't even pretend to inspect their men. "Private Madden, sir," said Sergeant Rudd, as if to say, "Who else?"

"Have that man sign a statemint of charges," said Sergeant Garrett, in a bored, it-shall-be-done voice, looking up. "And issue him a new cartridge belt."

After retreat had sounded over the Fort Jackson loudspeakers, and Lieutenant Glass had turned the company back to the sergeant major and his platoon leaders, Sergeant Rudd commanded, "Madden, step forward! Platoon, dismissed!"

Our platoon was first in the run for chow.

At attention, I looked up at Rudd.

"Soldier, for being out of uniform, you *will* report to the mess sergeant after chow. And you gonna ride that mother-humping range every night until you stand formation in uniform."

"Why?"

"Why, what?'"

"Why do I have to ride the range? It wasn't my fault somebody stole my cartridge belt. Sergeant Brasbee ordered us to stack arms and he failed to post a guard. Put *him* on KP."

"You a real smart-ass, ain't you, Madden? You better be glad this ain't Ko-rea. You wouldn't last a week."

"Heard they throwed your ass on KP." Allen Carter put his finger on his own name on the KP roster.

"Yeah."

"Young soldier, you better shape the hell up. Ol' Rudd's after your ass."

"Why don't you go ahead and sign, Madden?" asked Puckett. "Lost mine on maneuvers one time. All the hell they charged me was a dollar and eleven cents."

"It's not the money. How can a bunch of guys who steal from each other fight together? And for what?" I really wanted to know. They weren't interested in discussing it, not even academically.

All my life from the time I could think coherently, I had persistently stood up for the rights given me by the Constitution and other laws and for rights I did not actually have from any source, but only thought I had or thought I should have had. I had certain other rights of which I was ignorant. I stood up for moral and ethical rights that had no legal basis. I was always vaguely aware of that ambience of rights.

"You're crazy, Madden. You ought to be teaching Sunday school."

"He ort to have his nuts cut out," said Baggett, looking up from *Sheila of the Jungle* comic book.

"I don't see why we have to wear cartridge belts anyhow," said Jesse, sullenly.

"Yeah, what use are they?'" asked Rastelli. "Did you ever see a cartridge in a cartridge belt?"

"Technically," said Puckett, "it's so when we march, we're under arms."

Jesse sneered. "You got any more of them silly reasons?"

"See, you guys agree it's stupid," I said. "So why do you wear them? Why don't we all just turn up without cartridge belts, then maybe they'll see how silly it is."

"I ain't getting my ass throwed on KP, ner in the stockage neither. Ain't worth it."

On my 21st birthday, Momma's presents arrived. "An applesauce cake with orange icing, my favorite. And tan cashmere muffler, for when this heat turned to freezing cold," on sale, with a birthday card. "Sure wish I could see you on your 21st birthday. Now you can tell the world, 'Today I am a man!' Happy 21st Birthday, Love and a big kiss."

That night, the mess sergeant made me wash the walls of the mess hall, reminding me of painting the engine room going through the Panama Canal. A little before midnight, he released me.

I strolled across the street from the mess hall into the jungle, hit the trail running, lickety split, shedding my sweat-saturated fatigues, stopping to shuck off my combat boots and socks, hit a fast pace running again, stark naked, howling like a lone wolf.

Dressed again, I walked deeper into the forest, where a handsome Black soldier mysteriously emerged, neatly dressed in uniform, and we had a pleasant, interesting, conversation.

As we parted, I hoped to see him again. I never did.

Later that night, ugly sounds of a thief in the next tent over getting the blanket treatment — men flailing socks filled with bars of soap, beating him as he lay under his blanket — woke me.

"Sergeant," said Lieutenant Glass, in his quiet, penetrating voice, "there's a man in the ranks out of u-nee-form!"

When Sergeant Rudd couldn't believe his ears, he turned his eyes on me, and sure enough, I was out of uniform. Officially, not even the fatigues I had on were a uniform, because streaked with soot and soiled from the grease trap the mess sergeant had ordered me to clean, a filthy, nasty, dirty uniform is no longer a uniform.

"I want that man's name."

"Man out of uniform is Private Madden, sir."

"Why isn't he wearing a cartridge belt? Regulations state he must be wearing a cartridge belt."

"Says he lost it, sir."

"It was stolen!" I yelled, so Lt. Glass could hear me.

The platoon groaned.

"Why is his uniform dirty and wrinkled, Sergeant Dunn?"

"He ain't too good at personal grooming, sir. He's one of them Maddens from North Knoxville."

"I had to ride the range last night and — !"

"Silence in the ranks!" Sergeant Major Garrett's voice was louder than mine.

" — then the washhouse was off limits!"

"Nobody gave you permission to be at ease, soldier." Lieutenant Glass's quiet voice carried more clearly than a shout. "Sergeant Major, I will inspect the ranks after chow this morning. Every man will be in uniform. I don't want to see no discrapincies!"

My platoon snickered.

A little while later, I was standing at the urinal. Suddenly, Sergeant Rudd was right beside me.

"You wanna ride that black-ass range again tonight?"

"No."

"Supply Sergeant's opening up early."

"Sorry, Sergeant, I'm not going to sign."

"You fuck up my goddamn platoon, you fuckin' with me, soldier. I better not catch you out in Columbia. You lucky you got out of Camp Gordon alive, boy. I got friends was with me in Ko-rea down there. They told me all about you, you dirty little commie!"

Rudd sprayed piss on the toes of my dusty combat boots, as if signing his name with a flourish. As I yelled outrage at him, he violently shook the drops off the end of his prong, stowed it in his pants, and walked out, buttoning up.

In the chow line and at the table where I sat and from tables nearby, I got a barrage of advice to surrender, all of it the same caliber.

After chow, Lieutenant Glass inspected the ranks. A lot of guys needed haircuts. Some of them needed to apply Brasso to their buckles. "I got your name, soldier!" Brasbee had repeated occasion to say.

Lieutenant Glass stopped in front of me. "Sergeant, wasn't this man told to sign a state-mint of charges?"

"Yes, sir. I told him yesterday at noon formation. He refuses." Brasbee held his clipboard braced between his forearm and his hip, waiting.

"He refuses?" Lieutenant Glass's small, bony, rather handsome face was only a few feet from mine, looking down at me. It was odd to be discussed as if I were invisible.

"I reported it stolen, sir."

"Who give you permission to speak?" Sargent Brasbee was quietly curt.

Lieutenant Glass instructed Sargent Brasbee to "Have Private Madden sign a state-mint of charges. We must be cost-conscious, soldier," and moved on, pretending to inspect the rest of the platoon, the last, moving more quickly, until the front rank must have seemed like striding past a picket fence.

As we were marching out of the company area, shepherded by Sergeant Keats, I noticed Sergeant Major Garrett deployed in front the orderly room door, his fists stuck in the fat of his hips, behind him the sign I had painted for him several weeks before with its misspelled word that had proved to him that I was, just as he had thought, an educated fool.

"Madden, step out!"

He led me into the orderly room. Through the window screen, I watched the others march on down the street.

"Madden," said Garrett, pointing a loaded finger between my eyes, "You better shape the fuck up! You ain't gonna disrupt my company no more."

"I tried to do the right thing when I reported the theft to — "

"Don't you sass *me*. Soldier, when you talk to *me*, you keep your mouth shut."

Garrett told me Lieutenant Glass was very upset, and that I had better sign right now and be in uniform for the next formation.

"I want to be in uniform, but I can't until Sargeant Brasbee recovers my cartridge belt, sir."

"Come with me!" Sergeant Garrett chugged like a locomotive out the side door and straight up the steep path to the front steps of the supply room.

"Sergeant, issue this man a cartridge belt."

Corporal Marcos grinned, and imitated Brasso. "He ain't signed a state-mint of charges yet."

"Come on, come on."

Marcos slung a new, fresh-smelling belt on the counter.

"Put it on." I strapped it on, warily, allowing the feeling of triumph to rise. It fell when he said, "Marcos, where's that state-mint of charges?'" Marcos put it on the counter. "Now, sign that mother-fuckin' thing!"

"I'd sign it," I said, disgusted, as I always was, with that expression, "if I thought it would turn right around and fuck somebody's mother."

"A smart ass to the end." Marcos stopped grinning.

"This isn't the end. I'm not signing."

"You refuse my order?"

"This order, yes, because it's illegal."

"Take off that cartridge belt."

I unstrapped and draped it over the counter. It slithered off. I picked it up and put it down and Marcos snatched it up.

The sergeant major stormed out the door and down the path into the orderly room.

Shading my eyes with my hands, I looked through the screen door. "What do I do now, Corporal?"

"Report to the clerk-typist school. On the double!" As I walked past the window at the back of his chair, he swiveled. "On the double, Madden!"

On the blacktop at the crest of a rise just outside the company area, I saw Sergeant Keats striding toward me through heat waves, pointing his finger.

"You the one that started them calling me Shane and mooing at me when I walk away."

"You do look like Alan Ladd, Sergeant." I meant that as a compliment.

"You gonna look like a sieve tomorrow when I get you on that rifle range.'"

"Already had that in basic."

"You're due to re-qualify, soldier. I re-qualified every day in Korea, shootin' me some gooks."

I noticed but did not celebrate the anniversary of the October Revolution in Russia.

In typing class, during the break, I worked out some futuristic ideas I had developed while cleaning out the grease trap the night before.

"After the ravages of war are cleared from the face of the earth and this final disfiguration passes into the bloody pages of pre-Communist history, Mankind will move on in sublimity toward its destiny. It is not Russia who rules the world today. It is the people everywhere who rule. When America surrendered, Russia's role in the struggle for universal freedom played out, and she ceased to exist as a nation. Comrades, nations no longer exist anywhere in the world; there are now cities and countries within the world community. Never again will one nation wage war with another, simply because nations no longer exist.

"The factories of the world that produced bombs during the war will tomorrow provide the wretched of the world family with clothing, shoes, and means for construction. Out of tanks, we, each of us, working together in a labor of love and need, will make bridges and cars, and from battleships will come the everyday items with which to make life and work more pleasant. In a matter of a year, Comrades, not a single piece of war mechanism will exist to offend your eyes and enrage you at the stupidity of man. Never before has man been given or rather given himself the opportunity that today is his — that of shaping out of chaos with the technology that war can't erase a new, abundant, free, happy world."

At formation, nothing was said about my being out of uniform. Nor when we returned to the company area. But at formation after noon chow, Sergeant Dunn told me to report to the mess sergeant for KP after supper — punishment for wearing dirty fatigues, which "shows disrespect for the uniform of the United States Army."

That afternoon, Sergeant Major Garrett stood in for Lieutenant Glass at retreat. His absence and no mention of the cartridge belt made me feel the conflict was over, but still, I felt uneasy.

That night, I was cleaning out the giant cook stoves, when Sargent Brasbee stuck his helmeted head in the door and yelled, "Madden!"

"Present!'"

"Report to the orderly room on the double!"

I double-timed it to the orderly room. The night orderly looked up at me. "Report to the company commander."

What the hell was he doing in the area this late at night? Lieutenant Glass lived off post. I knocked on his door.

"Come in."

Absorbed in a large thick book, the company commander pretended to be oblivious to my presence. Facing me on his desk was a statement of charges, my name typed in.

"Private Madden reporting to the company commander as ordered, sir." The tribal way to pronounce "sir" on such occasions was "surp," but I liked the lieutenant and meant him no disrespect.

"At ease, Private Madden." He had a soft, gentle voice. On that hot August night, I felt in the room, with its mellow lamplight, a sort of intimacy. A young white Southern liberal, who always declared that Blacks are as intelligent as whites, and a Black officer from Arkansas.

We could talk now, and he would understand. We did talk, quietly, coolly, a flow of logical cogitation, and I even threw in a few parallels between my collisions with the Army and the injustices perpetrated against his people, daily assaults on their dignity, selfhood. But if he understood as a Black man, he refused, as an officer, to accept the consequences of my reasoning, which, I figured out, would mean his undermining the authority of his cadre, contributing to their defeat in the eyes of all those educated young men. The cadre was made up of grammar school graduates and high school dropouts who had served their country in World War II or Korea. Bigger things than a cartridge belt had been at stake. I realized that. I did not scorn it, but I was also convinced that to sign that statement of charges would be the first step toward becoming a casual in my private war with the Army. When the next small issue turned up, I could hardly resist on principle, and one small, trivial issue after another would follow, and then, sometime after I had ceased to split hairs or care, a major act of capitulation.

"Private Madden, you must sign this statement of charges."

"Sir, I must refuse."

Refusing to sign a statement of charges was unheard of. I felt scared and alone, standing there in that office, as Lieutenant Glass slammed the big red book shut and let it drop melodramatically on the desk.

Without raising his voice, but with a quiver of suppressed rage, he said, "Private Madden, I can have you court-martialed on five separate counts — maybe six. Repeat-itly showing disrespect for the uniform of the United States Army, repeat-itly refusing to obey the commands of non-commissioned officers, repeat-it insubordination, negligent loss of governmint property, and repeat-itly appearing in fo'mation out of unee-form.'"

"What's the sixth one?"

"Refusing to obey a direct order from your commanding officer."

"But you haven't given me a direct order, sir."

"I am now."

"You're giving me a direct order to sign a statement of charges?"

"That's right. I order you, Private Madden, to sign that statemint of charges."

Refusal to obey a direct order from one's commanding officer carried one of the most severe of penalties. "Where's a pen, sir?"

Smiling, he pulled a green fountain pen out of his middle drawer, uncapped and handed it to me. I noticed it was just like the one my modern poetry teacher had given me when I went into the merchant marine and that I filled with green ink, and I remembered, standing there, that I used it to write poems and stories and philosophical reflections and had lost it, then found it in a whore house in Antofagasta, Chile, the year before.

But it wouldn't write. I looked up, smiling. "Ironic, isn't it, sir? Out of ink."

In no mood for irony, he snatched it from my hand and shook it violently. "It can be filled with ink."

But ink won't come out of a khaki shirt. Looking down at the black ink he had splattered on his shirt, he cursed under his breath. Now, his wife, too, would hate me.

I signed with a flourish.

"A new cartridge belt will be ee-shooed to you at the supply room in the morning after reveille. That is all."

"Yes, sir."

Just as the boys on the regular roster were leaving, I returned to KP.

The mess sergeant was a red headed, good-hearted old fellow about to retire. "I left a light on for you, son. Sergeant Rudd said for me to save mopping the floor for you. I'm going to bed. Just lock up when you get done."

I schucked off all my clothes. Sweat streaming down from my scalp to my ankles, I mopped the floor. And then I got a huge round pot, filled it with cold water and dumped it over my head. The shock almost made me faint.

Defiantly, I wrote a passage by flashlight of the novel version of "Cassandra Singing" on my cot under my government issue wool blanket. Lone and Gypsy making love in the silo, their favorite place.

"Man in the ranks out of uni-form!" Sergeant Brasbee seemed not surprised.

Lieutenant Glass's face was stunned blank.

"Madden!" screamed Sergeant Major Garrett. "You was supposed to report to the supply sergeant right after chow this morning!"

"I did as I was ordered. I signed a statement of charges. But Lieutenant Glass didn't give me a direct order to appear in full uniform."

Lieutenant Glass saluted the sergeant major and, shaking his head, walked away, into the orderly room.

"Move 'em out!" Sergeant Major Garrett ordered. "Sergeant Rudd, order Private Madden report to the company commander."

He did. Happily.

"I was about to ask permission anyway."

"You got my permission to report to the mess sergeant after retreat for standing formation in a filthy uniform again."

Without speaking to me, Sergeant Major Garrett flung his arm toward Lieutenant Glass's door. I knocked, was admitted, came to attention, rendered a smart military salute, said, "Private Madden to see the company commander as ordered, surp."

"Private Madden, as your company commander, I give you a direct order to report to the supply sergeant and secure a cartridge belt and wear it at all times while you are in the company area."

"Yes, sir."

I did it.

Returning to the orderly room, I requested permission to see the company commander, was granted permission, knocked, was admitted, came to attention, rendered the proper military salute, intoned, "Private Madden requests permission to speak to the company commander, surp."

Permission granted, I entered his office. Lieutenant Glass returned the salute. "Yes?" His tone was friendlier, as if he not only knew what it was like to be humiliated and had wanted me to suffer it, too, but that he now felt a little remorse for having been the agent of that humiliation, subject himself at any time to suffer it all over again.

"I request permission to visit the inspector general."

He was stricken. He couldn't refuse, any more than I could refuse to execute a direct order from my commanding officer — not without severe consequences. He didn't refuse. In a sputtering rage, he blurted, "Permission granted!"

"Which way do I go?"

"Find it yourself.'" He wanted to stomp me.

As I passed the sergeant major's desk, he grouched, "Join the company at school, Madden. On the double."

"I have permission to visit the inspector general." I kept walking out the door, imagining the look on his face.

Not that I was eager to do it, not that I relished the irony. I was on my way to complain about the mistreatment of a trainee at the hands of a Black company commander, a former ranger, who had worked harder than most to reach the goal he had set for himself, a goal not achieved with only a lieutenant's bar.

The inspector general was a tall, lanky, bronzed, dark-haired Texan, who scrutinized me out of deep-set eyes, listening patiently to my story, including my complaint about the vicious circle of the uniform dirtied by KP, the impossibility of washing it before the next formation, then catching KP again for wearing a filthy uniform.

He told me to hand over the new cartridge belt I was wearing and dismissed me.

As I walked back, wondering what the inspector general would do, my triumph did not put a spring in my step.

When a staff car full of brass passed me three minutes after I left the I. G.'s office, I wondered where they could be going in such a hurry.

When I reached the mess hall at the lower end of the company area, I saw across the parade ground through the screen door into the orderly room where Sergeant Major Garrett stood at rigid attention, a colonel, a major, and two captains glaring at him as the Texan chewed him out.

With a swooshing movement, they all turned and burst through the side door and stalked up the path to the supply building, and as I reached my cabin door, I saw the colonel toss the cartridge belt over the counter and rip a piece of paper in two and throw the pieces on the floor as Corporal Marcos stood at attention, trying to decide whether to shit or go blind.

And then the brass brigade turned and descended the steps and got into the staff car and roared away in a cloud of sandy dust, climaxing the cleanest, sharpest group movement I had ever seen. Swift, exhilarating. But I disliked it almost as much as I enjoyed it. And I was glad that Lieutenant Glass had not been in his office.

After a few moments, knots in my stomach, I knocked lightly at the orderly room door, afraid to wake the dead. Slumped in his swivel chair, Sergeant Major Garrett said, in a cold, neutral voice, "Wait in your tent until I send for you."

In the mail came William Faulkner's A *Fable*. I unwrapped the package standing in chow line. It came in a slipcase, signed, number 748 of only 1,000, for $11.99 of my Army pay. The idea of soldiers mutinying appealed to me. I listened to men in front and back of me make fun of me for wasting good money on a book, for Christ's sake. Holding *A Fable*, I heard Faulkner's Nobel Prize speech, as I often remembered it throughout the past four years. "I refuse to accept the end of man . . . they shall endure."

Sitting on my bunk, I dipped in and out of Faulkner's *A Fable.*

Mama Bidet, the commander, has " . . . a pitiless preoccupation with man, not as an imperial implement, least of all as that gallant and puny creature bearing undismayed on his frail bones and flesh the vast burden of his long inexplicable incomprehensible tradition and journey, not even in fact as a functioning animal but as a functioning machine in the same sense that the earthworm is: alive purely and simply for the purpose of transporting, without itself actually moving, for the distance of its corporeal length, the medium in which it lives, which, given time, would shift the whole earth that infinitesimal inch, leaving at last its own blind insatiate jaws chewing nothing above the spinning abyss: that cold, scathing, contemptuous preoccupation with body vents and orifices and mucous membrane as though he himself owned neither, who declared that no Army was any better than its anus, since even without feet it could still crawl forward and fight." I was happy to see a close variation on Faulkner's 1950 Nobel Prize speech. "I believe that man will not merely endure. He will prevail."

Sergeant Brasbee's voice screeched out in the sun and sand. "Madden! Re-port to the orderly rooooom!"

I had almost reached the screen door when Lieutenant Glass walked out, in full uniform, looking terrific. A jeep was parked between the two pine trees just off the blacktop. Sergeant Keats was driving.

The lieutenant got into the back seat. He spoke quietly to Keats, who ordered me to "Get in."

I started to get in beside Lieutenant Glass, because I knew the sergeant didn't want me sitting beside him, but Keats knew protocol. "Up front!"

So, with the Black officer in the backseat of an open jeep in South Carolina, we peeled out.

We passed the company marching in from Clerk Typist School for evening chow. Out of his sleepy grin, Stinnet was calling cadence: "Hut, tew, threet, hoor, Madden keep in step!"

Lieutenant Glass and I had to wait, sitting side by side, a half hour before we were admitted into the inspector general's office.

Side by side, we rendered the proper military salute to the colonel from Texas who stood behind his desk, looking at tall, immaculate Lieutenant Glass from South Carolina and sawed-off, droopy Private Madden, from Tennessee. Us southerners. The colonel invited us to be seated side by side on the hard chairs.

The colonel informed Lieutenant Glass that Private Madden had registered certain complaints and told him what they were. With no trace of sullenness, the lieutenant listened carefully. "What do you say to those charges, Lieutenant?"

"Sir, I intend to have Private Madden court-martialed on six counts."

"You do that, Lieutenant Glass, and I will have *you* court-martialed on seven counts."

It was dramatic, it was impressive, it was just, but he was a Texan and Lieutenant Glass was an Arkansas "nigra," so David Madden, the southern liberal, felt ashamed. I had an urge to reproach my benefactor.

But the Texan didn't appear pleased with the situation, he did not gloat. Summing up, he spoke in a mild but firm tone. "Lieutenant Glass, I can see Private Madden is not a good soldier, but he has certain rights nevertheless, and it is my duty as inspector general to protect those rights, just as I would protect yours."

I felt an urge to ask him whether he would protect Lieutenant Glass's rights back home in Texas, but then that would have made this a different episode.

As I rode back with Lieutenant Glass, he seemed relaxed in the open jeep under the brutal South Carolina sun. Not at all tense or resentful. When he got out of the jeep, he walked easily into the orderly room. He hadn't won, but he had not contradicted, personally, Brasbee or Rudd or his other cadre, and they should appreciate that.

Returning to my tent, I opened *A Fable*, where I had saved my place with an envelope from one of Vera's letters.

A few minutes later, Keats's face appeared at the screen, framed by his hands, a burst of sun behind him. "Let's go," he said, in a funereal voice.

I followed him to the jeep. I got in beside him. As he peeled out of the sand and dust, I noticed, sticking out from under the seat between his legs, the blackish buckle of a cartridge belt.

When we passed the cutoff to Clerk Typist School, I wondered what the hell. Then a swamp rose on both sides of the blacktop. Was he going to take me out into the boondocks and beat me to death with that cartridge belt?

Hearing rifle fire, I remembered that the company was supposed to go out to re-qualify and I was relieved, until I recalled Keats saying he couldn't wait to get me on the rifle range.

I qualified again, making sharpshooter, and then Keats yelled an order.

"What?" we all asked.

"I distinctly said, police up the muddafuggin area, soldier up the area. Any you malingerers, your ass belongs to me."

To perform quickly and efficiently, we all dropped to our knees and moved forward.

"Hey, Madden!" Keats yelled, behind me.

Afraid his tone of sarcasm meant he would be aiming a rifle at me, I turned slowly. Just reading about William Bradford Hughie's *Execution of Private Eddie Slovak* made me, as a targeted communist sympathizer, quake.

The company, half of them on their knees in the tough, dry grass, half of them bent over at the waist, rose, turned expectantly, and looked at the new cartridge belt that dangled from Keats' upheld arm. "Found a stray cartridge belt. You can have it, if you want it."

All the guys started patting their waists to see if they had dropped their belts. Then, relieved, they all laughed.

Lugging my helmet liner full of spent rounds, I walked back toward Keats, smiling. I liked him. I hoped he was going to hand it over in good grace. I wanted him to like me.

Clamping my helmet liner between my knees, I took the cartridge belt from him, and as I snapped it on, he said, in a low voice, as quiet and smooth as Alan Ladd speaking to hired killer Wilson in *Shane*, "We're going to get your ass, Madden. You made a fool out of our company commander and all the NCO's. You better look behind you, boy."

I did, quite often, at night in the company area, on the fort, and everywhere I went in Columbia on the weekends. But nobody was ever there — not even Sgt. Rudd, who had put in for a transfer to a company nearby, but rumors drifted back to me that he still talked about beating my ass.

Three of us were taken out of class to jerk nails out of a huge slew of boards that had constituted a small building on the typing school campus. I stepped on a rusty nail. The friendly Black commander of the typing school insisted that I be taken to the infirmary for shots. I was ignorant of the effect on me of sulfa — a rash all over my body.

"CHRIST AS A PARANOID HOMOSEXUAL"

As I was nearing the end of the six-week course, my Clerk Typist School instructor, a very likeable, not very military fellow, instructed the class. "Now today, gentlemen, I want you to write me an essay right on your typewriters and hand it in. Okay, a good test of your ability, your progress, okay, is when you type something out of your head, in your own words, okay, as opposed to copying from the manual. So go at it, men. Make it as neat as you can. You *will* be graded. But I'm giving you the freedom to write whatever you want to. Just keep it clean."

"Hearts too soon made glad," I intoned. They all laughed.

His tone made me feel he was speaking directly to me, as if the Army was showing an interest in what was on my mind. What came to mind was a mind not necessarily my own, a mind I imagined. On the long, buff military typewriter paper, following a line of reasoning, using a kind of Socratic method of interrogation, I set out to give the Army something out of the ordinary to think about.

"'Christ as a Paranoid Homosexual'

"The paranoid is one of the most interesting of all psychotics, especially he whose complex exhibits the symptoms in their classic form. The most remarkable characteristic of paranoia which distinguishes it from most other psychological or psychosomatic disorders is the patient's level of intelligence, often far above that of the average person, and his use of almost flawless logic in systematically explicating the particulars of his persecution delusion. He builds from the raw material of this delusion an edifice far more elaborate than the most accomplished liar.

"Paranoia has a strong homosexual repression content. Paranoids charge the other with wanting to rob him of his normal sexual activities. The pronounced tendency of superiors in the army to suspect men of all kinds of misdemeanors comes under the headings Insidious Group Paranoia Manifestation and C.P.I.: Constitutional Psychotic Inferior. Somehow living the army life has gotten me thinking of such things.

"A friend of mine, an atheist, made the remark one day in the course of a discussion on religion, 'It seems to me not remarkable at all what Christ did. Isn't it clear that he was a hopeless paranoid homosexual?' The content of this striking statement, even from an atheist, interested me, an agnostic, for a reason out of its context. I had cause to believe that my friend was not so well informed in psychiatry that he could know of the strong homosexual compulsion that has been discovered to exist working subconsciously in the mind of the paranoid.

"That my friend used the two psychoses, commonly referred to separately, in conjunction, impressed me that the relationship isn't quite as obscure as is sometimes suspected. The remark turned my mind to the case of Jesus Christ himself. I wondered what my friend's line of reasoning might be. Questions arose.

"To our knowledge, did Christ, though he was a god impersonating a mortal, ever show so-called natural, sensual affection for a member of the opposite sex, and weren't his disciples all men for whom he often expressed a great show of love? Did he not turn his back on his mother and father? Could it have been a behavior manifestation of a repressed homosexual guilt feeling? Why was his only female confidante and friend a harlot, one who, because he was pure and she defiled, might replace the mother he couldn't face?

"Of course, the features of the paranoia my friend suspected are evident. Christ believed that the whole Roman Empire was against him and that he suffered for all mankind — a gross inflation of his ego as well as the most classic example of paranoia ever to influence history. Most importantly, he never tired of prophesying his own crucifixion which would not only atone for his own sins (which he denied) but those of all other men alive and to come. This is a typical characteristic of the paranoid's delusion — that of martyrdom anticipated, the final justification of his fears. How could he have possibly taken Pilate's generous offer of freedom if he would renounce his claims to being the Messiah? The elaborate structure of logical argument he had declared so often wouldn't then allow him to do other than take up the cross and fulfill the implications of his delusion.

"The case of Christ is undoubtedly the most complex but in a larger sense one that was beautiful and essentially most kind to its subject, and unfortunately for the paranoid, fortunately for mankind, most rare."

Private Howie, a slightly effeminate, precocious Harvard freshman, a philology major who looked no older than 15, often talked with me in the post library. Because his father was a friend of the regimental colonel, Howie was often invited to cocktail parties. He told me that my typing teacher, a nice fellow really, turned the finished copy of "Christ as a Paranoid Homosexual" over to the Black captain, a criminologist in civilian life, who headed the school. My essay, Howie said, was the topic of discussion for weeks among the officers.

The commander of Clerk Typist School called me to his office. Although he was appalled by my essay on Jesus Christ as paranoid homosexual, we had a serious, complex discussion about religion, literature, and creative writing. I refrained from telling him the whole story of Cassie and Lone. Because he was Black, a former criminologist, I assumed he was a liberal, but as I talked about God and communism, I learned that he was a tolerant conservative, or he was drawing me out at the request of Army Intelligence.

"Dear Vera, Saturday my clerk typist school class graduates and everyone ships out but me and some boys held over to testify in a Court Martial against a thief in our company. They're holding me because of the Counter-Intelligence Corps' interest in me, which I don't suppose is ever going to let up. I would gladly tell them anything they want to know. So, you see I have my worries. How I long to get the hell out of that disgusting company! They kick me around and then politely ask me to decorate their dayroom and I accept and win awards in base-wide competitions. But every time I buck them, it's within the law — the law of the Army — not my own law.

Love, David"

★

THE LOOMING EXECUTION OF CARYL CHESSMAN

In 1948, I had read that Caryl Chessman had committed twenty robberies and thefts throughout the Greater Los Angeles area. He was believed to be "The Red-Light Bandit," who robbed a couple as they were parked on a hill in West Pasadena, forcing Regina Johnson to perform oral and anal sex, threatening to kill her boyfriend if she did not surrender.

Captured and arrested after a high-speed chase, Chessman was interrogated for 72 hours. Claiming he was beaten and tortured, Chessman confessed to the "Red Light Bandit" crimes. The rape victims positively identified him.

Put on trial for 18 counts of robbery, kidnapping, and rape, Chessman was sentenced to death.

I followed the case of the world-famous Caryl Chessman on San Quentin's death row as he fought and overcame execution deadlines. He would be the first convict executed for kidnapping under the "Little Lindbergh law." His case had re-ignited anti-death penalty protests throughout the world.

My life-long opposition to the death penalty, and that I identified with him as an individualist, but with many reservations, led me to Chessman's memoir *Cell 2455, Death Row*.

"The problem remained one of finding reasons and not fault. Blame fixing for its own sake was a profitless practice," he wrote. "I was one of the trees in this dark and forbidding forest. I knew what it meant to live beyond the reach of other men or God. I have 'proved' everything I had felt the need to prove: that I couldn't be scared or broken or driven to my knees, that I didn't give a damn.

"But here is where the tragedy lies: this felt need is compulsive and negative only. It is a need to prove one can do without — without love, without faith, without belief, without warmth, without friends, without freedom. This negative need to prove becomes progressively greater and greater; a truthless tyrant, it comes to dominate; it grows brash and boldly demanding. If not checked, the ultimate conscious or unconscious need is to prove that one can do without even life itself."

Reading Camus' *The Stranger,* about Meursault's being on trial and executed, partly because he didn't cry at his mother's funeral, and his essay against the death penalty "Reflections on the Guillotine," enhanced my feelings about Chessman and others on death row. That Chessman read Nietzsche strengthened the bond.

His case reminded me of the execution of Julius and Ethel Rosenberg, and I had read about the earlier Sacco and Vanzetti case in *A Little Treasury of American Prose* at sea. I had just recently read about Private Eddie Slovak, the only American soldier executed in World War II, for desertion, by firing squad — a jury of twelve peers — in France. *Knock on Any Door* by Black novelist Willard Motley contributed to my opposition to the death penalty. The protagonist, Nick Romano, a likable hoodlum, said, "Live fast, die young, leave a good-looking corpse!" He was executed in the end.

Out of that many-faceted sense of association by conviction and, maybe, the fact that my brothers John and Dickie were criminals, I wrote to Chessman. That made up, a little, for my not having written to Julius and Ethel and Rosenberg before their execution for espionage as Russian spies.

"This letter may never reach you, Caryl. I am a 'soldier' doing time in scorching hot Georgia and news of the outside world is not easily accessible, so I do not know this evening when you are to be murdered by the state of California or even whether the insatiable hunger of this society for vengeance has already been catered to.

"Last week I saw the very bad movie based on your life in crime and tonight I finished your book. I do not know whether it is an honest book, as I do not know whether you are guilty of the crimes for which your life is scheduled to pay. The difference it makes to me is nominal. But I would rather the book were honest, except for its declaration of innocence, and you were guilty than for both the book and the plea to be untruthful.

"I am anything but optimistic, yet I prefer to believe in both the honesty of the book and the innocence of the charges against its author. Your book demonstrates to me — with its show of the understanding of human frailty, of the anatomy of both love and hate, of society's blundering, spiteful shallowness, and lack of responsibility for the spiritual well-being of its citizens — that you are an extraordinary person with uncanny creative talent, with a gift for analyzing the ills by which man is afflicted. For that alone you deserve to live.

"But I am not writing to praise you, to declare my faith in your innocence, to show pity, or to offer platitudes to dull however briefly your last hours (I certainly hope they shall not be). I do not really know exactly why I am writing to you, for certainly I have never before written such a letter or anything near it.

"It is not because I am myself a writer, because intellectually though not yet violently I am living outside the circumference of society, and so lucidly understand the things you admirably express in your book, nor is it because my own older brother has spent 1/4 of his life in custody and the last month celebrated his 25th birthday in a federal penal institution, nor that my younger brother spent nearly as much of his own life in the reform schools of Tennessee, nor because my mother too has suffered for their having been unable to respond to the rehabilitation treatments, nor is it because I was raised in an environment which bred crime and violence, from which I escaped without an arrest but with perhaps some mental effects.

"Of course, those reasons do play some small part in my motivation for writing to you, but the main urge comes from something else which I find inexpressible, a feeling not even well defined, but a feeling which is probably deeply rooted in every man but obscured by society and its impersonal complex of conditionings — a feeling of kinship, a simple but vital force in me which tells me that I have met and have recognized with the clear eyes of love a human being who is going to be senselessly murdered by the righteous bastard off-spring of that force of fundamental love which created every existing thing — that force which is God, indescribable, unnamable. It is not the God of the Christian barbarians but of the Buddha. You no doubt have read of this gentle man whose wisdom shone over the horizon of the spirit long before Christ's gaudy pyrotechnic display.

"No, I am not a follower of some California Buddhist cult, nor do I believe I have found the answers in Buddha that I have sought all my life. 'Go and seek thine own salvation with diligence,' he told his followers on his deathbed. But at this moment his philosophy and the ancient Brahmins cosmology best describe my own vague, intuitive ponderings.

"So I write to you not out of pity, for men have suffered worse and my heart isn't big enough to weep for them all, but because I cannot bear the thought of your dying without having known that somewhere in the world someone feels he has understood, on a level of comprehension at which you were probably trying to reach, those to whom you have told your story. And to feel that one has understood generates an inexplicable desire to communicate with that person. I feel it is vital to my own spiritual well-being to know that you know I understand in the deepest sense I am capable of.

"Society is putting you to death and it, in its arrogance and promiscuous blindness, numerically includes me. Since I cannot tolerate this outrage in silence, I must tell you that I have no part in it and am responsible only in so far as I am impotent to help you.

"Why do I not write to other condemned men? Because I do not know them as well as you have revealed yourself, and since I cannot know what is in their minds, the only level on which I could reach them is on the level of ugly pity. I cannot offer anyone that. In fact, I cannot offer you anything — not even a steadying hand should you stumble. If they kill you, remember in some far corner of your mind, that another fellow human being shall not forget you, as you wanted to be remembered.

"I hope you get another reprieve and if you do and if you have time, I suggest you read *The Stranger* by Albert Camus, a French existentialist. And, also, you may find some sort of cold comfort in the teachings of Buddha. I know of no man more ideally of the mind for it than you.

Good luck, David Madden."

★

"AGNES OF GLASGOW"

A Libretto for David Van Vactor

After I had eaten roast lamb and artichokes with lemon butter dip with the Van Vactors, Vera knocked at the beveled glass front door. When I opened it, she stepped awkwardly into my open arms.

Then Walton let himself in.

All assembled in the living room holding glasses of wine, I waited for an opening.

"Even when I was a little boy, I was free to explore Knoxville, and when I left home to live in Washington, DC and mostly in New York or travelling abroad, I was eager to explore the streets of towns as soon as possible after my arrival.

"Wanting to know about the state in which I was confined, espcecially, my having no car, the area close around Fort Jackson, I consulted the thick *WPA South Carolina Guide to the Palmetto State*, and discovered Agnes of Glasgow, who crossed the Atlantic Ocean in search of her beloved, serving under General Cornwallis during the American Revolution — reminding me of Henry Wadsworth Longfellow's Evangeline searching for her lover in Louisiana.

"So, I got on a bus to Camden, where Meeting Street led me into the old Quaker Cemetery. In a brick-enclosed plot, I knelt to read the tombstone. "Agnes of Glasgow 1760–1780. Here sleeps Agnes of Glasgow who tradition says followed her lover of the British Army across ocean and through wilderness to Camden. She was taken by death before she found him and buried here at night by "King" Haigler and his men. Agnes of Glasgow departed this life Feb. 11, 1780.

"In a romantic fever, I searched further in the Columbia Public Library and discovered that she became a legend of American folklore. She was born of noble birth. One account speculates, the Scotch lass fell in love with Lt. Angus McPherson, a brave British officer, who embarked to America with the British Army. Tidings from him came slowly, then ceased." I paused for effect.

"What happened next?" Raven was eager to know.

"He's pausing for effect." Walton read me like a book.

"How it was, without telling her parents, she stowed away on a sailing vessel bound from England to America?" I had aroused Vera's inquiring mind.

"Having survived storms, Agnes arrived in Charleston, South Carolina. Hearing that her lover may have been wounded and discovering that his unit was assigned near Camden, in Kershaw County, South Carolina, she wandered through towns and the wilderness hoping to encounter someone who knew him. Her lover's company was unknown, but after much searching, she was told that he was with General Rawdon at Camden.

"From Georgetown, she traveled by canoe with King Haigler, an American Indian leader who befriended her, to Camden. A soldier curtly told her that her lover was dead. Through a window, she saw a fresh grave. A fever seized her, and she died without having laid eyes on her lover. King Haigler buried her under cover of darkness.

"A different legend provides a variation on that story. Oh, you all don't wanna hear this story?" I drew upon one of Mammy's storytelling techniques for reinvigorating the listener's attention.

"Just tell it." Dave flicked a long ash off his cigarette into the smoldering fireplace.

"Because she followed his camp and accompanied him, some believed she was General Cornwallis' mistress, causing her to become a social pariah. Her beloved's body was carried on a stretcher made of muskets. Generals Cornwallis, Rawdon, and Tarleton led the burial procession, conducted with military precision over fields to the Quaker graveyard, in a silence broken only by a mockingbird. Soldiers dug the narrow grave with bayonets and mess dishes. Rocks and a broken bayonet were used to fashion the headstone and the inscription. Bricks from Cornwallis' house were later installed to keep the headstone from sinking. The headstone, it was said, was sent from Glasgow, but before it could be erected, the British moved out, and it was stored.

"Later, Camden citizens took it out and placed it.

"Because the grave did not point West, and because coins were found nearby, many people thought it pointed to buried treasure. People flocked to the grave and dug around it, many finding malarial fever but no treasure. Ghost hunters from around the country still visit her grave. Wildwood, Cherokee Rose, cedar, jasmine, and myrtle trees grow there.

"Local legend is that she searches for her lover still, and that her ghost haunts the 'Old Quaker Cemetery' where she was buried and the surrounding wooded area to the very day I stood there, body and mind thrumming in romantic ecstasy."

"David writes while talking." I was seldom sure whether such comments from Vera were loving, or what.

"Riding the bus back to Columbia, I imagined an opera libretto about Agnes of Glasgow and was eager to write a brief description to send you, Dave."

I had written two rather wild libretti for Dave before the Army Leviathan swallowed me up.

"I damn well want to see it soon, David, because I just finished a cello concerto and I'm between projects."

I kept up with Raven in New York. She confided in me the story of two current loves, John Cullum, who was forging a career in the theater, as Bill Howell, a darkly handsome fellow whose radio announcer voice was haunting and who had become a live television drama director, was bowing out.

John and I had acted in a few plays together at UT. I was most often cast as an old man, as in Clifford Odets' *Golden Boy*, in which I played an old Jewish man who often quoted Schopenhauer. John played the Golden Boy, a boxer. A captain returning to us, to UT Theater, he wept after doing a sight reading of J. B. Priestley's *Dangerous Corner*, a really great performance. He also starred in Eugene O'Neill's *Beyond the Horizon* and in *Petrified Forest* in which I played a telegraph lineman who spoke the first line, and few thereafter. Before leaving for New York, John was in love with the ballet teacher who taught Iva Lee.

I was partly the reason he went to New York to seek a career in acting because when he sought my advice, I urged him to "Go! But you will never be a romantic leading man."

★

HOPE SAVAGE

The Only Real Bohemian

On leave, December 15, 1954, strolling nostalgically among the open toy counters in the basement of Kress's, I saw the love of my life, walking toward me, a heart-stopping image. We said so few words that by the time I reached the gray daylight on Gay Street I could remember only that she testified that she was happily married to a man who worked for the telephone company — I always see him wearing spikes, climbing a telephone pole — she who had yearned to become a ballet dancer and choreographer and be married to an agnostic writer living in bohemian Greenwich Village.

Because Stanley Kenvin, my closest army friend, and I were so very different in most ways, and because he seemed intent upon going along with me into Columbia to share a room, apartment, or even a house, I wondered whether he might be spying on me for the CIC or the FBI because my refusal to sign a bogus Senator McCarthy-inspired loyalty oath put me under suspicion of being a communist.

An attractive real estate lady of about 35 had entrusted Kenvin and me with the keys to take a look by ourselves at a house for rent. "Return the keys Monday morning, please, without fail."

So Kenvin and I had corralled Kent, the very urbane company clerk, a Yale man, and M. L., a very young-looking kid majoring in liguistics at Harvard, well-met on Main Street, to spend the night, for a modest fee, on bare mattresses in the three bedrooms of the furnished house.

That night, Kenvin and I were watching Vittorio De Sica's *Miracle in Milan*, sitting in the back row of a rickety South Carolina University auditorium, reminding me of the one at the Black college in Knoxville where Vera and I used to walk five miles to see foreign movies.

When the lights came on so the student projectionist, set up in the middle of the auditorium, could see to change reels, we looked around, and saw to our right at the end of our row a lovely honey-blond young girl of about seventeen wearing a buckskin jacket with fringes on the sleeves.

"Goddamn!" we chimed. Our excitement made our seats creak. "Goddamn!"

We agreed in whispers that no girl who looked that lovely and whose aura was so aloof would ever respond to any attempt by lowly guys like us to speak to her.

As the lights went off, we kept looking over at her in the dark until the last reel.

When the lights came up again, there she sat, right next to Kenvin.

"You all look interesting." Her voice was high-pitched but distinctive, crystal clear.

Kenvin gave her his name, and I leaned across him to give her mine.

"Hope Savage is my name. But call me Sura. The word for South in India. . . . May I come with you all?"

At a pizza joint, Hope's own poems and her intensely passionate recitation astonished us.

I am soaked where I lie in a crimson flood,
I am bathed in the grass with my own red blood.

All is sorrow and grief, all is woe and pain,
and I by the watchers of the night am slain!

Two gleamings behind the darkness of sky:
Ah, Castor, ah Pollux, have you doomed me to die?

My Castor, my Pollux, I have loved, and I love!
For you has my gaze all my nights been above!

I have fallen on my knees with a face that was wet
with tears for my soul; but alas! You forget!

You never knew the love that you had!
You are naught! I must die! All my life I was mad!

You could not feel the love I did give;
save me not now, for I will not live!

On my garments of crimson let the mighty sea fall,
Oh, I kiss and caress it and welcome it all.

I HAVE YEARNED TO BE BURNED BY THE STARS

I have yearned to be burned by the stars,
Or to drown deep and deep down in the flood;
All the trees my soul sees are its bars,
And the rain is its pain and its blood.

Though the cry from on high is my wail,
White delight in its light my soul sings;
I fly forth toward the north through the hail,
I awake and I take mighty wings!

After we put her on a Trailways Bus to her hometown, Camden, thirty miles away, we were both more soaringly in love than body-wracking sexually aroused, yelling in unison, "Goddamn! Goddamn! Goddamn!" all the way on the city bus to the empty house we had invaded around noon that day.

As I lay on a bare mattress trying to stay awake to see Hope's goddess face, hearing her passionate, intense voice, curled up beside M. L., the boyish Harvard linguist who looked about 15, both of us in our jock shorts in the smotheringly humid bedroom, I heard Kenvin yell "Goddamn!" from the bare mattress he shared with company clerk Kent in the bedroom down the hall, sparking my yell, "Goddamn!" until Kenvin and I were a chorus repeating "Goddamn!" and "Hope Savage!" until Harvard and Yale who had joined us, from the third bedroom, yelled, "Shut the fuck up, for Christ's sake, you two maniacs!" and "Who the hell is Hope Savage?"

We woke up in the morning yelling, "Goddamn!" and "Hope Savage!"

The next morning, in uniform, the four of us got down on our knees and crawled through a hole we had made in the Fort Jackson fence that just happened to run along the side of the house, just in time for reveille.

Remembering Camden from the time a few weeks previous when I had gone there to find the grave of Agnes of Glasgow, I got on a Trailways Bus to pay an uninvited, surprise visit to Hope who had told us that that was her hometown.

When I asked the mailman where the Savages lived, he pointed out that Henry Savage was the mayor, and gave me the address. 1919 Lyttleton Avenue.

After a long walk, I stood in front of the white columned mansion of Henry Savage II, the mayor of Camden, delighted that it was only a block away from the neglected but fenced-in grave of Agnes of Glasgow in the Quaker graveyard.

Hope's elegant, sophisticated mother let me in and sat me down in her living room, a cut a little above the Van Vactors where I had passed many evenings over seven years in Knoxville.

Mrs. Savage, who made me think of a more deliberately sedate Ginger Van

Vactor, introduced me to Hope's two younger sisters and three brothers, all of them blond, as they drifted in and out, sitting briefly, hanging over the backs of chairs, the value of each of which probably exceeded my whole family's net worth. I assumed that her father the Mayor, a Civil Rights advocate, author of a few books, was at the town hall, governing.

"Virginia, please go up and tell Hope she has a visitor."

She went up, then skipping down the stairway, Virginia announced, "Hope is on her way down."

Hope appeared in the double doorway of the high-ceilinged living room. Surprised to see me, but smiling, and made a little shy by the human surroundings, she crossed the room at an unselfconscious gait.

As she turned to sit on a violet, satin-covered chair, I saw that the back of her skirt was hiked up. I imagined that this ethereal being had just gotten up from the toilet seat, unmindful of earthly cautions.

Her response to her embarrassed mother's subtle comment was obliviousness, a quality of temperament I had noticed in that pizza joint. I then supposed that obliviousness was a state of mind always on the surface of her deep interior life.

Suddenly, Hope gave me her explicit attention, startling me. "Let's walk outside."

As we walked around the house in the bright, very hot air, I set out to impress her with my knowledge of existentialism, assuming that she, as a strange being living awash in her imagination and in the imaginations of Swinburne, Shelley, and Keats, would also be open to a twentieth century kind of bizarre life. She had not heard of Albert Camus and, off my description of his philosophy of the absurd, she said, "I fear he is too concerned with ordinary life."

I tried harder and failed more miserably with each try.

Surely, living so close, she often visited the grave of that romantic young woman, Agnes of Glasgow.

"She was a fool to come all that way just to end up with a man, don't you think? Dead, as it turned out. Then to die of a broken heart, seems to me rather silly."

Not the humidity alone, of which she seemed oblivious, made me sweat.

Partly because she seemed more and more like her, I lunged into telling her about Cassie, as if she were a real person, living not in a mansion but in a rundown old house in Knoxville up on Sharp's ridge, but I shut up when I sensed Hope had drifted into her obliviousness mode.

I risked telling her, "Your face reminds me of Botticelli's 'Spring.'" But the image in my head was "Birth of Venus."

"I love Botticelli's 'Birth of Venus' nude because it sprang full blown from his imagination."

"But you are real, dressed or nude."

"Am I? I am disappointed in you, David Madden."

Even so, she walked me to the street. "Oh, wait." She pivoted slowly around and went swoopingly back into the house. I waited quite a while, suffering heat chill. She came out holding a book. "Here. I have it by heart."

My Sister and I by Nietzsche was what she placed in my hands.

During the bus trip back to Columbia, exhilaration for having seen her again swamped Hope's faintly negative impression of me.

Hope's very difference from Iva Lee made me see her face and hear her voice now and then as I went back over those luminous moments with Hope, a girl very unlike any I had ever met or even heard tell of. Except maybe Cassie, who was already taking on some essence of Hope's other-worldliness.

Simultaneously with dipping back into *The Anti-Christ*, I read Nietzsche's *My Sister And I*, about his incestuous relationship with his older sister, Elizabeth, and his complex relationship with his mother. They reminded me of Lone and Cassie and Lone and Momma in my novel and play that I was imagining every day. Nietzsche talks much about women he loved, Lou Salome, whose face in photographs resembles Vera's, and Cosima, Wagner's wife, Lou, and a prostitute. (I was ignorant then of the fact that Nietzsche scholars reviled that book as a hoax.) Reading about an outcast and exotic appealed to me and got into, but not literally, my depiction of the relationship of Lone and Cassie. They, like Hope Savage and Raven and Iva Lee, who was called "Puny" because of a long bout with fever such as Cassie suffered, along with other literary works, inspired elements of "Cassandra Singing" that were always shifting.

When Kenvin told me he was worried that the CIC might think he was a Communist because of his association with me, we parted semi-amicably.

So, I moved a third time, into an upstairs room in Columbia, in a big, two-story old house on Sumter Street among elegant mansions, close to South Carolina University. The landlady was very clean. A plant on the landing in the midst of Lysol fumes reminded me of Harry Haller in Hermann Hesse's *Steppenwolf*, who regards a plant on a landing and the household odor as expressive of the despairingly ordinary bourgeois life. He struggles between two sides of man's nature — the spiritual and the animalistic, the "wolf of the steppes." I liked him. And a short piece depicting a poet who was a prisoner who drew a train on the wall of his cell, and next morning the guard found his cell empty.

After a few days, Kenvin came by to visit and decided he wanted to rent the room down the hall, the dark one.

Kent, a clerk in my company, the very cultured, haughty Yale man who the Harvard fellows treated haughtily, rented a room next to Kenvin's. Seeing him shaving in the bathtub faintly disgusted me, even though I had admired Clifton Webb doing that in *Laura*. Kenvin's reappearance where I lived, augmented by Kent's arrival, intensified my suspicion that the two of them were assigned to keep an eye on Madden the Red every morning, I rode into Fort Jackson with Kenvin in another old car he had bought, pulling over when the guns went off, the bugles blew, and, as required, getting out of the car to salute, as we did, leaving the post at taps. Kenvin's salute was crisp, mine was half-assed.

Deep in the aura of the Lonsdale neighborhood just below Sharp's Ridge in Knoxville, creating a life for Cassie and Lone and their momma and Daddy and Blackie, I heard Kenvin's thrusting footsteps and his voice and, faintly, a high-pitched female voice, coming up the stairs. He opened my door without knocking, stepped aside to present, grinning, the shocking sight of Hope Savage in the doorway, perversely wearing a simple blue winter coat.

"Hope! I was just writing about you, Cassie as sort of you, and there you stand in the shivering flesh."

"More or less." Seeing the way she and Kenvin looked together hurt, but I saw that she was glad to see me, well, sort of, at least. "Well, until I perhaps see you again, David." That high, quivering voice was very like Cassie's as I imagined her talking — on the verge of mild hysteria.

Kenvin didn't shut my door, but he shut the door to his own room, likely so that I could hear and suspect.

They showed up in my open doorway again later, and he told me he was driving Hope home to Camden.

When he returned that night, I asked him what had happened. I got that horn-rimmed, sleepy-eyed look and pursed-lipped, half-mocking, half-supercilious smile of his. Rather mockingly, he insinuated that he had made love to her.

On his next visit to Hope's home, Kenvin willingly took me along.

But the auspicious event turned out to be Hope and Kenvin walking around the grounds of the estate, me walking close behind, playing hard to get.

Confined to the military training milieu, I felt that the "News of the Day" reached me from an alien realm out there in the world.

I was fascinated to read in the Columbia paper about a fifteen-year-old, Pauline Parker, who set out to break all the ten commandments. She lived in Christchurch, New Zealand of all places. Pauline's family was lower middle class, her friend Juliet's family was rich and highly educated.

Pauline kept a diary describing their strange friendship. Juliet and her divorced father were leaving shortly for South Africa, and Pauline's mother refused to allow her to go with them, so Pauline and her friend Juliet beat her mother to death. They knew what they had done was wrong, but they considered themselves more intelligent, more talented, almost of a rare species, and thus outside the law. Pauline proudly broke all Ten Commandments, but Juliet broke only nine.

I told Hope Savage, whose imagination thrived on the bizarre, about Juliet and Pauline.

Under the shadow of the C. I. C., in chow line, I read, flauntingly, I confess, H. L. Mencken's translation of Nietzsche's *The Anti-Christ.*

Private Reverend Frye protested. The company sergeant told me to stop reading that thing in his chow line. I invoked a constitutional right to read, and won, because, I suspected, he had only a vague idea of that phrase.

More than ever, I was voraciously reading, in every genre.

Listening to Nietzsche's starkly lucid voice as I read *My Sister and I* that Hope Savage had put in my hands, sometimes hearing *her* voice, I decided to emulate the aphorisms that were included in a separate section at the end. I had always been partial to brief passages, epiphanies, and aphorisms, and so I fashioned some of my own.

Thoughts After Reading Nietzsche While in the Army

(1) I long to have, more than peace of mind, a vivid, living, organic sense of history, acting out of which I may extend the boundaries of my intellectual awareness far beyond conscious realization, intuitively achieve a union of the Heraclitan flow and flux of my being with that of the timeless, combined Jungian being of the race and beyond into the universe.

(2) An atheist or his cousin the agnostic needs many Christs. The cross of human suffering is crowded with martyrs of wisdom and truth. The blood of one Christ drowns many more and nourishes only those chosen who know its bitter taste. Many people go up on a cross of some sort, but too many like it for all the wrong reasons and too few go up for the right cause. For the mob, one Christ is too many, but from the atheist's perspective, not enough "Christs" have made good the agony.

(3) Our culture in its dictatorial capacity is like the radio announcer who holds up to the audience a card telling it when to laugh, when to cry, when to applaud, when not to. But in that cultural studio, the audience is not as polite and obedient. It laughs, cries, and applauds at the wrong places, and some of its members are *planted* to create a disturbance. Maybe it needs an awesome sponsor, its equivalent to Ex-lax.

(4) Cassandra of the present, Screecher of Doom, is dead. The silence of those to whom she spoke killed her.

(5) To believe in oneself, three things one must know: who one is; who one isn't; and that others are often not as one sees them.

(6) All music is lamentation.
(7) Out of sorrow, despair, remorse, insanity come either self-disintegration or genius. What comes between these poles is a messy fusion of the two.
(8) Any study of religion is time better spent with reason and beauty. Theologians are engaged in the unlovely task of making profoundly obscure what is simply obscure.
(9) Genuine laughter is a sorrowful sound. Do tears often accompany raucous, sympathetic laughter because the subconscious is weeping?
(10) These modern democratic asses, who would chop off the head of real democracy if it reared, go on affirming in their electoral orgies the same old illusions, falsehoods, and cultural poisons that have down the years become completely, unrecognizably sanctified.
(11) It is the irony of history that hoaxes forced quietly or violently upon the stupid of ages past become deified by the intelligent of the present and future.
(12) Unlike Nietzsche, I do not condemn Christianity. Why should I do ineptly what Nietzsche and Christianity itself do so effectively?
(13) Why do I have such utopian hopes for man when I need but walk down a street to see lucidly how utterly hopeless this creature really is.
(14) Nietzsche's lamentations, screaming out of his utter loneliness, his vivid sense of immediate doom, the pain of lunatic self-denial, embody the essence of my present state of mind, though to a lesser intensity. I quite naturally affirm and doubt in one breath, as I inhale, and exhale.
(15) I want to elevate man. Sometimes I say I want merely to do my part. But deep inside I have an explosive compulsion to be the detonator of a blast, which might uproot man from his firm implantation in the basalt of immobility, irresolution, stagnant morality.
(16) The body of a woman is the only void in which it is sublime to lose oneself.
(17) I am leaving this space open to further thought.

For a while, my intellectual atmosphere was somewhat Nietzschean. His very titles were like monuments one passes by from time to time. *The Will to Power, Thus Spake Zarathustra, The Anti-Christ, Beyond Good and Evil, Twilight of the Gods.* "The old Gods are dead." Although as an agnostic, I was not anti-Christ, I enjoyed knowing he, too, was attacking Christians. I liked thinking about the idea of the superman, while regretting that it appealed to Hitler, and I liked Nietzsche's role as rebel outcast, but learning that he died of syphilis, the great terror of midcentury fornicators, shocked me sadly.

"David Madden," my typing teacher used to tell me in an accusatory tone, "*you* are just an iconoclast."

"I like being called an iconoclast because I like the sound the word makes. Say, it again."

Along with Albert Camus, my conviction was that agnostics had a secular obligation to act as a guide for wayward Christians into a more profound religious realm for the sake of all mankind.

As nascent agnostic priest, I preached Jesus the humanist in the latrine while questioning his divinity.

The guy on latrine duty followed a stunned silence with a declaration. "Latrine detail is a crock of shit, if you was to ast *me*."

Another time, I was sorting spent rifle shells at a raised table with some other Government issues — why, I don't remember — scrutinizing pros and cons about God and Jesus, when a Black fellow I liked looked up and quietly asked, "What? You don't believe in no motha-fuckin' Christ?"

"No, I don't."

"Man, I ort a cut your motha-fuckin' balls off, man!"

"Well, that would be one for-certain way of converting me to Christianity."

January 15, 1955, the London Festival Ballet came to Columbia, with Tamara Toumanova in *The Dying Swan* by Camille Saint-Saens, choreography by Michel Fokine.

I was deeply affected watching ballet and modern dance although, as with opera when I could not distinguish the words, even in English, for the overwhelming action of the music, I never could identify what was being expressed by the movements of the two very different genres of dance, not even Tamara Toumanova as the dying swan or Valerie Bettis' *A Streetcar Named Desire.* Passing an open doorway, I saw a Black woman sitting inside on a bench, taking a smoking break, and imagining she was Martha Graham, I sat beside her, and it turned out she was Martha Graham.

Outside, against the wall beside the wide wine-colored doors, between Greek columns, stood Hope Savage, as sudden a sight as when the lights went up after *Miracle in Milan* and there she suddenly was, sitting beside Kenvin and me. "Thrilled" was the most apt word to describe how seeing her again, alone, made me feel.

Our conversation was rather ordinary, considering who I imagined we were and what I imagined and hoped we were to each other.

I saw her off on the bus to Camden.

On a December night, I was dancing drunk, solo, in place, at the bar in Casa Manana, in Columbia, when in walked Walton Rawls, my old friend, my literary critic at Knoxville High and in the Van Vactor living room, who, even then, resembled young James Joyce, a cloistered Harvard intellectual now, a good friend of Newell Anderson, double haughty impression when I saw them together, each a striking contrast to Ralph Carr, best friend of my teenage years, proletarian, who had a confident aloof air of his own, then serving in Occupied Germany.

"David, perhaps most interesting to you is the fact that I now have a mistress. This has greatly complicated my life, because the woman is married, supposedly happily so.

"Noting your predilection toward the vaginal kiss I have been moved on occasions to give it a try. Unfortunately for the experience, my appetite for such a delicacy has been quelled each time by certain savage smells emanating from the vicinity. Perhaps the fault is my fastidiousness in taste. But perhaps I wait too late in the game; you may be able to instruct me in the practice. In this realm I bow most humbly to your mastery. Ars Gratia 'Arse'tis. Walton"

Enviously happy for him, I never imagined soft-spoken Walton a cocksman like Ralph Carr.

Trapped in an institution so neutered that sex was on everyone's mind constantly, it was somehow a natural irony that for me Army-time was a no-love-making time.

I sent to Walton my Nietzsche inspired aphorisms and a revised version of "Rosanna."

A few weeks later, a letter from Walton Rawls in hand, I was keenly aware of its having come to me from the atmosphere of Harvard University as I remembered it.

But Harvard and Cambridge would never be the same, because Hope had told me that her family spent more time there in a fine house near Longfellow's house than in Camden.

As I was describing Cassie putting on her dead brother's motorcycle gear, my landlady knocked on my door to tell me some girl named Hope Savage "of all things" was calling me on her phone from the Trailways Bus station to say she urgently wanted me to meet her on the State Capitol grounds.

Up ahead, she was pacing up and down, wearing a blue beret and a trench coat. Inside, I hoped, was a living, breathing Botticelli nude.

She had already, at the sight of me, I supposed, come up out of the prevailing twilight interior of her psyche, agitated, talking loud, maybe sounding hysterical to anyone around in the night spaces, although I knew she was simply in her own unbroken zone.

But the uniformed guard who patrolled the grounds, the very one who had told the Black kid I was sketching one Sunday, "No niggers allowed," now asked 18-year-old Hope, who looked 15, whether "this man" was molesting her.

"Quite the contrary, officer, he is a dear, dear friend from long, long ago."

Disappointed, the guard ambled off among the hovering Confederate statues.

The great torrent of words Hope uttered boiled down to this: "My mother told me that if I cut my hair, so embarrassing to the family in a town like Camden, as she put it, she would give me one hundred dollars. Tell me, dear David, should I shear off my hair?"

Shorn of her long, long honey-colored hair, she definitely would no longer resemble the face of a Botticelli or Hope Savage or Sura. Came to mind Elizabeth Taylor cutting her hair to look like a boy jockey in *National Velvet* and Ingrid Bergman cutting her hair to a curly bob in *For Whom the Bell Tolls.*

"What makes your mother want to be so mean to you?"

"Oh, no, not mean, she's very caring, very liberal, like my father, just very much of this world, I fear."

"Cut it, Hope. Then take the hundred dollars and get on a bus to Greenwich Village where you belong."

As she ascended the steps of the bus that would take her back to Camden, she remembered, and handed back down to me her ragged copy of Baudelaire's *Flowers of Evil.*

From behind a grimy window, Hope wanly waved goodbye, faintly smiling, as I imagined the Greyhound took her toward Greenwich Village.

IMAGINING "CASSANDRA SINGING" ON AND OFF KEY

Writing and reading were my own private paradise, and what I read affected my responses to characters in some of the novels that I read and some movies I saw before and during life within the realm of military limbo and participated in acts of my imagination, my dreaming, thinking about, and creating Cassandra and Lone's lives together back home in the impoverished Lonsdale neighborhood at the city limits along Sharp's Ridge, and the rock quarry, the creek, and an abattoir below.

Phaedra by Racine, about an older woman in love with a younger man, had an unusually erotic allure. But the incestuous brother and sister in Jean Cocteau's *Les Enfants Terribles,* and his movie adaptation *The Holy Terrors,* was a major influence as I was writing about Cassie and Lone. I turned to more Cocteau, *Orphee.* And *The Infernal Machine.* "The gods exist; that's the devil of it" is the epigraph.

I reached for Shirley Jackson's *Hangsaman.* The folk song epigraph took hold of me. "Slack your rope, Hangman, O slack it for a while, I think I see my true love coming, coming many a mile." I imagined Cassie singing the song itself for Lone to overhear, as a warning. The strange title and the psychological suspense involving a teenage "young girl lost in a dark and terrifying labyrinth," somewhat like Cassie, was the lure.

With the very first paragraph, Jean Stafford's *The Mountain Lion* affected my creation of the brother-sister relationship in "Cassandra Singing." "Ralph was ten and Molly was eight when they had scarlet fever."

I had great affection for fourteen-year-old Mick Kelly in Carson McCullers' *The Heart Is a Lonely Hunter*. Mick's tomboy ways and audacious manner of speaking resembled Cassie's. Mick, like Cassie, moved among the people in the town, stealthily in the night, spying on other lives and sitting under the window of one house often, listening to Mozart. One night, Mick listens to a Beethoven symphony, "Like God strutting in the night. . . . Wonderful music like this was the worst hurt there could be. The whole world was this symphony, and there was not enough of her to listen." She beat her thigh with her fists and scraped the same spot with sharp rocks until her hands bled. Listening to such music with Iva Lee, another model for Cassie, I squeezed her hand until it hurt a little.

Holding that book, I enjoyed the feel of it, the woven texture of the cover, and often intoned the title, to hear it. "*The Heart Is a Lonely Hunter* by Carson McCullers." I held such books out in front of me to gaze upon them, as I day-dreamed of holding *Cassandra Singing* as a published book, which I imagined would make me world famous before I reached 21. Frankie in McCullers's *A Member of the Wedding* also suggested Cassie.

Those books, plays, and movies constituted a kind of memory ambience that hovered over the development of "Cassandra Singing."

To make her more vivid in my mind as I wrote about her, I imagined Cassie not only as an exotic girl like Raven, an ideal figure like Hope Savage, but in the raunchiest, somewhat grotesque, dark terms. My sometimes, somewhat perverse perception was authorized in a way by James Joyce's having Stephen in *A Portrait of the Artist as a Young Man* relish the smell of horse manure, more broadly by Victor Hugo's exhortation that writers deal not only with the sublime but with the grotesque to some extent, the same streak in my imagination of the somewhat perverse bizarre had taken hold of me as I tried to catch in the excess an essence of Cassie.

The active delineation of the art of creative writing itself was one of my main purposes as I kept to my main focus, which was on the development of "Cassandra Singing," as novel and play, and perhaps as a film script.

★

"CASSANDRA SINGING" WINS PLAYWRITING CONTEST

In Clerk Typist School, between lessons and Miss Hovey's assignments, I had written many versions of the opening, warming up to write the first full draft of the novel version of "Cassandra Singing."

The beginning: "Awake all night imagining Lone and Gypsy and Blackie having wild, careening adventures on their motorcycles, causing the Law to chase them up and down the steep hills and round and round the twisting, hairpen curves of Harlan, Cassie listened to Lone's motorcycle, at long last, close the distance between the highway and the swinging bridge that would bring him back to his cot across from her bed."

Momma sent me a clipping announcing UT's annual statewide one-act play contest in which I had won second place with "Call Herman in to Supper" when I was still in high school.

For advice, I tracked down Joe Baldwin, the instructor at UT who had allowed me, still in high school, to participate in his unofficial nighttime playwriting workshop.

I worked hard and fast improving the one-act play version of "Cassandra Singing" for the one-act play contest.

I wrote a working scenario for "Cassandra Singing" in three scenes.

I made many drawings of Cassie and Lone and of their mother and father and of scenes and stage designs. Re-reading the scenario and scenes for the novel enabled me to imagine Cassie and Lone on stage, an audience watching, and so see them more vividly alive.

February 1954,

At the end of a year in the Army, Momma sent me clippings from the Knoxville *News-Sentinel* announcing that "Cassandra Singing" won third place.

"Mr. Madden is now serving in the Army and is on his way this week to Alaska." The news story informed readers that Madden had played a fairy beach bum in "Season in the Sun" at Carousel and an old Mayor in *The Enchanted* by Jean Giraudoux, adapted by Maurice Valency, and an old Jewish philosopher in *Golden Boy* by Clifford Odets on the stage of the Bijou where he had been an usher at age 13."

★

"MADDEN, YOUR RED ASS IS ALASKA BOUND!"

Even as I was fitfully creatively and intellectually afire, or even when embers in the grate of my brain smoldered, I was quite simply melancholy most hours of most days. Coming and going un-conjurable in the novel version, Cassie and Lone seemed to continue to live and breathe up on Sharp's Ridge in Knoxville with little need of my consciously stimulating my imagination to breathe life into them.

Looking at Marlon Brando in the *On the Waterfront* stills in the stand set up out front of the Palmetto Theater on Columbia's Main Street, I remembered Marlon Brando vividly in *A Streetcar Named Desire, Viva Zapata,* and *The Wild One.* Having heard he was homosexual, I was supposing that Marlon Brando, masculine-feminine beauty ideal, and my favorite living playwright Tennessee Williams, known to be "queer," made love, when suddenly, the smart-assed Sergeant Carlyle in Personnel was standing beside me.

After he had treated me mean-spiritedly when I repeatedly tried to see my personnel records, his manner that night was overtly friendly. Suspecting that he was trying to pick me up, I executed a smart about face and faded into the theater.

By January 1955, the Army's CIC had still not adjudicated my case, so I assumed I was still in danger. I was sent out on various types of work details that drew me down into a funk.

Hope Savage's voice reached me in a letter from Greenwich Village.

"David, darling, if they humiliate you anymore just leave. We'll go to Mexico together where revolutions come and go, and every fifth tourist is liable to get hit by machine gun bullets. I'll commit a felony too so it will be as dangerous to repatriate me as it would you. But I know you would have deserted long ago but you had your reasons. Even so, just think — only a month to go and you desert — what a magnificent piece of insolence!"

I wrote to Momma, who had offered to go to the Governor to get me out of the army, as she had worked for years to help John and Dickie get out of prisons. "Hope Savage. What a magnificent girl! She tempts me. But never fear momma, you are *one* of the good reasons I don't abscond."

Hope sent me a large, matted picture of her that looked like the Greek Cassandra — wild hair, dark eyes, a morbid stare, a look that said, "Who are you and what do you matter to me!" And her fingers like a child's touching her cheek.

She was much more eccentric than Raven ever dreamt of being, and she read my letters to people all over New York so that when I return people will know what I am about. Dickie and John would laugh at her ideas about prison. She thinks of it as a place to be alone, to write and read and meditate.

"Someday, David, when you want solitude, you should commit a crime.

"I can see it now. The judge sternly sentences you to a year — society inflicting its pathetic wrath upon its mal-conformists — and you standing there with an insolent grin on your face."

Clearly, this girl so enchants me, her witchcraft may get me into trouble someday. But I am already in prison — a crowded, vulgar, dull, meaningless one. Yet to *choose* prison — that is *true* freedom.

Finally, I received "SPECIAL ORDERS, 11 FEB. 1955," ordering me to show up at Fort Lewis, Washington, to arrive on 1 March.

Every soldier I ever met so trembled at horror stories about being stationed in Alaska that the mere possibility of ending up there terrified them, and so, being assigned to service in Alaska terrified me the way stories about the reform school, where my brothers and most of my playmates ended up, gave me shivers. Simultaneously, I yearned to go to Alaska someday, on my own. I was in the fifth grade when I first put a story into writing, compared with more often telling stories orally. "Across the Snow," was about a life-saving serum run by dogsled from Anchorage to Nome, inspired by the movie version of Jack London's *The Call of the Wild.*

I shuddered to imagine not so much Alaska itself as the bare-faced fact that to correct my behavior in that land of glaciers, the Army might conduct me into the stockade. Or that communist Russia might act to fulfill its mission in life by invading some dark night. One theater in The Cold War conflict played out in Russia's neighbor-cold, cold-assed Alaska.

"Madden, your red ass is Alaska bound, you little commie!"

Almost strangling the red folder in which they kept my disgraceful records, personnel Sergeant Carlyle broke into stagey giggling gyrations of delight. The very one who had tried to pick me up in front of the *On the Waterfront* poster outside the Palmetto theater in Columbia.

"Your new assignment's our revenge for all the trouble you've put the department through."

Personally, I imagined, to get me out of tale-telling range.

I didn't say what Br'er Rabbit said, "Please don't throw me into the briar patch!" but like Br'er Rabbit that was where I had always yearned to go, a romantic desire, until I heard all those stories about duty in Alaska.

My facial and body expressions of abject terror thrilled Personnel Sergeant Carlyle all over again.

Arming myself for months of total darkness and months of total light, my creative life in the army in Alaska, I set out for the romantic, fearsome unknown, with scenes and notes on the novel version of "Cassandra Singing."

In the Army, I somehow read 100 novels, plays, and nonfiction. A few of the books I intended to read in Alaska were Sigmund Freud's *The Future of an Illusion*, Herman Hesse's *Siddhartha*, that C. P. Lee recommended a few years before, Faulkner's *The Sound and the Fury*, T. S. Eliot's verse play *Murder in the Cathedral*, and Herbert Muller's *The Uses of the Past*, a few passages of which already inspired my fervent desire to go to Istanbul and see St. Sophia Mosque, now a Cathedral. Gilbert Highet's *The Art of Teaching*, after having been subjected to far too much artless public school teaching, which moved me to aspire to teach innovative appreciation courses in English and all the other arts in high school, of all places. Aldous Huxley's *Doors of Perception*, about his personal psychedelic experiments with peyote, which I fearfully intended to try someday, seemed a little scary.

I wanted to read Gore Vidal's *Williwaw*, because it is set at sea in Alaska's Aleutian Islands and was his first novel, published when he was only 21, my own age as I was writing my own first novel, "*Cassandra Singing.*"

About to move out of one physical phase of my life into a starkly different landscape that might well affect in some ways my creative life, I set down my creative convictions, along with a few other notes.

"From childhood's hour," I have always been confident, with the ego of a child, that there is a place for my writing in the literary firmament. Imagination had the starring role in my life and literature.

Inspiration is a single flow sustained from concept on into revision.

In revision, I am most mindful of style and technique, of imagery.

I experienced the immediacy of the creative sensibility in conflict with stark experiences in the military.

In the very moment as I live my life, I simultaneously imagine it. Even, I like to imagine, in my mother's womb.

I write three or four things in various genres at once, and read in, but sometimes fail to finish, four or five books at once.

Having written in all genres since the fifth grade, I continue to be immersed in those reaches of the imagination.

Now, I was setting forth to Alaska with a keen awareness that during the time that the Army of the United States of America held me in thrall, I had been becoming a much more mature writer.

And having seriously pursued the imaginative, emotional, and intellectual pleasures of the Southern oral storytelling tradition and of all the arts — movies, radio and television dramas, plays, music, dance, photography, painting, and sculpture, and in all their sub-genres — I remembered them lucidly and actively, and subconsciously experienced them each day in the Army. I was myriad-minded.

American soldier as archivist, I crammed my empty duffle bag with all my worldly goods, mostly books and manuscripts, and hit the highway.

The big "They" granted me "five days delay in-route, chargeable as leave, plus five days travel time."

To say goodbye to my family and friends, especially the vivid Van Vactors, I hitchhiked north through the mountains on a substandard two-lane highway through Black Mountain, 20 miles before Asheville, becoming aware of the famous experimental college of the arts there, where I thought I might like to study or teach someday. On through Asheville, where I did long to visit Thomas Wolfe's house again, but it was just closing, and on to Hot Springs, North Carolina, and Newport and Dandridge, Tennessee to the streets of Knoxville.

I had followed news of the lives of John and Dickie who, when out of prison, were always on the move, here and there, potentially everywhere, quick snapshots in Momma's and Mammy's letters, and in the living room of the old home place, Momma and Mammy told the latest about Dickie and John, setting memories of them off in a flood upon me.

Planted like a sapling in military ground, slowly wilting, I read letters from Dickie, hearing Groucho Marx's voice. From his prison cell in Brushy Mountain near Petros, big brother Dickie spoke to me in letters. I dreaded exposure to the clichés with which Dickie, like John, always salted his letters.

"Hi, Bud. Just a few lines to let you know I received the two dollars you sent me. It sure was a godsend. I'm sorry I haven't written before now, but I'm only allowed three letters a week. And I have to take turns in writing home to my wife Anne and to Momma and Mammy. My wife was up to see me Saturday and Sun. But mom didn't get to make it. I sure was disappointed. Well David I guess I finally met the girl who'll really meet all specifications. One who really loves me. And I don't think you'll find me into trouble again."

When we played army, he always played General Rommel, the Desert Rat. So, I reckon marrying Anne, the daughter of a Nazi Colonel, was in the cards. I imagined what Anne looked like. She had desired earlier to come to see him in the states. It might be forcing it to liken her search to Evangeline or Agnes of Glasgow.

Davie asked whether Dickie packed a gun or beat somebody within an inch of their life.

"No, Dickie was never a violent criminal, not even a common thief, always just a low-level check-passing conman.

"John's face was always childlike, an awed expression, and his voice was sonorous.

"Dickie, forced to sit still, wrote often. John, in and out of the Marines and the Navy, discovered to be underage, always on the move, crisscrossing the continent, wrote less often.

"In life and in letters, Dickie exploited clichés as a con man cynic. John exploited clichés as a true believer."

My family and I were so often mindful about Dickie and John as mysterious wanderers who came and went that before I opened letters from Momma or Mammy or the very few from Daddy, memories and auras of my brothers pervaded my consciousness.

I spent time with my family, minus Dickie, still in prison, and John, wandering again, at that time in an antique Hudson, a big dog in the passenger seat, money from a church charity in his pocket, or a fancy restaurant where he was, he loudly charged, served Porterhouse steak with a hair in it, or from conning folks into buying his cheap-assed jewelry.

The visit to good ol' 206 Henegar Street was on the fly, but good enough for remembering fondly for a while later on in Alaska.

At Mammy's, I rooted in the barrels to handle and peruse my old manuscripts, stored in the old red kid's desk in the garage.

Going into the army, I cut away the scotch tape and took off the walls of my rented room my art and photograph prints and stored them along with my books and other stuff at Mammy's.

I waited outside Knox High to catch a glimpse of Iva Lee as she emerged to go home. She must have used a different exit.

Good ol' boy Billy Tindall, an agent for Blue Cross, told me he saw her often because she handled insurance for the Knoxville School system.

I went on pilgrimage to see the sights I loved for the last time before being sent to Alaska.

I walked Gay Street from north of the Southern Railway viaduct all the way to the south end of the Gay Street Bridge over the river. Gay Street Bridge was almost a mystical place, on which Iva Lee and I often stood, looking down upon Front Street slums. Standing on Gay Street Bridge again, I felt a personal and historical version of the ideal of beauty that standing on Brooklyn Bridge made me — and Hart Crane, "O harp and altar" — feel. More powerful, more often, standing on it, and remembering feeling mystical alone, remembering standing there sharing the vision with Iva Lee.

Looking out at the views from the bridges of Knoxville across the Tennessee River, across First Creek and Second Creek, and in Manhattan and towns to which the Seatrains and to which other ships took me in foreign countries seemed to have a mythic status.

And I explored the ground under bridges and viaducts.

I paused to contemplate the facade of the Bijou, now showing *East of Eden*.

Standing on Union Street facing Market Square and the three-story Market House, I walked all around the block-long building, imagining the pick-up trucks offering vegetables and berries in season, past the Gold Sun Cafe, the Rialto and the Crystal, slummy theaters, White Store, where I used to meet Momma after she got off work at Millers' and help carry the week's groceries, and around the corner, I saluted the front of the Roxy theater, covered with movie stills for three features, a cartoon, a Zorro chapter play, and a burlesque show.

I took the long walk along the river to the UT area and visited WUOT and the room where Vera used to work as a paid student worker cataloging recordings. And stepped next door and visited C. P. and Robert briefly in their Ayres Hall basement offices.

I strolled over and took one last look inside Carousel Theater, where I had acted, no longer under a tent but still a theater in the round, and I was surprised, delighted to see Dave Van Vactor there and watch him conduct again, this time the University of Tennessee Training Orchestra, aware that Dave had created the Department of Fine Arts, situated in an old Mansion on Kingston Pike within the embrace of the University grounds. The music was by classical composer Telemann and Eric Delamater, American composer, conductor of the Chicago Symphony, in which Dave used to play the flute and which had put out recordings of some of Dave's compositions.

I am so inclined to indulge in nostalgia that I feel it even before some things get gone. Riding a streetcar, I got nostalgic for the times Dickie and I, as kids, rode past rich folks' houses way out to the end of the line in Lyons View where it turned around Dalton's store and we went inside and bought a Grapette that we shared.

A few years later, steeped in nostalgia, Iva Lee and I had made that trip more than once, aware that the East Tennessee Asylum for the Insane was close by.

I had ridden on every streetcar in Knoxville and every bus after the Lincoln Park car ended its last run. April 12, 1945, when I was twelve, I boarded a streetcar in which the conductor and the sparse riders were weeping for the sudden loss of President Franklin Delano Roosevelt. All the streetcars were rusty now, on display upon a hillside on Maryville Highway in Vestal.

Around about age 12, my impression of "Buzzard Roost," where South Knoxville Negroes lived on the slopes of Sharp's Ridge, as a scary, exotic place, forbidden to most white people diminished.

I was on the streetcar going to town glad to see a Black soldier sitting across the aisle. A huge lug of a man walked up to the soldier and demanded that he get up and give a white man a seat. The soldier refused. The man shouted racist comments. I got up and offered the white man my seat. His response was to beat hell out of me and the soldier, but finally he stormed off to the front and hung on a strap, fuming.

I walked Gay Street from its intersection to Fifth Avenue all the way across the river bridge to the South Knoxville end.

I got off the bus at the end of Cedar Street, took a good look at Lincoln Park Methodist, especially the upstairs Sunday school classroom where I first thrilled to the very sight of Jonnie Lou and Iva Lee.

I climbed the hill on Cedar Street and down the other side past Tilly's Pond, up another hill past Troutman's Grocery Store, now abandoned, and dwelled upon the sights in the block where my childhood was richest in imagination and experiences but not quite yet at all in writing. The front door at 316 was shut, the window shades down.

I took a notion to walk McMurray Street up the very steep hill to Buddy Smith's house, where only his mother lived now, then back down and on to the end to look again at the red clay bank where four or five of us boys waited for trains to slow down so we could hop a freight to Black Oak and wander around Sterghi's vast farm and swim in Bull Run creek.

I sat on a wall to start listing the places I had visited and would visit:

Lincoln Park, the neighborhood more full of vivid memories than any other, 316 Cedar Street and two houses where we lived during the war, and the next block over on Atlantic Avenue, from which we walked to Mammy's house, then we moved on down on the corner of Atlantic and Pershing, where I began to write stories.

Lincoln Park Elementary School, where I adored Jonny Lou Gilmer for 5 years.

Christenberry Junior High, a block from Mammy's, where I loved Jenny Bowling and Iva Lee, formed lifelong friendships, and wrote stories in class.

Knox High School, a huge three-story building, with an impressive World War I statue facing Fifth Avenue, where I was known as a likeable but strange agnostic.

The University of Tennessee, called The Hill, where I met Jerry Thomas in art class.

Three-story market house in Market Square where I saw movies at the Roxy Burlesques three-feature movies theater, and the Rialto, the Crystal —

I listed:

The two houses in the Fort Sanders neighborhood on Holston Avenue where I rented three different rooms in three different houses near UT.

Lawson McGhee Library, where Iva Lee and I kissed in the stacks, and listened to music on earphones, and had a good view of East Knoxville.

The used books and magazine store on Gay at the river bridge, and the used bookstore on South Gay Street, that moved to Union Street, and classy Matheny's new bookstore on Clinch.

Bearden Street where Iva Lee and I first made love, and I found an old copy of *Look Homeward, Angel* in the crawl space under the house.

McCalla Avenue where Iva Lee and I made love often and I created a very cramped study I called my "sanctuary," and in two years wrote poems, stories, plays, and movie scenarios.

Passing the old corner of North Broadway and Walker Boulevard where the Knoxville *News-Sentinel* for our routes were dropped, I remembered my responses to bad news were often gut-wrenching, as when Japanese fishermen were on camera expressing their fear of effects of hydrogen bomb tests. My lingering horror of Hiroshima and that my conviction the bombing was wrong in uniquely tremendous ways provided a context for my response to the fishermen's nightmarish fears. Every time I read something about the atomic bombing of Hiroshima and Nagasaki, I was abysmally sad and outraged all over again, as when I read that the center of the Nagasaki blast was a poor neighborhood, and that as an ironic justice many Christians lived there. I sold the extra newspaper that announced the dropping of the "Adam Bomb," as I pronounced it, ignorant of what it really was.

No one answered the doorbell at the Van Vactor mansion. Dave, Ginger, Raven, and Davie, all dispersed, all somewhere out into a world they knew well and embraced exuberantly, I imagined.

Out of Knoxville, I hitchhiked on up into Chicago, where I found a newsstand that sold the Sunday, March 5, 1955 Knoxville *News Sentinel*, and was excited and proud to see an article by Sarah Booth Conroy that informed the world that my one-act play "Cassandra Singing" would be produced, along with two other plays, March 10, 11, 12, which meant that light would go up on my play on opening night during my long trip on a troop ship to Alaska.

I flew out of Chicago in a new-style two-story TWA, my first time to fly, to Tacoma, Washington. From there, I moseyed nine miles south by Greyhound bus to my transitory destination, Fort Lewis, Washington.

Arriving at Fort Lewis, way station en route to Alaska, I found Walton's verdict on first chapters of C*assandra Singing*, passed on from Fort Jackson.

"I think your 'Cassandra Singing' chapters are fine. You just do not yet have the idea clearly in mind — that is essential though.

"As for parting advice from ol' Uncle Walton as you set out for your Alaskan adventure, a major chapter in your creative life in the Army, stick this in your pipe and smoke it: F. Scott Fitzgerald's 'test of a first-rate intelligence is the ability to hold two opposed ideas in the mind at the same time and still retain the ability to function.'

Your pal, Walton."

On furnace duty, I felt brotherly with William Faulkner who wrote *As I Lay Dying* on a barrelhead, working nights at the University of Mississippi power plant. I wrote next to nothing the week I was on furnace duty.

By bus to Tacoma, I had a desultory visit with my old acting buddy Brendan, ex-monk, now jet pilot, and his rather homely, but, even so, striking wife Charlotte, Raven's best friend in Knoxville who had played the violin under Dave's baton in the Knoxville Symphony Orchestra.

His letters to me were stuffed into my duffle-bag along with all the others.

Getting letters from ex-monk, UT graduate student in philosophy, Brendan Liddell, felt strange, his being a jet pilot, compared with my rank as private first class in the Army.

Brendan had acted in Sidney Kingsley's *Detective Story* at UT with me and became one of my best friends for a while — frank, abrasive, irritating, but a vital stimulus to my argumentative nature. His diction and rhetoric, talking or writing, consistently drew upon the Elizabethan era.

He confided in me that his mother defensively killed his father with a pressing iron. He gave me a photograph of his lovely sister in her nun's habit.

In one of his letters, he informed me that rampant sex had undone him.

"David — Sex! About which I spend many a thoughtful hour. The lovely Lieut. in California has probably seen the last of me, but not through my desires. Just Air Force desires.

"I'm afraid that of late I have given vent to my baser animalistic instincts. To wit, a warm woman and a soft bed after a goblet of Manischewitz is quite a pleasure, as you know. In Tacoma there is an apartment, a woman, a bed — and I'm coming back to work greatly relaxed certain mornings. Let it rest —

"And leave Raven alone. I think half of her trouble is you. Not that you're so bad for her, but she doesn't keep up with you, nor you with her, so there you are.

"I had a pretty pornographic idea for a short story . . . And I've been painting lately . . . A few nude studies, a horrible thing of Raven. No poems . . . Actually, I've been too busy with air alert, and fornicating, to do anything creative. Alert is very exacting, in a way. Right now, my Sabre jet is sitting downstairs, its power unit plugged in, needing only a switch to start and take off. I have all my flying equipment in the plane. My Mae West on, and here I sit, ready to dash. The rockets are loaded and ready to fire. All we need is the enemy and the buzzer, and I'll leap to fly in five minutes airborne. Never had a scramble yet, but it may be in a minute, hour, week, or month, one never can tell. Just depends what unknown comes along . . .

"I go & farewell. God love you — Brendan"

Before catching a bus back to my company area, I indulged my passion for cityscapes, walking all over Tacoma.

I hoped I would escape the stockade for asking "why" one time too many, hoping everybody who had sent me such a multitude of letters since I entered the military would populate my imagination and subconscious with many more, especially mystical Hope Savage.

I became increasingly aware of the ways Hope Savage was like Cassie.

I hoped she would write illustrated letters inciting me to rebellion, and I imagined and intended to climb mountains, exploring everything Alaskan, while continuing to avoid the stockade.

★

"CASSANDRA SINGING" IN ALASKA AND BEYOND

Not at all certain that Alaska would be far enough to escape Senator Joe McCarthy's reach, feeling somewhat like Larry Darrell, as portrayed by Tyrone Power, at the end of the movie adaptation of W. Somerset Maugham's *The Razor's Edge*, sailing to India in search of the meaning of life, sea spray dashing full-body against him, I felt rough seas in the Gulf of Alaska toss me around on my third-tier bunk, my ears plugged with chewing gum, among hundreds of bunks on a troop ship Anchorage-bound — where I was destined to serve the last half of my Army moments — most of the soldiers seasick, vomiting, groaning, some yelling bloody murder, while I, erstwhile seaman, lay somewhat sedately, eyes closed, imagining opening night, Thursday, March 10, 1955, of my prize-winning one-act play, "Cassandra Singing," lights going up on the then-innovative theater-in-the-round, imagining Momma, Daddy, Mammy and Cap, maybe even Phil, but not likely John or Dickie, but, yes, the Van Vactors, Dave, Ginger, and Raven, and my favorite teachers, C.P. Lee and Robert Daniel, maybe Jenny, Iva Lee, and Vera in the twilight of the darkened tent, Rosemary Sherrod, my red-headed, freckle-faced Knox High classmate, who I first saw tap dancing on the Bijou Stage at the Saturday morning Bugs Bunny Club, as Cassie says, "Lone, honey, who put this X-mark on the toe of your boot? Was it that girl you call Gypsy?" I hoped to arrive on the shores of Alaska in a blinding snowstorm, white like the mystical whiteness of the whale in *Moby Dick*, into a perilous realm of vast possibilities, and, simultaneously, total immersion in "Cassandra Singing" as three-act play and novel.

www.ingramcontent.com/pod-product-compliance
Lightning Source LLC
La Vergne TN
LVHW010926220826
846260LV00041B/1080

* 9 7 9 8 8 9 5 2 7 1 0 0 1 *